T0133708

Image Processing and Machine Learning, Volume 2

Image processing and machine learning are used in conjunction to analyze and understand images. Where image processing is used to pre-process images using techniques such as filtering, segmentation, and feature extraction, machine learning algorithms are used to interpret the processed data through classification, clustering, and object detection. This book serves as a textbook for students and instructors of image processing, covering the theoretical foundations and practical applications of some of the most prevalent image processing methods and approaches.

Divided into two volumes, this second installment explores the more advanced concepts and techniques in image processing, including morphological filters, color image processing, image matching, feature-based segmentation utilizing the mean shift algorithm, and the application of singular value decomposition for image compression. This second volume also incorporates several important machine learning techniques applied to image processing, building on the foundational knowledge introduced in Volume 1.

Written with instructors and students of image processing in mind, this book's intuitive organization also contains appeal for app developers and engineers.

Image Processing and Machine Learning, Volume 2

Advanced Topics in Image Analysis and Machine Learning

Erik Cuevas and Alma Nayeli Rodríguez

CRC Press
Taylor & Francis Group
Boca Raton London New York

CRC Press is an imprint of the
Taylor & Francis Group, an **informa** business

A CHAPMAN & HALL BOOK

MATLAB® is a trademark of The MathWorks, Inc. and is used with permission. The MathWorks does not warrant the accuracy of the text or exercises in this book. This book's use or discussion of MATLAB® software or related products does not constitute endorsement or sponsorship by The MathWorks of a particular pedagogical approach or particular use of the MATLAB® software.

First edition published 2024
by CRC Press
2385 NW Executive Center Drive, Suite 320, Boca Raton FL 33431

and by CRC Press
4 Park Square, Milton Park, Abingdon, Oxon, OX14 4RN

CRC Press is an imprint of Taylor & Francis Group, LLC

ISBN: 978-1-032-66032-5 (hbk)
ISBN: 978-1-032-66245-9 (pbk)
ISBN: 978-1-032-66246-6 (ebk)

DOI: 10.1201/9781032662466

Typeset in Palatino
by codeMantra

Contents

Preface Volume II

Image processing holds significant importance as it enables the enhancement and manipulation of images across various domains. One prominent field where image processing plays a pivotal role is in Medical Imaging. Here, it contributes significantly to the analysis and diagnosis of medical images, including X-rays, CT scans, and MRI images. By employing image processing techniques, healthcare professionals can extract valuable information, aiding in accurate diagnoses and treatment planning. Surveillance systems also heavily rely on image processing algorithms. These algorithms facilitate object detection, tracking, and the enhancement of image quality, thereby bolstering the effectiveness of surveillance operations. Additionally, image processing algorithms enable facial recognition, bolstering security measures in various applications. Remote sensing applications greatly benefit from image processing techniques as well. By employing these techniques, satellite and aerial images can be analyzed to monitor the environment, manage resources, and gain valuable insights for scientific research and decision-making. Multimedia applications, including photo editing software and video games, leverage image processing to enhance and manipulate images for optimal display quality. These applications utilize algorithms to adjust brightness, contrast, color, and other visual attributes, providing an enhanced visual experience to users.

Machine learning (ML) is a branch of artificial intelligence (AI) that enables systems to learn from data and make informed predictions or decisions without the need for explicit programming. ML finds extensive applications in various domains. For instance, in automation, ML algorithms can automate tasks that would otherwise rely on human intervention, thereby reducing errors and enhancing overall efficiency. Predictive analytics is another area where ML plays a crucial role. By analyzing vast datasets, ML models can detect patterns and make predictions, facilitating applications such as stock market analysis, fraud detection, and customer behavior analysis. ML also aids in decision-making processes, as its algorithms provide valuable insights and recommendations based on data, helping organizations make more informed and optimal decisions. Overall, ML is a powerful field within AI that offers immense potential for automating tasks, generating predictions, and supporting decision-making processes across various domains.

The integration of image processing and ML involves the utilization of techniques from both domains to analyze and comprehend images. Image processing techniques, including filtering, segmentation, and feature extraction, are employed to preprocess the images. Subsequently, ML algorithms come into play to analyze and interpret the processed data through tasks such as classification, clustering, and object detection. The ultimate objective is to harness the strengths of each field in order to construct computer vision systems capable of autonomously understanding and analyzing images without human intervention. This fusion allows image processing techniques to enhance image quality, thereby improving the performance of ML algorithms. Simultaneously, ML algorithms automate the analysis and interpretation of images, thereby reducing the reliance on manual intervention. By combining these two fields, a powerful synergy is achieved, enabling the development of robust and efficient systems for image analysis and understanding.

Our primary objective was to create a comprehensive textbook that serves as an invaluable resource for an image processing class. With this goal in mind, we carefully crafted a book that encompasses both the theoretical foundations and practical applications of the most prevalent image processing methods. From pixel operations to geometric transformations, spatial filtering to image segmentation, and edge detection to color image processing, we have meticulously covered a wide range of topics essential to understanding and working with images. Moreover, recognizing the increasing relevance of ML in image processing, we have also incorporated fundamental ML concepts and their application in this field. By introducing readers to these concepts, we aim to equip them with the necessary knowledge to leverage ML techniques for various image processing tasks. Our ultimate aspiration is for this book to be a valuable companion for students and practitioners alike, providing them with a solid understanding of image processing fundamentals and empowering them to apply these techniques in real-world scenarios.

In order to encompass all the crucial information, it was necessary to include numerous chapters and programming examples. Consequently, the resultant book became extensive, comprising a substantial amount of content and programming code. However, acknowledging that a single-volume book encompassing numerous chapters and programs might overwhelm readers, the decision was made to divide the book into two volumes. This division was undertaken with the primary goal of ensuring that readers could appropriately handle and comprehend the material. By splitting the content into two volumes, the book becomes more accessible and manageable, alleviating readers from feeling overwhelmed by the sheer volume of information. This deliberate division fosters a smoother learning experience, allowing readers to navigate through the content more effectively, explore the material in depth, and absorb concepts and techniques at their own pace. Ultimately, the decision to divide the book into two volumes is driven by the intention to optimize readers' understanding and engagement with the comprehensive materials and programs presented within its pages.

With the objective of ensuring that the book can be effectively navigated and comprehended by readers, we have made the decision to divide it into two volumes. Volume I: "Foundations of Image Processing" and Volume II: "Advanced Topics in Image Analysis and Machine Learning".

Volume I considers the fundamental concepts and techniques of image processing, encompassing pixel operations, spatial filtering, edge detection, image segmentation, corner detection, and geometric transformations. It serves as a strong foundation for readers seeking to comprehend the core principles and practical applications of image processing. By focusing on these initial six chapters, Volume I establishes the essential groundwork necessary for further exploration in the field. Building upon the knowledge acquired from Volume I, Volume II tackles more advanced topics in image analysis. It delves into subjects such as morphological filters, color image processing, image matching, feature-based segmentation utilizing the mean shift (MS) algorithm, and the application of singular value decomposition (SVD) for image compression. In addition to covering these advanced concepts and techniques, Volume II also incorporates several important ML techniques as applied to image processing. Recognizing the growing significance of ML in image analysis and its potential to enhance image processing tasks, relevant ML approaches are integrated throughout Volume II. This comprehensive volume expands upon the foundational knowledge from Volume I, enabling readers to delve into more sophisticated aspects of image processing while also incorporating the power of ML techniques.

The purpose behind dividing the book into two volumes was to ensure that each volume can function as a standalone and self-contained resource. This allows readers to review and study each volume independently, without requiring the other volume for context or comprehension. The self-contained structure enables readers to adopt a modular approach, focusing on specific topics or revisiting particular chapters as desired. This division grants readers the flexibility to engage with the material according to their individual needs and preferences, enhancing their learning experience and facilitating a more targeted exploration of the content.

Welcome to Volume II of our book on image processing and ML. This volume considers more advanced topics in image analysis, building upon the foundational knowledge acquired from Volume I. It also explores the inter-relationship between these advanced topics and the powerful techniques of ML. In addition to these advanced image processing concepts and techniques, Volume II also explores the integration of ML techniques within image analysis. Recognizing the growing significance of ML in the field, we have incorporated relevant ML approaches throughout this volume. By understanding and applying these ML techniques, you will unlock new dimensions of image analysis and enhance the capabilities of your image processing workflows.

After reviewing numerous books that consider image processing techniques and ML concepts, the authors identified a common trend of targeting readers with a solid mathematical background. Recognizing the need for a more inclusive and less technically focused approach, the authors embarked on creating a book that appeals to a wider audience of readers and students. This book encompasses all the essential topics found in other comparable literature, but with a distinctive emphasis on clear explanations, practical implementation, and real-world utilization of the methods. The intention is to minimize the emphasis on intricate mathematical details while prioritizing a comprehensive understanding and practical application of the concepts. By adopting this approach, the book aims to make image processing techniques and ML concepts more accessible and engaging to a broader range of readers, ensuring a fulfilling and enlightening learning experience.

This book not only encompasses advanced concepts and techniques in image processing and ML, but it also emphasizes the inclusion of substantial code and implementations. The authors recognize the significance of this aspect in facilitating a comprehensive understanding of the material. Even readers with strong mathematical skills may encounter challenges in fully grasping a particular approach until they observe it implemented in code. By providing code implementations of algorithms and methods, any confusion or uncertainty is alleviated, leading to enhanced understanding and knowledge transfer. This approach enables readers to progress through this book, starting with simpler methods and gradually advancing to more complex ones. By focusing on the computational aspect through implemented code, readers can visually observe the various models, reinforcing their mathematical comprehension and fostering a deeper understanding of the subject matter.

While other comparable books often prioritize the theoretical aspect of the subject or provide a general approach to algorithm development, our book takes a different approach based on our teaching experience. We have observed that students grasp the material more effectively when they have access to code that they can manipulate and experiment with. In line with this, our book utilizes MATLAB® as the programming language for implementing the systems. MATLAB is widely popular among engineers and offers an extensive library collection for various disciplines. Although other programming languages like Java, R, C++, and Python are also utilized in engineering, MATLAB stands out due to its unique features and the familiarity it holds among practitioners in the field. By employing MATLAB, we aim to provide readers with a practical and hands-on experience, enabling them to modify and explore the code, further enhancing their understanding of the concepts and fostering their ability to apply the techniques in real-world scenarios.

The multitude of computational methods employed in image processing and ML can be overwhelming for beginner readers, primarily due to the extensive array of mathematical concepts and techniques involved. While some practical books attempt to address this challenge by presenting pre-existing recipes, they may not adequately cater to cases where the problem assumptions are not met, necessitating algorithm modification or adaptation. To address this limitation, it becomes crucial for a book to provide the conceptual understanding required to appreciate and comprehend the underlying mathematics. The objective of this book is to strike a balance by offering a comprehensive yet approachable exploration of commonly used computational algorithms and popular image processing and ML approaches, with an emphasis on maintaining rigor. By achieving this balance, the book aims to equip readers with the necessary conceptual foundation, enabling them to navigate the complex landscape of image processing and ML while fostering their ability to modify and adapt algorithms to suit specific requirements.

While image processing methods often involve intricate mathematical concepts, it is feasible to utilize these models even without a deep understanding of their mathematical foundations. For many readers, a more attainable approach to learning image processing and ML is through programming rather than complex mathematical equations. Recognizing this, our book is designed to cater to this objective, providing a practical and accessible learning experience. By emphasizing programming implementations and applications, we strive to empower readers to grasp the concepts and techniques of image processing and ML in a more approachable manner. Our aim is to bridge the gap between theory and practice, enabling readers to effectively apply these methods in real-world scenarios, even if their mathematical understanding may be limited.

To effectively teach image processing and ML, it is beneficial to combine theoretical knowledge with practical computer exercises that enable students to write their own code for processing image data. This hands-on approach allows students to gain a deeper understanding of the principles and techniques involved. Given that image processing principles find application in various fields such as ML and data analysis, there is an increasing demand for engineers proficient in these concepts. Consequently, many universities have responded to this demand by offering comprehensive courses that cover the most commonly used image processing techniques. Image processing is widely regarded as a highly practical subject that inspires students by showcasing how image transformations can be translated into code, resulting in visually appealing effects. By integrating theory with practical exercises, students are equipped with the necessary skills and knowledge to effectively apply image processing techniques in real-world scenarios, preparing them for the challenges and opportunities in the field.

The content of this book has been thoughtfully thought through with a focus on its applicability in teaching contexts. As a result, it serves as a comprehensive textbook tailored for undergraduate and postgraduate students in the fields of science, electrical engineering, and computational mathematics. It is particularly suitable for courses such as image processing, computer vision, artificial vision, advanced methods, and image understanding. Designed to encompass a full semester, the book provides the necessary material to support an entire course, ensuring a comprehensive learning experience for students pursuing these subjects.

The book is organized in a way that allows readers to easily understand the goal of each chapter and reinforces their understanding through practical exercises using MATLAB programs. Volume II consists of six chapters; the details of each chapter are described below.

Chapter 1 analyzes, applies, and manipulates morphological filters, which alter image structures using a structural element. These filters are utilized on both binary and grayscale images.

In **Chapter 2**, the processing of color images is discussed. The central point of this chapter is the treatment of existing programming techniques for the representation and conversion of images to color.

In **Chapter 3**, the geometric operations among the pixels of an image are described. Using geometric operations, it is possible to distort the images. In other words, the values of the pixels can change their positions. Examples of this type of operation are displacement, rotation, scaling, or distortion. Geometric operations are widely used in practice, particularly in current and modern graphical user interfaces and video games.

The second part of the book considers the integration of image processing with ML. This section explores how image processing formulations can be solved using ML algorithms. This part of this book consists of three chapters; the details of each chapter are described below.

Chapter 4 discusses the problem of image matching or locating a known part of the image, which is usually described as a pattern. To detect the patterns, the correlation method was selected. This type of problem is typical in applications such as the search for reference points in stereovision, the location of a certain object in a scene, or the tracking of objectives in a sequence of images.

In **Chapter 5**, image segmentation from the perspective of features is presented. The MS scheme corresponds to a clustering method that has been extensively used for segmentation. In this chapter, the method in which the MS algorithm is employed for segmentation purposes is discussed.

Finally, in **Chapter 6**, SVD is considered for image compression. SVD is one of the most important matrix factorization paradigms used in computing. SVD provides a numerically stable matrix decomposition that can be used for a wide variety of purposes and is guaranteed to exist. These ML concepts can be applied to image processing, such as compression and pattern identification.

For more than five years, we tested multiple ways of exposing this material to dissimilar audiences. In addition, we have had invaluable tolerance from our students, mainly from the CUCEI at the University of Guadalajara, Mexico. All collaborations, assistance, and discussions with colleagues would deserve an additional chapter. To all, our testimony of gratitude.

Erik Cuevas
Alma Nayeli Rodriguez
Guadalajara, Jalisco, Mexico

1

Morphological Operations

The median filter has the ability to modify the two-dimensional structures present in the image. Among these changes, we can mention the elimination of the corners of structures, rounding them, or eliminating points or thin structures such as lines or small artifacts (see Figure 1.1). Therefore, the median filter selectively reacts to the shape of local image structures. However, the operation of this filter cannot be used in a controlled way; that is, it cannot be used to modify structures considering a particular method.

Morphological filters were originally conceived to be used on binary images, that is, on images whose pixels only have two possible values, 1 and 0, white and black [1]. Binary images are found in a large number of applications, especially in document processing.

In the following, we will define the pixels of the structure as those corresponding to one and the pixels of the background as those corresponding to zero.

1.1 Shrinkage and Growth of Structures

Starting from the fact mentioned above, the median filter 3×3 can be applied to binary images to reduce large structures and eliminate small ones. Therefore, the median filter can be used to eliminate structures whose size is smaller than the size of the median filter (in the case of example 3×3).

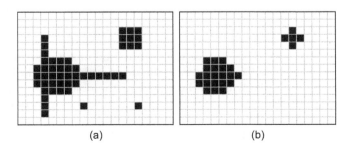

(a)   (b)

FIGURE 1.1
Median filter 3×3 used on a binary image. (a) Original image and (b) result after filter operation.

DOI: 10.1201/9781032662466-1

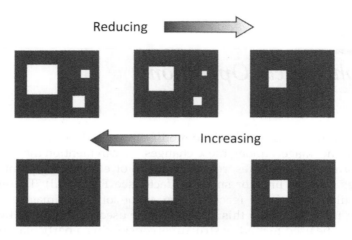

FIGURE 1.2
By successively reducing and subsequently enlarging structures in an image, it is possible to remove small elements.

From these results, the question arises: Is there an operation that can be used to modify elements within an image through the use of the size and shape of a defined structure?

The effects of the median filter can be considered interesting. However, its effect on the image, although it can eliminate small structures, is also capable of affecting large structures. Another approach that can be considered better and capable of controlling the image structures is based on the following principle (see Figure 1.2):

1. First, all structures in the image are reduced, with the result that small structures are simply eliminated.
2. Through shrinkage, small structures are eliminated while large ones remain.
3. Later, the reduced structures are enlarged until the large structures recover their original size.

From Figure 1.2, it is evident that for the elimination of small structures, it is only necessary to define two different operations: reduction and increment. Reduction allows the pixels of the last layer of the object that is in contact with the background to be eliminated (Figure 1.3). In the operation of increment, a layer of pixels (belonging to the background) is added to the structure in such a way that it grows in size (Figure 1.4).

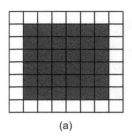 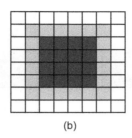 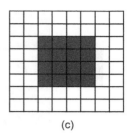

(a)   (b)   (c)

FIGURE 1.3
Reduction of a region through the removal of the pixel boundary structure. (a) Original image, (b) highlighting the boundary pixels, and (c) removal of frame boundary pixels.

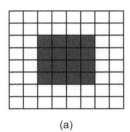 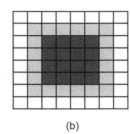 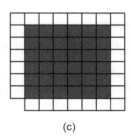

(a)   (b)   (c)

FIGURE 1.4
Incrementing the region of the image through the growth of the border of pixels of the structure that belongs to the background. (a) Original image, (b) highlighting the border of the structure that belongs to the background, and (c) final structure.

1.1.1 Neighborhood Types between Pixels

In both types of operations, it is necessary to determine the way in which two pixels establish a neighborhood relationship between them. Two types of neighborhoods can commonly be distinguished.

- **Neighborhood 4.** Under this approach, a neighborhood is considered to exist if a pixel is in direct relation to a neighboring pixel that is above, below, to the left, or to the right of the pixel in question (Figure 1.5a).
- **Neighborhood 8.** Under this approach, a neighborhood is considered to exist if a pixel, in addition to the relationships specified by neighborhood 4, also has a direct relationship with the pixels diagonal to it (Figure 1.5b).

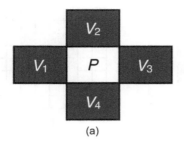 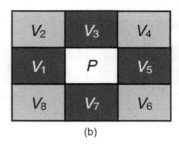

(a)   (b)

FIGURE 1.5
Definition of the neighborhood of a pixel P. (a) Neighborhood-4, defined on P and (b) neighborhood-8, defined on P.

1.2 Fundamental Morphological Operations

The operations of reduction and increment are two of the fundamental morphological operations performed by filters, which are closely related to the physical processes of erosion and dilation [2]. There is an interesting relationship between both processes and those described qualitatively in the last section. Since dilation is conceived as growth and erosion as the loss of area or volume, they would be perfect analogies of the operations. Under such conditions, it could be said that adding a layer of pixels to a structure in an image would dilate the structure, while removing a layer of pixels from a structure would erode it.

1.2.1 The Structure of Reference

Similar to the operation of a linear filter, it is necessary to define a matrix of coefficients for the operation of a morphological filter. Therefore, it is necessary to characterize a matrix called a reference structure. The reference structure contains only elements 0 and 1. The content of this structure can be defined as follows:

$$H(i, j) \in \{0, 1\} \tag{1.1}$$

This structure has, like the filter coefficient matrix, its own coordinate system, with the reference point (see Figure 1.6) at its origin.[1]

1.2.2 Point Set

For the formal description of morphological operations, it is more practical to describe images as sets whose elements can be referenced by two-dimensional coordinates. For example, a binary image $I(x, y)$ consists of a set of points

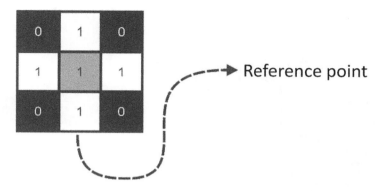

FIGURE 1.6
Example of a reference structure for binary morphological operations.

P_I with coordinate pairs corresponding to points whose pixel value is 1. This set can be defined as follows:

$$P_I = \{(x,y)\mid I(x,y)=1\} \tag{1.2}$$

As shown in Figure 1.7, not only an image but also a reference structure can be described by the set notation defined above.

Using this description, the operations performed on binary images can be defined in a simple way. For example, the inversion of a binary image that swaps pixel values from 1 to 0 and vice versa can be defined as the complement set, such that

$$P_{-I} = \overline{P_I} \tag{1.3}$$

where $-I$ defines the inverse of I. In the same way, if two binary images I_1 and I_2 are element by element, joined through the logical function OR, then the definition of this operation in set format can be expressed as follows:

$$P_{I_1 \cup I_2} = P_{I_1} \bigcup P_{I_2} \tag{1.4}$$

Due to the fact that the set notation is an alternative representation of binary operations, this notation is used alternately, taking into account the economy of the description and understanding of the operation, depending on the case. For example, the operation $I_1 \bigcup I_2$ will mean the same thing as $P_{I_1} \bigcup P_{I_2}$ or $\overline{P_1}$ and $\overline{P_2}$.

1.2.3 Dilation

Dilation is a morphological operation corresponding to the intuitive idea of growing or adding a layer of pixels to the structure of the image [3].

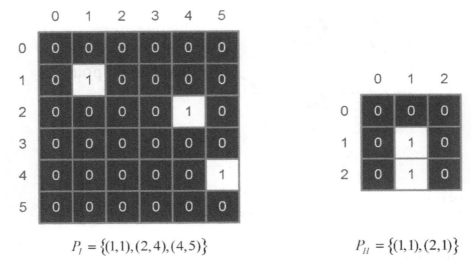

$$P_I = \{(1,1),(2,4),(4,5)\} \qquad\qquad P_{II} = \{(1,1),(2,1)\}$$

FIGURE 1.7
Description of a binary image *I* and a reference structure *H* as sets of coordinates P_I and P_H.

The specific growing mechanism is controlled by the reference structure. This operation is defined in the set notation as follows:

$$I \oplus H = \left\{ (x',y') = (x+i, y+j) \mid (x',y') \in P_1, (i,j) \in P_H \right\} \qquad (1.5)$$

As indicated by expression 1.5, the set of points that involves the dilation of an image *I* and its reference structure *H* is defined by all the possible combinations of the pairs of coordinates of the sets of points P_1 and P_H. The dilation operation could also be interpreted as the result of adding a set of pixels with value 1 to the image (P_1). The shape corresponding to the new layer of elements depends on the reference structure. This can be illustrated in Figure 1.8.

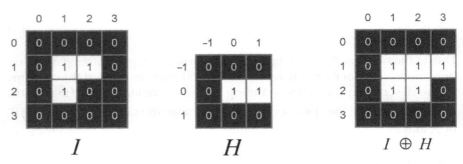

FIGURE 1.8
Example of dilation. The dilation operation is applied to the binary image *I*, using *H* as the reference structure. The structural element *H* is added to each pixel 1 of the image *I*.

1.2.4 Erosion

The quasi-inverse operation of dilation is erosion [4], which is expressed in set notation as follows:

$$I \ominus H = \left\{ (x',y') = (x'+i, y'+j) \in P_1(i,j), \forall(i,j) \in P_H \right\} \tag{1.6}$$

This formulation refers to the fact that for each point (x', y') in the image, the result involves the points for which all possible values $(x'+i, y'+j)$ are found in I. Figure 1.9 shows an example of the erosion performed between an image I and the reference structure H.

$$I \oplus H = \left\{ (1,1)+(0,0), (1,1)+(0,1), \right.$$

$$(1,2), (0,0)+(1,2)+(0,1),$$

$$\left. (2,1)+(0,0), (2,1)+(0,1) \right\}$$

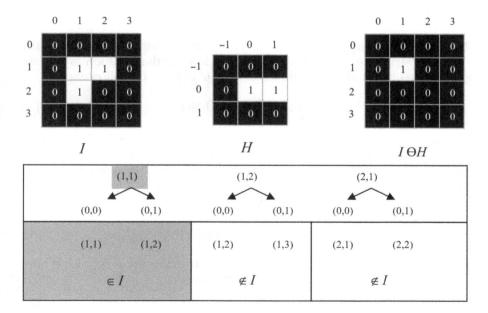

FIGURE 1.9
Example of erosion. The image I is eroded through the reference structure H. From this process, it can be seen how the pixel in I with coordinates (1,1), when it is added to the elements (0,0) and (0,1) of the reference structure, obtains. As a result, points (1,1) and (1, 2) are part of image I. Therefore, the outcome of the erosion will be one at position (1,1). For the other pixels of the image, this condition is not fulfilled.

This process can be interpreted as follows: A pixel (x', y') resulting from erosion is one whose reference structure centered on this pixel coincides in shape with the content of the image. Figure 1.9 shows how the reference structure centered on the pixel (1,1) of the image coincides in shape with the content of the image, so that the erosion result for this pixel is 1.

1.2.5 Properties of Dilatation and Erosion

The dilation and erosion operations cannot be considered inverse in the strict sense because it is not possible to completely reconstruct an eroded image through the successive application of dilations. The same applies in the opposite direction. However, they have a close, dual relationship. Since a dilation of the pixels with a value of 1 in an image can be carried out by eroding the background and adding pixels with a value of zero, this can be expressed as follows:

$$\overline{I} \ominus H = \overline{I \oplus H} \tag{1.7}$$

Dilation is also commutative, so it is valid to formulate:

$$I \oplus H = H \oplus I \tag{1.8}$$

Therefore, as in convolution, it is possible to interchange the image and the reference structure. From this property, it follows that dilation is also an associative operation. Due to this, it is valid to express the following:

$$(I_1 \oplus I_2) \oplus I_3 = I_1 \oplus (I_2 \oplus I_3) \tag{1.9}$$

The sequence in which the operations are performed is not relevant. This property is useful since, in this way, the reference structure can be divided into smaller structures in such a way that the speed of the complete operation is faster, as there are a smaller number of operations. Under such conditions, the dilation operation could be expressed as follows:

$$I \oplus H = ((I \oplus H_1) \oplus H_2) \tag{1.10}$$

where H_1 and H_2 correspond to the reference structures in which H has been divided. Erosion, however, is not commutative, so:

$$I \ominus H \neq H \ominus I \tag{1.11}$$

1.2.6 Design of Morphological Filters

Morphological filters are specified by defining two elements, the operation they perform (erosion or dilation), and their corresponding reference structure.

The size and shape of the reference structure are application-dependent. In practice, the reference structures shown in Figure 1.10 are the most frequently used. A disk-shaped reference structure with a radius r adds a layer of r pixels to objects in the image when it is used through the dilation operation. The opposite effect happens when the same structure is used with the erode operation, so in this case, a layer r of pixels is extracted from the objects in the image. Considering Figure 1.11a as the original image and Figure 1.11b as the reference structure, the results of the dilation and erosion of the image are obtained. They are shown in Figure 1.12, considering different values of r.

Other results of the morphological erosion and dilation operations for reference structures of different shapes are shown in Figure 1.13.

Different from spatial filters (Chapter 2), it is generally impossible to create two-dimensional isotropic[2] filters H from one-dimensional reference structures H_x and H_y. This is due to the fact that the morphological operation that is established between both reference structures always produces a new square reference structure and is, therefore, not isotropic.

The most commonly used method for the implementation of morphological filters in large dimensions is the iterative application of the same reference structure in small dimensions. Under such conditions, the result of one operation is again used to apply the operation with the same reference structure. This would give approximately the same result as if a large reference structure were used (see Figure 1.14).

(a)   (b)   (c)

FIGURE 1.10
Typical reference structures of different sizes. (a) 4-neighbor structure, (b) 8-neighbor structure, and (c) small disk structure.

 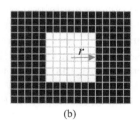

(a)   (b)

FIGURE 1.11
(a) Original image and (b) reference structure used in the examples to illustrate the effect of dilation and erosion for different values of r, where r defines the size of the disk.

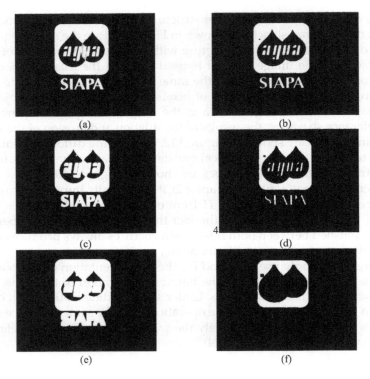

FIGURE 1.12
(a) Dilation at $r = 2$, (b) erosion at $r = 2$, (c) dilation $r = 5$, (d) erosion at $r = 5$, (e) dilation at $r = 10$, and (f) erosion at $r = 10$.

1.3 Edge Detection in Binary Images

A typical application of morphological operations is the extraction of the edges of the objects contained in a binary image [5]. The process for detection, which is described in Algorithm 1.1, begins with applying the morphological operation of erosion (1) to the image, using as a reference structure any of those defined in Figure 1.10. The objective of applying erosion is to remove from the original image the outer layer (edge) of objects within the image.

Then, the edge of the objects in the image can be found if, for the image that was eroded, its inverse is obtained (2). Therefore, we will have an image where the objects have a value of zero, while the background of the image and the edges of the objects are one. Therefore, if an AND operation is applied between the original image and the inverse (3) of the eroded version

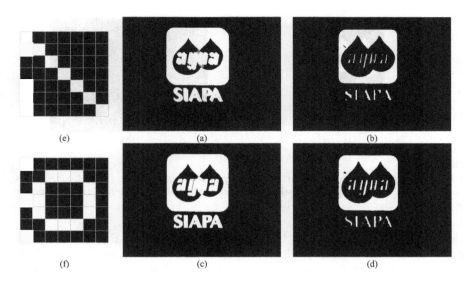

FIGURE 1.13
Binary dilation and erosion, considering the reference structures (e) and (f). (a) Dilation and (b) erosion using (e) with values of 1 on the main diagonal as reference structure and (c) dilation and (d) erosion using (f), a circular pattern as the reference structure.

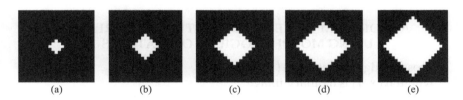

FIGURE 1.14
Operation of large filters by the iterative application of the operators on the image. (a) H, (b) $H \oplus H$, (c) $H \oplus H \oplus H$, (d) $H \oplus H \oplus H \oplus H$, and (e) $H \oplus H \oplus H \oplus H \oplus H$.

of the image, the edges of the objects are obtained. This result is because only common pixels between both images are considered. Figure 1.15 shows edge detection using Algorithm 1.1.

1.4 Combination of Morphological Operations

In practical image processing applications, dilation and erosion are used in most cases in different combinations. In this section, we consider three of the most common combinations of erosion and dilation, such as opening,

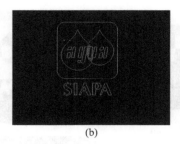

(a)   (b)

FIGURE 1.15
Edge detection using the erosion morphology operation. (a) Image I_{inv} (x, y) obtained from Algorithm 1.1, considering as original image Figure 1.11a and (b) image I_{border} (x, y), the edges obtained after executing Algorithm 1.1.

closing, and the hit-or-miss transformation [6]. Due to the quasi-duality existing between the morphological operations of dilation and erosion, they can be used in combination. Of the existing combinations, two are of special importance and have special names and symbols. These operations are called opening and closing.

**ALGORITHM 1.1.   EDGE DETECTION ALGORITHM
USING MORPHOLOGICAL OPERATIONS**

Erosion edge detection $(I_b(x, y))$
where $I_b(x, y)$ is a binary image

1. Erosion of $I_b(x, y)$ is done by using one of the following reference structures, obtaining I'.

$$I'(x, y) = I \ominus H$$

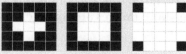

2. The image that was eroded is inverted:

$$I_{inv}(x, y) = \overline{I'(x, y)}$$

3. The AND operation is applied between $I_{inv}(x, y)$ and $I_b(x, y)$:

$$I_{borde}(x, y) = I_{inv}(x, y) \vee I_b(x, y)$$

1.4.1 Opening

The opening is defined as an erosion followed by a dilation, using the same reference structure for both operations [6]. The opening operation is defined as follows:

$$I \circ H = (I \ominus H) \oplus H \tag{1.12}$$

In the openening, the first operation (erosion) causes all the pixels in the image with a value of one (that are smaller than the reference structure) to be removed. Structures remaining in the image will, through dilation, be smoothed and enlarged to approximately equal to their original size (before applying erosion). Figure 1.16 shows the effect of the opening operation using a disk-shaped reference structure when considering different disk sizes r (see Figure 1.16b).

1.4.2 Closing

The sequence of dilation followed by erosion, using the same reference structure, is called the closing [6]. This operation is formally defined as follows:

$$I \bullet H = (I \oplus H) \ominus H \tag{1.13}$$

Through the closing operation, the holes detected inside the objects of the image, which are also smaller than the reference structure, are filled. Figure 1.16 shows the effect of the closing operation using a disk-shaped reference structure when considering different sizes of the disk r (see Figure 1.16b).

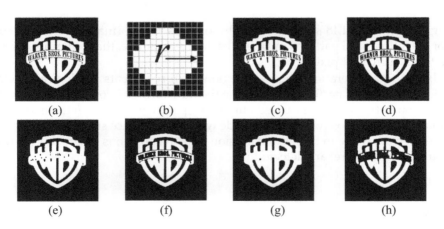

(a)   (b)   (c)   (d)

(e)   (f)   (g)   (h)

FIGURE 1.16
Effects of opening and closing operations with different sizes of the reference structure.
(a) Original image, (b) reference structure and the parameter r that modifies its size, (c) opening operation considering $r = 5$, (d) closing operation with $r = 5$, (e) opening for $r = 10$, (f) closing for $r = 10$, (g) opening for $r = 15$, and (h) closing for $r = 15$.

1.4.3 Properties of the Open and Close Operations

Both opening and closing operations are idempotent. This means that you could perform the operation multiple times and still get the same result as if you performed it just once, that is:

$$(I \circ H) \circ H = I \circ H$$
$$(I \bullet H) \bullet H = I \bullet H \tag{1.14}$$

Another important property that both operations possess is duality. This property means that an opening operation with values of one (1) is equivalent to applying the closing operation with values of zero (0). This is defined as follows:

$$I \circ H = \overline{\left(\overline{I} \bullet H \right)}$$
$$I \bullet H = \overline{\left(\overline{I} \circ H \right)} \tag{1.15}$$

1.4.4 The Hit-or-Miss Transformation

This transformation is useful for identifying certain pixel configurations. The hit-or-miss transform of I and H is denoted as $I \otimes H$. In the expression, H is a reference structure that involves a pair of reference structures $H = (H_1, H_2)$. The hit-or-miss transform is defined in terms of two reference structures as follows:

$$I \otimes H = (I \ominus H_1) \bigcap (I' \ominus H_2) \tag{1.16}$$

Figures 1.17 and 1.18 show how the hit-or-miss transformation can be used for detecting pixel patterns in an image. In this example, the configuration to detect is a cross of pixels.

In the final operation, the intersection ($\bigcap$) represents the logical AND operation. The name "hit-or-miss" that the transform has comes from the fact of the operations that are carried out in the operation. That is, in the first erosion (H_1), all the positions that coincide with the reference structure (success) are detected, while in the second erosion (H_1), the positions where there is no coincidence (failure) are detected.

1.5 Morphological Filters for Grayscale Images

Morphological operations are not restricted to their use with binary images but can be defined for grayscale images as well. All the morphological operations considered so far, with the exception of the hit-or-miss

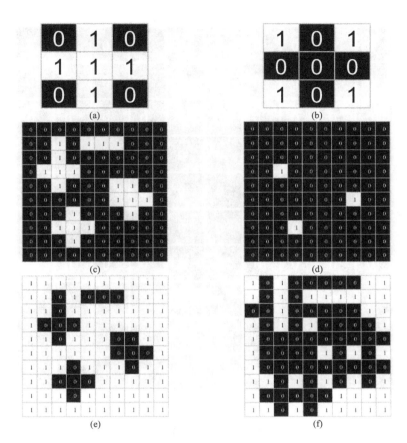

FIGURE 1.17
Illustration of the process of using the hit-or-miss transform. (a) Reference structure H_1, (b) reference structure H_1, (c) original image, (d) result of $I \ominus H_1$, (e) inverted original image I^c, and (f) the result of $I^c \ominus H_2$.

transformation, have natural extensions to grayscale images. Similarly, morphological operations can operate on color images by processing each plane as if it were an image of independent intensity. Although the morphological operations have the same name and use the same symbology, their definition for intensity images varies strongly compared to binary images.

1.5.1 Reference Structure

The first difference between morphological operations for the different image types is the reference structure. The reference structure not only represents a matrix of "ones" and "zeros" that describe the shape and dimension of the structure that will operate on the binary images, but now it is also a matrix

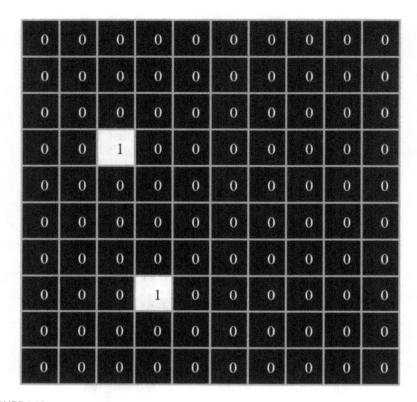

FIGURE 1.18

Result of the hit-or-miss transform $I \otimes H = (I \ominus H_1) \bigcap (I^c \ominus H_2)$ of Figure 1.17.

of coefficients "similar" to those defined by linear filters. Therefore, the reference structure is described as a two-dimensional function of real values defined as follows:

$$H(i, j) \in \mathbb{R} \tag{1.17}$$

The reference structure values $H(i, j)$ can be positive, negative, or zero. However, unlike the coefficient matrix of a spatial filter, the zeros also influence the final result of the calculation.

1.5.2 Dilation and Erosion for Intensity Images

The dilation for grayscale images ($\oplus$) is defined as the maximum of the sum produced by the values of the reference structure and the region of the image with which it corresponds. That is defined as follows:

$$(I \oplus H)(x, y) = \max_{(i,j) \in H} \{I(x + i, y + j) + H(i, j)\} \tag{1.18}$$

On the other hand, erosion is defined as the minimum of the subtraction operation between the values of the reference structure and the region of the image to which it corresponds. The operation can be formulated as follows:

$$(I \ominus H)(x,y) = \min_{(i,j)\in H}\{I(x+i,y+j) - H(i,j)\} \qquad (1.19)$$

Figure 1.19 shows an example of the effect of dilation on grayscale images. Figure 1.20 illustrates the result of applying the erosion operation. In both operations, it may happen that there are values outside the normal range used to represent the image data (0–255). If this situation happens, then its limit value is simply taken. Therefore, if the number is negative, the value of zero is considered as the result, and if the value of the operation is higher than 255, the result 255 is considered (this operation of considering limits is better known as "Clamping").

Dilation and erosion can be combined to produce a variety of effects. For example, subtracting the operation of the erosion version of an image from its dilated operation is called "morphological gradient." It is defined as follows:

$$\partial M = (I \oplus H) - (I \ominus H) \qquad (1.20)$$

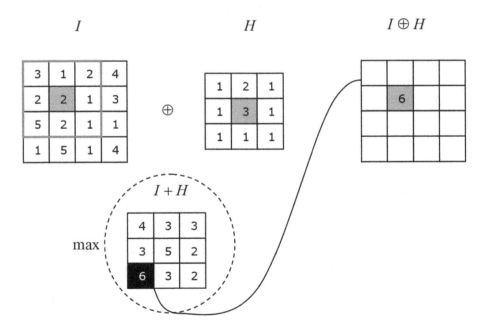

FIGURE 1.19
Dilation on grayscale images $I \oplus H$. The reference structure 3×3 is centered on image I. The values of the image are added element by element with the corresponding values of H, from the sum $I+H$. The maximum is chosen, which is considered the result of this process.

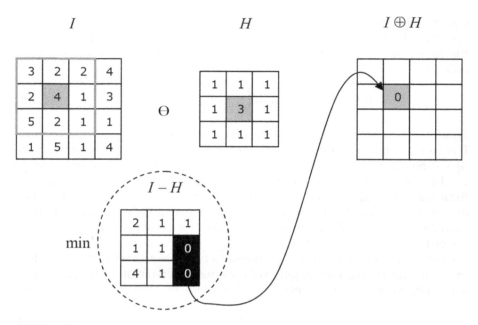

FIGURE 1.20

Dilation over grayscale images $I \ominus H$. The reference structure 3×3 is centered on the image I. The values of the image I are subtracted element by element from the corresponding values of H. From the subtraction $I - H$, the minimum is selected, which is considered as the result of this process.

Results of the morphological dilation and erosion operations on grayscale images are shown in Figure 1.21, also considering the operation of the morphological gradient.

1.5.3 Open and Close Operations with Grayscale Images

The expressions for opening and closing grayscale images have the same form as their binary counterparts. Both operations have a simple geometric interpretation. Figure 1.22 shows this interpretation considering an image profile (the grayscale values of a line). For the case of the opening operation, it is as if a horizontal structure (Figure 1.22b) would be added to the curve of Figure 1.22a that connects to the inside of the trace. As can be seen, the size of the structure does not allow it to fit within the presented peak in such a way that this maximum is eliminated as a result of the operation (Figure 1.22c).

In general, the opening operation is used to remove small peaks of light elements in the image, while the other gray levels remain practically unchanged.

Figure 1.22d gives an illustration of the closing operation. Note that, unlike the opening operation, the structure is placed in the profile at the top so that

(a)

(b)

(c)

(d)

FIGURE 1.21
Morphological operations performed on grayscale images. (a) Original image, (b) eroded image, (c) dilated image, and (d) morphological gradient.

the valleys, if they are smaller than the structure, will be filled. Figure 1.22e shows the result of the closing operation.

Contrary to the opening operation, the closing operation allows the cancellation of small, obscured values present in the image, which are smaller than the size of the used reference structure, leaving the other intensity values without significant change.

Because the opening operation suppresses bright details smaller than the reference structure and the closing operation removes dark artifacts, both operations are used in combination to smooth and denoise images.

The filter product of the combination of the opening and closing operations is called the opening and closing filter; such a filter has the ability to simultaneously remove bright and dark artifacts from images, similar to salt and pepper noise. In the filter operation, the grayscale image is opened (removing bright artifacts), and the result of this process is then closed (removing dark artifacts). Figure 1.23 shows the effect of the opening and closing operations on a grayscale image, to which salt and pepper-type noise was added. Likewise, the result of using the opening and closing filters is also shown.

Another way to use the opening and closing filters is to apply them repetitively, varying the size of the reference structure in each iteration.

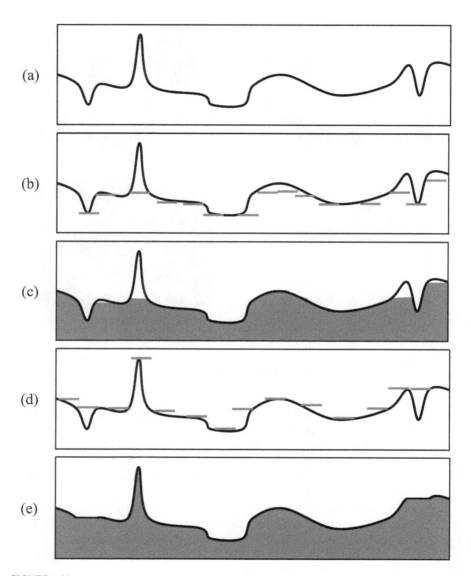

FIGURE 1.22
Interpretation of opening and closing operations on grayscale images. (a) Profile of a grayscale image, (b) application of the structure to the profile according to the opening, (c) result of the opening operation, (d) application of the structure to the profile according to the closing, and (e) result of the closing operation.

FIGURE 1.23
Results of the opening and closing operations on grayscale images. (a) Original image, (b) image with salt and pepper noise, (c) result of the opening operation on (b), (d) result of the closing operation on (b), and (e) result of the filter of opening and closing on (b).

This process is known as a 'sequential filter'. The effect of this filter on grayscale images allows for smoother results than those obtained by simply opening and closing the filter (Figure 1.24). Algorithm 1.2 shows the process of implementing the sequential filter.

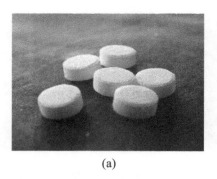
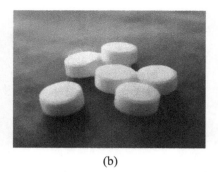

(a)   (b)

FIGURE 1.24
Effect of the sequential filter. (a) Original image and (b) the result of the filter, obtained from a repetition of three stages varying r from 1 to 3.

ALGORITHM 1.2   SEQUENTIAL FILTER

Sequential filter $\left(I(x,y)\right)$

Where $I(x,y)$ is an intensity image

1.   **for** r=1:t

2.   Opening operation $I_1 = I \bullet H$
3.   Closing operation $I_2 = I_1 \bullet H$
4. $I = I_2$
5.   end **for**
6.   The final result of the complete process is I

1.5.4 Top-Hat and Bottom-Hat Transformation

This operation is defined by the subtraction of the original grayscale image minus the opening of that image [7]. This operation can be defined as follows:

$$I_{TopH} = I - (I \circ H) \tag{1.21}$$

The operation takes its name from the shape of the reference structure in this operation, which, as Figure 1.25 shows, is similar to a hat.

This operation is useful for enhancing details in the presence of shadows. Figure 1.26 shows the result of this operation in images. The bottom-hat

1	1	1	1	1	1	1
1	1	1	1	1	1	1
0	0	1	1	1	0	0
0	0	1	1	1	0	0
0	0	1	1	1	0	0
0	0	1	1	1	0	0
0	0	1	1	1	0	0

FIGURE 1.25
Reference structure used in the top-hat transformation.

(a)   (b)

FIGURE 1.26
Result of the top-hat transformation. (a) Original image and (b) result of the top-hat transformation.

operation is defined as the subtraction between the closure of an image and the original image, such that:

$$I_{BottomH} = (I \circ H) - I \qquad (1.22)$$

1.6 MATLAB Functions for Morphological Operations

MATLAB® has a large number of functions that allow the implementation of most of the morphological operations discussed in this chapter [8]. This section explains one by one the functions that allow executing morphological operations as well as some auxiliary functions.

1.6.1 Strel Function

All morphological operations perform their function on images using a structural element called the reference structure. MATLAB has the `strel` function, which allows building reference structures of different sizes and shapes. Its basic syntax is:

```
esref=strel (shape, parameters);
```

where `shape` is a string chain that specifies the shape to implement, of which there are several predefined options, while `parameters` is a list of data that specifies the properties of the form. For example, `strel('disk', 3)` returns a disk-shaped reference structure with dimension ±3 pixels. Table 1.1 summarizes the shapes and parameters that the `strel` function can implement.

In this chapter, the property of dividing a reference structure into several parts has been considered to implement the morphological operation of dilation when a large-dimensional reference structure is involved. In order to speed up the execution of operations when using morphological functions, `strel` produces a set of composite reference structures that allow an associative representation of a large reference structure.

If we consider the case previously treated as an example, we have:

```
>> esref=strel ('disk',3)

esref =

Flat STREL object containing 25 neighbors.
Decomposition: 6 STREL objects containing a total of 14
neighbors
Neighborhood:
    1       1       1       1       1
    1       1       1       1       1
    1       1       1       1       1
    1       1       1       1       1
    1       1       1       1       1
```

From the above, it can be seen that `esref` is not considered as a normal array but as a special structure called a `strel` object. This object includes different elements. The `Neighborhood` element is an array of ones and zeros that defines the reference structure. Another element reports the number of elements contained in the structure, which in this case is 25. An important part of the object is the number of elements into which the reference structure can be divided (in the case of this example, it is 6). Therefore, if these elements are associated, they could formulate a larger reference structure. Within the `strel` object, there is a set of ones (14 elements) present in the structures into which the reference structure has been decomposed. Table 1.1 describes the shapes and structures that can be implemented using the MATLAB `strel` function.

TABLE 1.1

Shapes and Structures That Can Be Implemented Using the MATLAB® `strel` Function

Syntax	Description
`esref=strel('diamond',r)`	Creates a diamond-shaped structure, where the value of *r* specifies the distance from the end of the shape to the center

`esref=strel('disk',r)`	Create a disk-shaped structure where *r* specifies the radius of the disk

`esref=strel('line',long,grad)`	Constructs a structure in the form of a line, where the parameter long represents the length of the line, while deg defines the direction of the line

`esref=strel('octagon',r)`	Create an octagonal frame, where *r* specifies the distance from the center to one of the sides

`esref=strel('square',w)`	Create a square structure of width defined by *w*

(Continued)

TABLE 1.1 (*Continued*)

Shapes and Structures That Can Be Implemented Using the MATLAB® `strel` Function

Syntax	Description
esref=strel('arbitrary', Matriz)	Constructs a structure of an arbitrary shape defined by an array whose elements are "zeroes" and "ones"

The `whos` command delivers the number of variables that are present in the MATLAB environment. When this command is applied after inquiring about the components of `esref`, six elements are displayed. They represent the elements used to decompose the final structure. These commands are as follows:

```
>> components=getsequence(esref);
>> whos
Name                Size        Bytes       Class       Attributes
    components      6x1         1870        strel
    esref           1x1         2599        strel
```

```
>> components(1)
ans =
Flat STREL object containing 3 neighbors.
Neighborhood:
     1
     1
     1
```

1.6.2 MATLAB Functions for Dilation and Erosion

The `imdilate` function implements the dilation operation, and its basic syntax is as follows:

```
IR=imdilate(I,H)
```

where *I* is the image to which the dilation is applied using *H* as the reference structure. *IR* is the dilated image. If *I* is a binary image, then *IR* will also be binary, while if *I* is an image of intensity *IR*, it will be too. Therefore, by using the same function, we can perform this operation for binary images and for grayscale images. The reference structure *H* can be obtained by using the strel function.

The imerode function implements the erosion operation, and its basic syntax is as follows:

```
IR=imerode(I,H)
```

where *I* is the image to which the erosion is applied using *H* as the reference structure. *IR* is the eroded image. If *I* is a binary image, then *IR* will also be binary, while if *I* is an image of *IR* intensity, it will be too.

In order to show how to use the dilation and erosion functions, an example has been conducted. In this example, the morphological gradient (Section 1.5.2) of a grayscale image is implemented. Assuming that *I* is the image from which you want to extract the morphological gradient, the following commands are used:

```
>>H=strel('square',3);
>>I1=imdilate(I,H);
>>I2=imerode(I,H);
>>IG=I1-I2;
```

where *H* is the reference structure that is generated considering a square shape of dimension 3. When dilation and erosion are obtained using the same image and the same reference structure, a subtraction is produced between the dilated and eroded versions of the image, thus finding the morphological gradient of *I*.

1.6.3 MATLAB Functions Involving the Open and Close Operations

The imopen and imclose functions implement the opening and closing operations. The basic syntaxes of these functions are as follows:

```
IR=imopen(I,H)
IR=imclose(I,H)
```

where *I* is the image to which the opening or closing is applied using *H* as a reference structure. *IR* is the resulting image, if *I* is a binary image, then the result *IR* is binary, while if *I* is a grayscale image, the resulting *IR* element is also an intensity image. The reference structure *H* can be obtained by using the strel function.

1.6.4 The Transformation of Success or Failure ('Hit-or-Miss')

In the hit-or-miss transformation (Section 1.4.4), a reference structure composed of two elements (H_1 and H_2) is used. Under such conditions, the hit-or-miss transformation is defined as follows:

$$I \otimes H = (I \ominus H_1) \bigcap (I^c \ominus H_2) \qquad (1.23)$$

The image processing toolbox implements the hit-or-miss transform using the bwhitmiss function, whose syntax is described by:

```
IR=bwhitmiss(I, H1, H2);
```

where *IR* is the image obtained as a result of this transformation, while H_1 and H_2 are the reference structures described in Equation 1.19.

1.6.5 The bwmorph Function

The bwmorph function implements a variety of useful operations based on combinations of dilations and erosions. The basic syntax of this function is:

```
IR= bwmorph(I, operación, n);
```

where IR is a binary image. operation is a string element that specifies the operation to be performed. n is a positive integer that indicates the number of times the operation is repeated. The term n is optional, and when it is omitted, it means that the operation is performed only once. Table 1.2 describes the set of operations that can be executed under the bwmorph function. Several of these operations have already been discussed in this chapter. The bwmorph function can also be considered as a function that quickly implements several morphological operations without the need to separately build the reference structure. Conversely, in the case of erosion and dilation, the operations are performed, defining explicitly the reference structure.

1.6.6 Labeling of Convex Components

The convex components are all the pixels that have a binary value of one and are connected to each other based on some neighborhood criterion. Each of the detected objects forms regions that are assigned a unique label that identifies them.

The algorithms for labeling are mainly based on a connectivity criterion. The types of connectivity are three: connectivity-4, connectivity-8, and diagonal connectivity. In connectivity-4, the pixel (P0) is 4-connected (Figure 1.27a) if that pixel has one as a neighbor on the top (P2), bottom (P7), right side (P5), or left side (P4). On the other hand, a pixel is 8-connected (Figure 1.27b) if the pixel (P0) has a neighbor located diagonally (in addition to the positions in

TABLE 1.2

Different Operations That Can Be Implemented Using the MATLAB® Function
`bwmorph`

Operation	Description
`bothat`	Performs the bottom-hat operation using a reference structure of size 3×3. This function uses imbohat to perform the operation

`bridge`	Connect pixels that are separated by gaps of one pixel

`clean`	Removes lone pixels contained in the image

`diag`	Fill the pixels around diagonally connected white pixels to remove the connectivity of the background pixels

(*Continued*)

TABLE 1.2 (*Continued*)

Different Operations That Can Be Implemented Using the MATLAB® Function
bwmorph

Operation	Description
fill	It fills the gaps present in the structures of objects present in images

Operation	Description
hbreak	It removes the *H* structures of objects from the image so that a greater number of objects can exist in this way

Operation	Description
majority	Set the pixel to "one" if more than 4 pixels within a neighborhood of 3 × 3 are "ones"

Operation	Description
remove	Sets the pixel to zero if the 4-connected pixels are "ones"

(*Continued*)

TABLE 1.2 (*Continued*)

Different Operations That Can Be Implemented Using the MATLAB® Function
`bwmorph`

Operation	Description
`shrink`	If n=inf, the objects are reduced to points. Objects without holes are reduced to points, while objects with holes form rings. This operation maintains the Euler number

`skel`	If n=inf remove all pixels, reducing them to their lowest expression, lines. This process is called skeletonization

`thicken`	Add pixels to objects, only placing pixels that are connected

(*Continued*)

TABLE 1.2 *(Continued)*

Different Operations That Can Be Implemented Using the MATLAB® Function
bwmorph

Operation	Description
thin	Reduce objects without holes to lines and with holes to rings

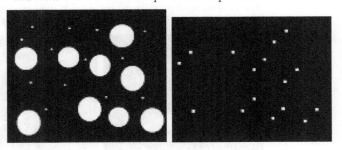

Operation	Description
tophat	Performs the bottom-hat operation using a reference structure of size 3 × 3. This function uses imbohat to perform the operation

P1	P2	P3		P1	P2	P3		P1	P2	P3
P4	P0	P5		P4	P0	P5		P4	P0	P5
P6	P7	P8		P6	P7	P8		P6	P7	P8
(a)				(b)				(c)		

FIGURE 1.27

Neighborhood criteria between pixels. (a) 4-Connected neighborhood, (b) 8-connected neighborhood, and (c) diagonally connected.

the 4-connected neighborhood), these diagonal elements include (P1), (P3), (P6), and (P8). Figure 1.27c shows the diagonal connectivity.

The neighborhood criterion has a great implication for the result of the detected objects in the image. Figure 1.28 illustrates the difference in object labeling depending on the neighborhood criterion. Figure 1.28a shows the

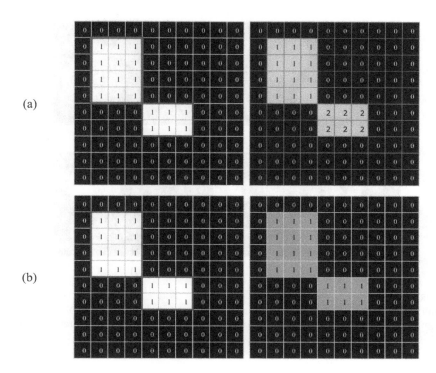

FIGURE 1.28
Object labeling results when considering different neighborhood criteria. (a) Result when it is considered a 4-connected neighborhood and (b) result when it is considered the 8-connected neighborhood.

objects found when the 4-connected neighborhood is used, while Figure 1.28b shows the result when the criterion used is 8-connected. As can be seen from both figures, it is clear that when the 4-connected criterion is used, there will be more objects since the connection criterion between objects will be more restrictive. On the other hand, in the case of 8-connected, the neighborhood criterion presents more flexibility, being able to absorb pixels and consider two objects as one.

MATLAB's image processing toolbox has the bwlabel function, which labels the detected elements with certain connectivity in an image. The syntax of this function is:

```
[L, num]=bwlabel(I, con);
```

where I is a binary image that contains the identified objects to be labeled. con specifies the type of neighborhood criterion considered (4 or 8). L is an array that contains the labeled elements, while num (this parameter is optional) specifies the number of objects contained in the image. If the value

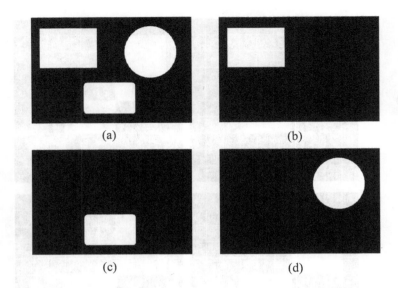

FIGURE 1.29
Result of the application of the bwlabel function for the labeling of objects. (a) Original binary image from which we want to detect the objects, (b) result of using $L = 1$, (c) result of using $L = 2$, and (d) result of using $L = 3$.

of con is omitted, the default connectivity of 8-connected is considered. The objects contained in L are labeled from one to the number of the object found n.

If Figure 1.29a is considered the binary image to be labeled, the result of applying the bwlabel function is three different objects or labels. To select each of the contained labels, a logic function can be used that allows obtaining the label in question. For example, to select label 2, we consider the following commands:

```
L=bwlabel(I,4);
I2=L==2;
```

After these commands, it is possible to observe the image shown in Figure 1.29c.

Notes

1. It is called the reference point because it is not necessarily the center, unlike the coefficient matrix of a filter.
2. Invariant to rotation.

References

[1] Jain, A. K. (1989). *Fundamentals of digital image processing*. Prentice Hall.

[2] Dougherty, E. R., & Lotufo, R. A. (2003). *Hands-on morphological image processing* (Vol. 59). SPIE press.

[3] Soille, P. (1999). *Morphological image analysis: Principles and applications* (Vol. 2, No. 3, pp. 170–171). Berlin: Springer.

[4] Serra, J., & Soille, P. (Eds.). (2012). *Mathematical morphology and its applications to image processing* (Vol. 2). Springer Science & Business Media.

[5] Gonzalez, R. C., & Woods, R. E. (2008). *Digital image processing* (3rd ed.). Prentice Hall.

[6] Soille, P. (2004). Opening and closing. In *Morphological image analysis: Principles and applications* (pp. 105–137). Springer, Berlin, Heidelberg. https://doi.org/10.1007/978-3-662-05088-0_4. Print ISBN 978-3-642-07696-1

[7] Kushol, R., Kabir, M. H., Salekin, M. S., & Rahman, A. A. (2017). Contrast enhancement by top-hat and bottom-hat transform with optimal structuring element: Application to retinal vessel segmentation. In Image analysis and recognition: 14th international conference, ICIAR 2017, *Montreal, QC*, Canada, July 5–7, 2017, *Proceedings 14* (pp. 533–540). Springer International Publishing.

[8] Gonzalez, R. C., Woods, R. E., & Eddins, S. L. (2004). *Digital image processing using MATLAB*. Prentice Hall.

2

Color Images

2.1 RGB Images

The RGB color model is based on the combination of the primary colors red **(R)**, green **(G)**, and blue **(B)** [1]. The origin of this model is in television technology and can be considered the fundamental representation of color in computers, digital cameras, and scanners, as well as in image storage [2]. Most image processing and rendering programs use this model for internal color representation.

The RGB model is an additive color format, which means that the combination of colors is based on the addition of the individual components with black as the base. This process can be understood as the overlapping of three light rays of red, green, and blue colors that are directed toward a white sheet of paper and whose intensity can be continuously controlled [3]. The intensity of the different color components determines both the resulting color hue and illumination. White and gray or levels of gray are produced in the same way through the combination of the three corresponding RGB primary colors.

The RGB model forms a cube whose coordinate axes correspond to the three primary colors R, G, and B. RGB values are positive, and their values are restricted to the interval $[0, V_{max}]$, where normally $[0, V_{max}] = 255$. Each possible C_i color corresponds to a point inside the RGB cube, with the components:

$$C_i = (R_i, G_i, B_i) \tag{2.1}$$

where $0 \leq R, G, B \leq V_{max}$. Normally, the range of values of the color components is normalized in the interval [0,1] in such a way that the color space would be represented by the unit cube shown in Figure 2.1. Point $N = (0,0,0)$ corresponds to black, $W = (1,1,1)$ corresponds to white, and all points on the line between **S** and **W** are the grayscale hues where the R, G, and B components have the same value.

Figure 2.2 shows a color image, which will be used as a test image several times in the chapter. In the same way, the respective RGB components of the image are also shown in Figure 2.2.

  DOI: 10.1201/9781032662466-2

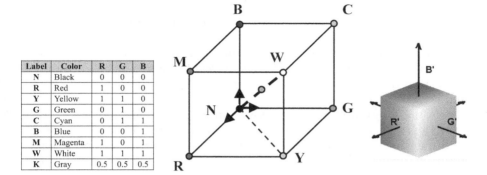

Label	Color	R	G	B
N	Black	0	0	0
R	Red	1	0	0
Y	Yellow	1	1	0
G	Green	0	1	0
C	Cyan	0	1	1
B	Blue	0	0	1
M	Magenta	1	0	1
W	White	1	1	1
K	Gray	0.5	0.5	0.5

FIGURE 2.1

Representation of the RGB color space as a unit cube. The primary colors red (R), green (G), and blue (B) constitute the coordinate axes. The individual colors red (R), green (G) and blue (B), cyan (C), magenta (M), and yellow (Y) are located in the corners of the color cube. All gray intensity values, such as (K), are located on the diagonal drawn from (N) to (W).

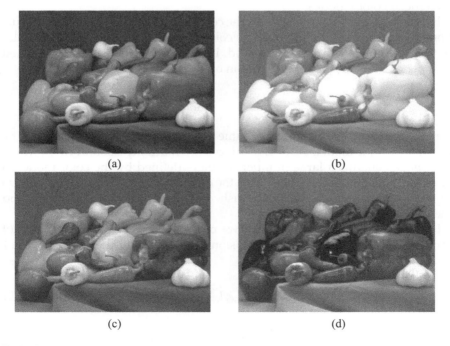

FIGURE 2.2

Color image in the RGB model and its respective planes *R*, *G*, and *B*. (a) RGB image, (b) plane *R*, (c) plane *G*, and (d) plane *B*. From the analysis of the different planes, it should be noted that peppers with a high red content acquire large (bright) values in the *R* plane.

RGB is a very simple color model. It is sufficient for color processing or when it is necessary to transform to a different color model, as will be seen later. For now, problems such as the correspondence between an RGB pixel and its true color or the meaning of the physical representation of the primary colors red, green, or blue will not be considered. Interesting details relating to color and the CIE color space will be covered later.

From the programmer point of view, an RGB color image is an array of size $M \times N \times 3$, where $M \times N$ defines the dimensions of the planes, while the dimension corresponding to 3 defines each of them R, G, and B. Based on the above, an RGB image can be considered an array of three grayscale images [4].

2.1.1 Composition of Color Images

Color images are characterized, like grayscale images, as pixel arrays, where different types of models can be used to compose the different color components that together form the total color. Two types of color images can be distinguished: the so-called full-color images and the so-called indexed or referenced color palettes.

Full-color images completely use the color space. That is, for their construction, the entire space defined for the color model is used for the representation of the image. On the other hand, indexed color images use a reduced number of colors in the representation of the image.

2.1.2 Full-Color Images

A pixel in a full-color image can assume any value in the space defined in the referenced color model. Full-color images are normally used in cases where the image contains a large number of colors defined by the color model in question, such as photographs [5]. In the composition of the color image, two types of associations can be distinguished: the composition of the planes and the composition of the packaging.

By the composition of the planes, we mean the separation of the different arrangements with the same dimension that constitute the image. A color image

$$I = (I_R, I_G, I_B) \tag{2.2}$$

can be considered as a related set of images of intensity $I_R(x,y)$, $I_G(x,y)$ and $I_B(x,y)$ (see Figure 2.3), where the RGB value of a pixel of the color image is obtained by accessing each of the arrays that constitute the combination in the form:

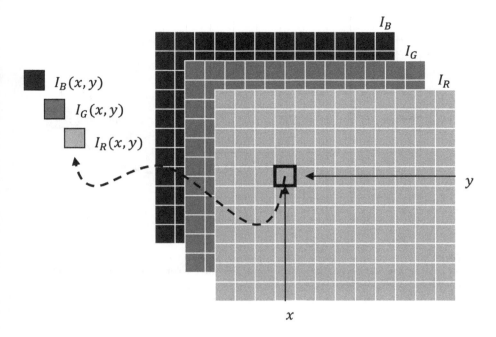

FIGURE 2.3
Composition of an RGB color image. Color or plane components are in separate arrays of the same dimension.

$$
\begin{pmatrix} R \\ G \\ B \end{pmatrix} = \begin{pmatrix} I_R(x,y) \\ I_G(x,y) \\ I_B(x,y) \end{pmatrix} \tag{2.3}
$$

The composition of the packing refers to the way in which the color components represent an individual pixel and the way in which it is stored in the structure (see Figure 2.4). That is:

$$
I(x,y) = (R,G,B) \tag{2.4}
$$

The values of the RGB color components can be obtained from a packed image at position (x,y) through access to the individual components of the color pixels, as

$$
\begin{pmatrix} R \\ G \\ B \end{pmatrix} \rightarrow \begin{pmatrix} R(I(x,y)) \\ G(I(x,y)) \\ B(I(x,y)) \end{pmatrix} \tag{2.5}
$$

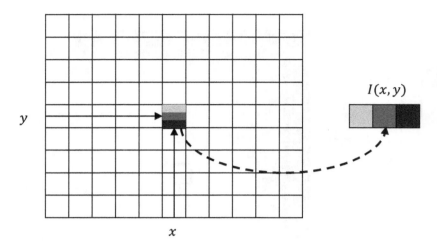

FIGURE 2.4
RGB color image and packaging composition. The three-color components R, G, and B are embedded in a single array.

where $R(I(x,y))$, $G(I(x,y))$ and $B(I(x,y))$ represent the color plane access functions.

2.1.3 Indexed Images

An indexed image can contain a restricted number of colors, making this type of image attractive for the representation of graphics or images of the GIF or PNG type, which are characterized by being light from the point of view of storage [5]. An indexed image has two components: a data array and a color map. The color map is a matrix of dimensions $n \times 3$. The length n of the palette is equal to the number of colors that it defines. They refer to the colors used to define the images. At the same time, each column specifies the value of the RGB color components defined in that line. Considering the above, an indexed image uses a direct mapping of the intensity pixels contained in the data matrix to the values contained by the color palette. The color of each pixel is determined by the integer value of the data array, which will actually be the index pointing to the colormap.

An indexed image is stored using the data array and the palette that defines its contained colors. This is important as the values contained in the data array have no meaning in the absence of the color palette. Figure 2.5 shows the relationship between the data matrix and the color palette.

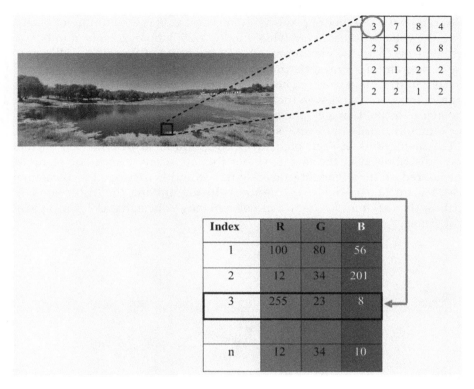

FIGURE 2.5
Relationship between the data matrix and the color map for the formation of indexed color images.

2.2 Histogram of an RGB Image

Histograms are distributions that describe the frequency with which the values contained in the image occur [6]. Each value of the histogram is defined as

$h(i)$ = the number of pixels in the image with the defined value i

for all $0 \leq i < K$ values, where K is the maximum permissible value to describe the data present in the image. This is formally expressed as follows[1]:

$$h(i) = \text{card}\left\{(u,v) \mid I(u,v) = i\right\}$$

$h(0)$ is then the number of pixels with the value 0, $h(1)$ the number of pixels with the value 1, successively, while finally, $h(255)$ represents the number of white pixels (with the maximum value of intensity) of the image. Although the histogram of a grayscale image considers all color components, errors present in the image may not be considered. For example, the lightness histogram may look good even though some of the color planes present inconsistencies. In RGB images, the blue plane usually contributes very little to the total luminosity of the grayscale image calculated from the color image.

The histograms of each plane also give additional information on the color distribution in the image. Under this approach, each color plane is considered an independent grayscale image and is displayed in the same way. Figure 2.6 shows the h_{Lum} lightness histogram and the histograms of each of the different h_R, h_G and h_B color planes, concatenated for a typical RGB image.

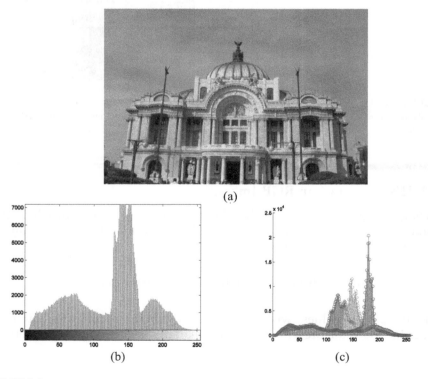

(a)

(b)   (c)

FIGURE 2.6
Histogram for RGB images. (a) Original image, (b) luminosity histogram (histogram of the grayscale version of the RGB image), and (c) concatenated histograms of the different R, G, and B planes.

2.2.1 Histogram of RGB Images in MATLAB

When analyzing RGB images, it is particularly important to be able to display the color content, characterized as the distribution of the data contained in each of the different R, G, and B planes. The traditional way of performing this task would be to find the histogram of each one of the planes, just as if it were an image of intensity. However, although this process allows us to find out important characteristics of the color distribution, it is not possible to adequately observe this distribution so that the contents of the different planes can be compared. Therefore, it is suggested to perform a function that allows the histogram of the different planes to be graphed in a concatenated manner. Program 2.1 shows the configuration of this function.

> **PROGRAM 2.1   THE PROGRAM IN MATLAB**
> **TO PLOT THE HISTOGRAM OF THE *R*, *G*, AND**
> ***B* PLANES IN AN INTERCALATED WAY**
>
> ```
> %%%%%%%%%%%%%%%%%%%%%%%%%%%%%%%%%%%%%%%%%%%%%%%%%%%%%%%%%%%%
> %Function that allows graphing the histograms of
> %the different planes R, G and B in a concatenated way
> %%%%%%%%%%%%%%%%%%%%%%%%%%%%%%%%%%%%%%%%%%%%%%%%%%%%%%%%%%%%
> function varargout = rgbhist(I)
> %It is verified that image I is
> %RGB, that is, that it has 3 planes
> if (size(I, 3) ~= 3)
>     error('The image must be RGB')
> end
> %256 values are set representing
> %the allowable data type depth
> nBins = 256;
> %Find the histograms for each plane R G B
> rHist = imhist(I(:,:,1), nBins);
> gHist = imhist(I(:,:,2), nBins);
> bHist = imhist(I(:,:,3), nBins);
> %the graphic object is created
> figure
> hold on
> %Histogram information is displayed.
> h(1) = stem(1:256, rHist);
> h(2) = stem(1:256 + 1/3, gHist);
> h(3) = stem(1:256 + 2/3, bHist);
> %A color is established for each of them
> %that correspond to the value they represent.
> set(h(1), 'color', [1 0 0])
> set(h(2), 'color', [0 1 0])
> set(h(3), 'color', [0 0 1])
> ```

2.3 Color Models and Color Space Conversions

The RGB color model, from the programmer perspective, is a simple way of representing data, which is totally oriented to the way colors are displayed on a computer. Although the RGB model is very simple, it hardly considers how colors are captured, in addition to being highly sensitive to changes in lighting [7].

Because important color characteristics such as hue, lighting, and others are implicitly defined in the RGB model, it makes it difficult to consider these factors in images that are specified in this color model. Alternative models such as HSV facilitate the characterization of these properties since, in HSV, features such as saturation, lightness, and hue are explicitly found as parts of the model.

Figure 2.7 shows, as an example, the distribution of colors in an image in the RGB and HSV color models. The description of their relationships, common characteristics, and differences will be discussed later.

2.3.1 Converting an RGB Image to Grayscale

The conversion from an RGB image to a grayscale is done through a calculation that results from considering an equivalent combination of the values

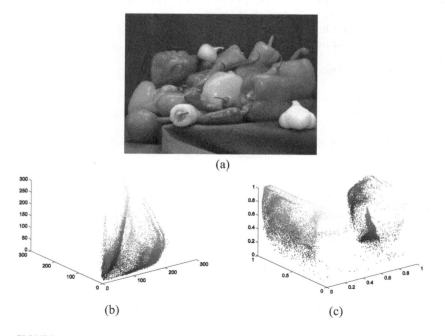

FIGURE 2.7
Color distributions of an image in different color models. (a) Original image, (b) distribution in the RGB model, and (c) distribution in the HSV model.

contained in each color plane that constitutes it. In its simplest form, this equivalent value could be established as the average of the values of the three-color components, such that:

$$E_p(x,y) = \frac{R(x,y) + G(x,y) + B(x,y)}{3} \tag{2.6}$$

The subjective lighting, typical of the RGB model, makes images with a large value in the red and/or green component have a dark appearance (in the grayscale image converted by Equation 2.6). The opposite effect occurs in those pixels where the content of the blue plane is large, showing a lighter appearance in its grayscale version. In order to solve this problem, it is considered as a better approximation to Equation 2.6 to calculate a linear combination of all the planes, defined as follows:

$$E_{lin}(x,y) = w_R R(x,y) + w_G G(x,y) + w_B B(x,y) \tag{2.7}$$

where w_R, w_G, and w_B are the coefficients that define the transformation, which according to the criteria used in TV for color signals are considered as follows:

$$w_R = 0.299 \quad w_G = 0.587 \quad w_B = 0.114 \tag{2.8}$$

Another suggested alternative in ITU-BT.709 for digital color coding considers:

$$w_R = 0.2125 \quad w_G = 0.7154 \quad w_B = 0.072 \tag{2.9}$$

Being formal, Equation 2.6 can be considered a special case of Equation 2.7.

An important consideration is the Gamma distortion produced in the TV signals that affect in a non-linear way, making the values shown in Equations 2.8 and 2.9 not correct. In numerous works, this problem is faced by defining the weights of the linear transformation as follows:

$$w_R = 0.309 \quad w_G = 0.609 \quad w_B = 0.082 \tag{2.10}$$

2.3.2 RGB Images without Color

Sometimes it is important to represent grayscale images in RGB format, mainly when you want to highlight some region of intensity with a color that contrasts and identifies. To generate this type of image, the grayscale value obtained (by using one of the models listed in Equations 2.6–2.10) is assigned to each of the planes in such a way that:

$$R(x,y) = E(x,y)$$

$$G(x,y) = E(x,y) \qquad (2.11)$$

$$B(x,y) = E(x,y)$$

2.3.3 Reducing Saturation of a Color Image

To reduce the saturation of an RGB image, the grayscale image is extracted, and a linear interpolation is performed on the differences between the color plane and the intensity version. Such a process can be expressed as follows:

$$\begin{pmatrix} R_D(x,y) \\ G_D(x,y) \\ B_D(x,y) \end{pmatrix} = \begin{pmatrix} E(x,y) \\ E(x,y) \\ E(x,y) \end{pmatrix} + Fac \cdot \begin{pmatrix} R(x,y) - E(x,y) \\ G(x,y) - E(x,y) \\ B(x,y) - E(x,y) \end{pmatrix} \qquad (2.12)$$

where $Fac \in [0,1]$ is a factor that controls the result obtained. The gradual increase in Fac characterizes the desaturation of the color image. A value of $Fac = 0$ removes each coloration and produces an image of intensity; with a value of $Fac = 1$, the plane values remain unchanged. Figure 2.8 shows examples of color images that have had their saturation reduced using different values of the factor Fac.

2.3.4 HSV and HSL Color Model

In the HSV color model, color information is represented through three components: Tonality (Hue), Saturation (Saturation), and Value (Value). This color model is also known as HSV and is mainly used by Adobe products [8]. The HSV model is traditionally represented through an inverted pyramid (Figure 2.9), where the vertical axis represents the value (V), the horizontal distance taking the V-axis as a reference corresponds to the saturation, and the angle that is established as a point of rotation by the V-axis defines the tonality. The point that corresponds to black in the HSV model is located at the peak of the inverted pyramid, and the point that corresponds to white is located in the central part of the base of the pyramid. The three basic colors, red, green, and blue, and their respective combinations of yellow, cyan, and magenta, are distributed at the base of the pyramid.

The HSL color model (Hue, Luminance, and Saturation, "Hue," "Luminance," "Saturation") is very similar to the HSV model, even identical in the Hue value. The luminance and saturation parameters correspond to the vertical axis and the radius that is established between the luminance axis and the value of the color in question. Despite the similarity of both models, the way of calculating the value of the parameters is very different

(a) (b)

(c) (d)

FIGURE 2.8
Saturation reduction in color images. (a) Original image, (b) image with *Fac* = 0, (c) image with *Fac* = 0.2, and (d) image with *Fac* = 0.5.

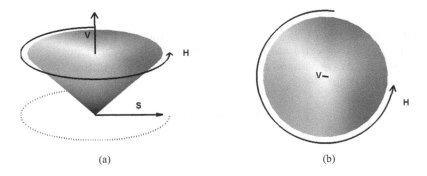

(a) (b)

FIGURE 2.9
HSV color model. (a) Color model and (b) the base of the pyramid.

(with the exception of *S*). The representation of this HSL model that is commonly found is that of the double pyramid (Figure 2.10), where the black and white points in this model are located at the bottom and top of both pyramids. The basic colors red, green, and blue, as well as their combinations, are located at the base where both pyramids meet.

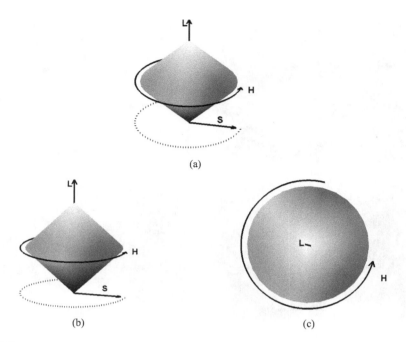

FIGURE 2.10
HSL color model. (a) HSL model in top perspective, (b) HSL model in front perspective, and
(c) base of both pyramids of the HSL model.

2.3.5 Conversion from RGB to HSV

For the conversion of the RGB to HSV color model, the values of the RGB
color planes are determined, which are typically between 0 and 255. The calculations for the conversion consider the following procedure.

Assuming that:

$$C = \max(R, G, B)$$

$$C = \min(R, G, B) \tag{2.13}$$

$$C_{dif} = C_{max} - C_{min}$$

If all the *R*, *G*, and *B* color components have the same value, then it is a grayscale element. Considering this C_{dif} so $S = 0$, with this, the value of the hue is
indeterminate.

If the values of the color planes are normalized such that:

$$R' = \frac{C_{max} - R}{C_{dif}} \quad G' = \frac{C_{max} - G}{C_{dif}} \quad B' = \frac{C_{max} - B}{C_{dif}} \tag{2.14}$$

Depending on which of the color planes has a higher value, an auxiliary variable H' can be calculated such that:

$$H' = \begin{cases} B' - G', & \text{if } R = C_{max} \\ R' - B' + 2, & \text{if } G = C_{max} \\ G' - R' + 4, & \text{if } B = C_{max} \end{cases} \tag{2.15}$$

The resulting value of H' is in the interval from [–1 to 5], for which it will be necessary to normalize this variable, whose auxiliary represents the tonality, so that its interval is from 0 to 1. Under such conditions, the following process is applied:

$$H = \frac{1}{6} \cdot \begin{cases} (H' + 6), & \text{if } H' < 0 \\ H', & \text{otherwise} \end{cases} \tag{2.16}$$

After these calculations, the values of the HSV components are obtained from the color planes of the RGB model. The values of the calculated HSV planes fall within the interval [0,1]. Obviously, it would be more natural to consider as the value of H an interval that specifies the full rotation [0,360°] instead of [0.1].

Through the previous procedure, the cube that defines the RGB color model is converted to a cylinder of length 1 and radius 1 (Figure 2.11). Unlike the traditional representation of the HSV model presented in Figure 2.9, in the cylindrical representation, all points lie within the geometric model. The transformation generated for the conversion from RGB to HSV has a non-linear character, where, interestingly, the black value of the model corresponds to the entire surface of the base of the cylinder. In Figure 2.11, the basic colors and some shades of red are shown with some

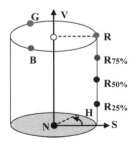

FIGURE 2.11
HSV model converted from RGB model. The black color corresponds to the entire surface of the base of the cylinder, while the basic colors R, G, and B are distributed in different parts of the upper perimeter of the cylinder. The white point is located at the top of the cylinder. On the side of the cylinder, the red color and different shades distributed along the V-axis are represented.

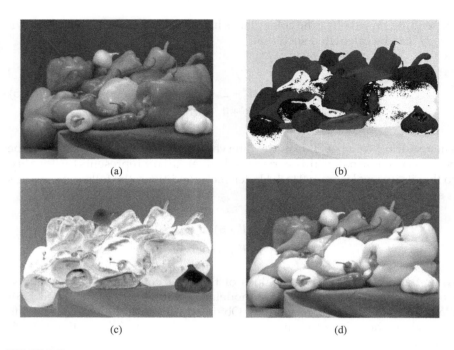

FIGURE 2.12
HSV planes are represented in grayscale. (a) RGB image, (b) H plane, (c) S plane, and (d) V plane.

markings, which are easier to specify in this model. Figure 2.12 shows the HSV components of an image, represented in grayscale.

2.3.6 Conversion from HSV to RGB

To conduct the conversion, it is first assumed that the values of the HSV planes present data within the interval [0,1]. For the calculation of the values of the RGB color planes starting from the information of an image defined in the HSV color model, an auxiliary variable is calculated, defining that:

$$A' = (6 \cdot H) \bmod 6 \qquad (2.17)$$

This expression returns a value ranging from 0 to 6. With this value, other variables are determined as follows:

$$
\begin{aligned}
c_1 &= A' \quad x = (1-S) \cdot V \\
c_2 &= (6 \cdot H) - c_1 \quad y = \left(1 - (S \cdot c_2)\right) \cdot V \\
z &= \left(1 - \left(S \cdot (1-c_2)\right)\right) \cdot V
\end{aligned}
\qquad (2.18)
$$

It can be calculated from the previous values, the normalized values of the R', G', and B' planes, whose values are within the interval [0,1]. The values of these planes are dependent on the values c_1, V, x, y and z, assuming that their respective values are defined as follows:

$$(R',G',B') = \begin{cases} (V,z,x), & \text{if } c_2 = 0 \\ (y,V,x), & \text{if } c_2 = 1 \\ (x,V,z), & \text{if } c_2 = 2 \\ (x,y,V), & \text{if } c_2 = 3 \\ (z,x,V), & \text{if } c_2 = 4 \\ (V,x,y), & \text{if } c_2 = 5 \end{cases} \tag{2.19}$$

The scaling is necessary to convert the normalized plane values to the maximum allowable value for the normally used data type N (which is normally 255). The following operations are performed for scaling:

$$R = \text{round}(255 \cdot R')$$

$$G = \text{round}(255 \cdot G') \tag{2.20}$$

$$B = \text{round}(255 \cdot B')$$

2.3.7 Conversion from RGB to HLS

To convert the RGB model to HLS, the calculation of the H component is the same as for the HSV case, so the same procedure dictated by Equations 2.13–2.16 must be used.

The remaining parameters, S and L, are calculated as follows:
First, for L,

$$L = \frac{C_{max} + C_{min}}{2} \tag{2.21}$$

Then for S,

$$S = \begin{cases} 0, & \text{if } L = 0 \\ 0.5 \cdot \dfrac{C_{dif}}{L}, & \text{if } 0 < L \leq 0.5 \\ 0.5 \cdot \dfrac{C_{dif}}{1-L}, & \text{if } 0.5 < L < 1 \\ 0, & \text{if } L = 1 \end{cases} \tag{2.22}$$

Figure 2.13 shows the HSL components of an image, represented in grayscale.

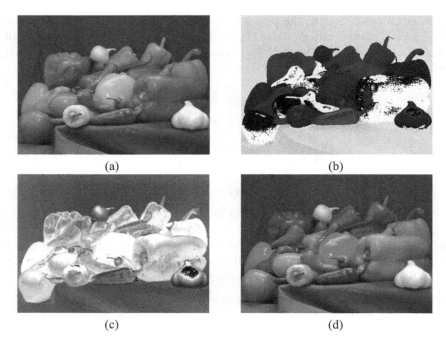

(a)   (b)

(c)   (d)

FIGURE 2.13
HSL planes are represented in grayscale. (a) RGB image, (b) H plane, (c) S plane, and (d) L plane. In (b), the dark regions correspond to the colors red and yellow, whose values are close to zero.

2.3.8 Conversion from HLS to RGB

For the conversion of the HLS color model to RGB, it is assumed that the values that define each plane H, L, or S are within the interval [0,1]. If $L = 0$ or $L = 1$, then the calculation of the auxiliary variables that define the different color planes R', G', and B' is simplified, such that:

$$(R',G',B') = \begin{cases} (0,0,0), & \text{if } L = 0 \\ (1,1,1), & \text{if } L = 1 \end{cases} \tag{2.23}$$

If L does not acquire either of these two values, the calculation for determining the respective RGB color planes is performed based on the following process. If it is considered that:

$$A' = (6 \cdot H) \bmod 6 \tag{2.24}$$

It would produce a value that falls within the interval $(0 \le A' < 0)$. Then, some parameters are calculated, such that:

$$c_1 = A' \quad d = \begin{cases} S \cdot L & \text{if } L \le 0.5 \\ S \cdot (L-1) & \text{if } L > 0.5 \end{cases}$$

$$c_2 = (6 \cdot H) - c_1 \quad y = w(w - x) \cdot c_2 \tag{2.25}$$

$$w = L + d \quad z = x + (w - x) \cdot c_2$$

$$x = L - d$$

With the previous values, the normalized values R', G', and B' of the planes are calculated, applying the following model:

$$(R', G', B') = \begin{cases} (w, z, x), & \text{if } c_2 = 0 \\ (y, w, x), & \text{if } c_2 = 1 \\ (x, w, z), & \text{if } c_2 = 2 \\ (x, y, w), & \text{if } c_2 = 3 \\ (z, x, w), & \text{if } c_2 = 4 \\ (w, x, y), & \text{if } c_2 = 5 \end{cases} \tag{2.26}$$

These values will be in the interval [0,1], so the only thing to be calculated is the scale of the values to the maximum allowable for the type of image, which is normally 255, so when applying:

$$R = \text{round}(255 \cdot R')$$

$$G = \text{round}(255 \cdot G') \tag{2.27}$$

$$B = \text{round}(255 \cdot B')$$

The values that define the image in the RGB model will have been found.

2.3.9 Comparison of HSV and HSL Models

Despite the similarities between both color spaces, there are also notable differences between the V/L and S planes (in both spaces, the H plane is the same). These differences are shown in Figure 2.14. The main difference between the HSV and HLS color models is the way the colors are organized. That is, the way the basic colors red, green, and blue are combined. To illustrate this difference, Figures 2.15–2.17 show how some points are distributed between the RGB, HSV, and HLS color models. The comparison is based on an initial uniform distribution of 1,331 points in the RGB model (Figure 2.15), where the distance of each point in each dimension has a resolution of 0.1 ($11 \times 11 \times 11$). From Figure 2.16, it is noticeable that the uniform

FIGURE 2.14
Comparison between the components of the HSV and HLS color models. The saturation plane in the HLS color model represents bright regions of the image with a larger value, so negative values of the image correspond to these points. The H tonality planes of both models are the same, so there is no difference.

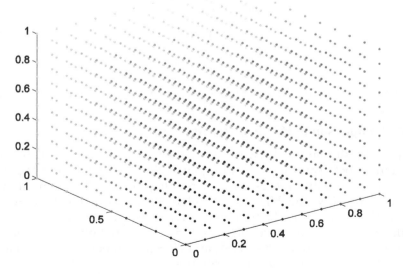

FIGURE 2.15
Uniform RGB distribution used in comparison with HSV and HLS model.

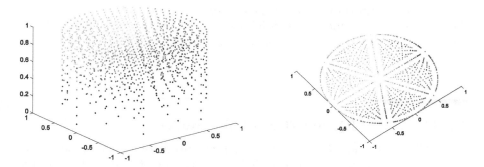

FIGURE 2.16
HSV distribution is produced by transforming the uniform RGB distribution of Figure 2.15. The resulting distribution in this model is distributed asymmetrically in circles, presenting a higher density as the value of plane *V* increases.

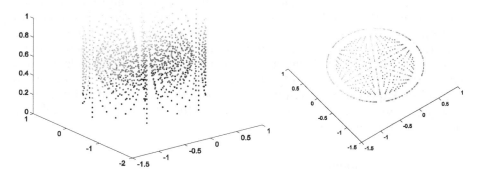

FIGURE 2.17
HLS distribution is produced by transforming the uniform RGB distribution of Figure 2.15. The resulting distribution in this model is distributed symmetrically within a cylinder-shaped space.

RGB distribution generates in HSV a distribution that forms a circular path, increasing the density of points as it approaches the upper surface of the cube. Contrary to the HSL model (Figure 2.17), the points are distributed symmetrically with respect to the center, while the density of points is very small, especially in the white region. Considering the above, a certain movement made in the white area would produce a virtually undetectable color change.

In practice, both HSV and HLS color spaces are widely used in both digital image processing and graphics programming. In digital image processing, the segmentation of the background of color images (Color keying) is particularly interesting, as is the processing of the remaining planes after having separated the H plane.

Something important that must be taken into account is that with the decrease of the saturation plane S, it is difficult to determine the angle H. The most critical case is when the value of $S=0$, where the value of H is undefined.

2.4 The YUV, YIQ, and YCbCr Color Models

The YUV, YIQ, and YC_bC_r color models are used for image standardization in the field of television. The YUV and YIQ models are the basis of the color encoding used in the NTSC and PAL systems, while the YC_bC_r model is part of the standard for digital television. In all these color models, the components that define it consist of three planes: that of light and two other so-called chromatic components, which encode color differences in them. Through this definition of color, it is possible to have compatibility with previous black-and-white television systems and, at the same time, allow the use of signals that handle color images. Because the human eye is unable to distinguish sharpness in colors with such precision and, conversely, is more sensitive to brightness, the bandwidth for defining color components can be significantly reduced. This situation is used by color compression algorithms, such as the JPEG format, which has an RGB to YC_bC_r converter as part of the algorithm. However, although the YC_bC_r model is widely used in image processing, mainly in compression applications, the YUV and YIQ models are not used to the same degree.

2.4.1 The YUV Model

The YUV model represents the basis for color coding in both America's NTSC and Europe's PAL video systems. The luminance component is defined from the RGB components by the equation:

$$Y(x,y) = 0.299R(x,y) + 0.587G(x,y) + 0.114B(x,y) \tag{2.28}$$

where it is considered that the RGB values were already corrected by the Gamma factors $\mathrm{Gamma}(\gamma_{PAL} = 2.2$ and $\gamma_{NTSC} = 2.8)$ necessary for television reproduction. The UV components are linear factors of the difference between the luminance value and the red and blue color planes of the RGB model. These values are defined as follows:

$$U(x,y) = 0.492(B(x,y) - Y(x,y)) \quad V(x,y) = 0.877(R(x,y) - Y(x,y)) \tag{2.29}$$

Considering the equations defined both for the luminance $(Y(x,y))$ as well as for the chromatic components $(U(x,y), V(x,y))$, it can be defined as the transformation matrix:

$$
\begin{bmatrix} Y(x,y) \\ U(x,y) \\ V(x,y) \end{bmatrix} = \begin{bmatrix} 0.299 & 0.587 & 0.114 \\ -0.147 & -0.289 & 0.436 \\ 0.615 & -0.515 & -0.100 \end{bmatrix} \begin{bmatrix} R(x,y) \\ G(x,y) \\ B(x,y) \end{bmatrix} \quad (2.30)
$$

The transformation from YUV to RGB can be obtained through the inversion of the matrix defined in Equation 2.30, producing the following model:

$$
\begin{bmatrix} R(x,y) \\ G(x,y) \\ B(x,y) \end{bmatrix} = \begin{bmatrix} 1.000 & 0.000 & 1.140 \\ 1.000 & -0.395 & -0.581 \\ 1.000 & 2.032 & 0.000 \end{bmatrix} \begin{bmatrix} Y(x,y) \\ U(x,y) \\ V(x,y) \end{bmatrix} \quad (2.31)
$$

2.4.2 The YIQ Model

A variant of the YUV system is the YIQ system, where I implies the phase and Q the quadrature. The values of I and Q are derived from the values of U and V, applying a geometric transformation, where the U and V planes are rotated 33° and mirror-inverted. This is defined as follows:

$$
\begin{bmatrix} I(x,y) \\ Q(x,y) \end{bmatrix} = \begin{bmatrix} 0 & 1 \\ 1 & 0 \end{bmatrix} \begin{bmatrix} \cos\beta & \sin\beta \\ -\sin\beta & \cos\beta \end{bmatrix} \begin{bmatrix} U(x,y) \\ V(x,y) \end{bmatrix} \quad (2.32)
$$

where $\beta = 0.576$ (33). The component represents the same value as the one defined in the YUV model. This YIQ model is better compared to the bandwidth needed for YUV color rendering. However, its use was practically eliminated by the YUV model.

2.4.3 The YC$_b$C$_r$ Model

The YCbCr color space is a variant of the YUV model used as a standard for color coding in digital television. The chromatic components are similar to their U and V counterparts. That is, they are conceived as differences between the luminance value and the R and B color planes. However, unlike the U and V planes, different factors are used that affect the existing difference. The equations used to calculate this color model are the following:

$$
Y(x,y) = w_R R(x,y) + (1 - w_B - w_R) G(x,y) + w_B B(x,y)
$$

$$
C_b = \frac{0.5}{1 - w_B}(B(x,y) - Y(x,y)) \quad (2.33)
$$

$$
C_r = \frac{0.5}{1 - w_R}(R(x,y) - Y(x,y))
$$

Similarly, the transformation from YC_bC_r to RGB is defined as follows:

$$R(x,y) = Y(x,y) + \frac{1 - w_R}{0.5} C_r$$

$$G = Y - \frac{w_B(1 - w_B)}{0.5(1 - w_B - w_R)} C_b - \frac{w_G(1 - w_G)}{0.5(1 - w_B - w_R)} C_r \tag{2.34}$$

$$B = Y(x,y) + \frac{1 - w_B}{0.5} C_b$$

The International Telecommunications Union (ITU) specifies the values of $W_R = 0.299$, $W_B = 0.114$, and $W_G = 0.587$ for carrying out the transformation. With the previous values, the following transformation matrices can be defined:

$$\begin{bmatrix} Y(x,y) \\ C_b(x,y) \\ C_r(x,y) \end{bmatrix} = \begin{bmatrix} 0.299 & 0.587 & 0.114 \\ -0.169 & -0.331 & -0.500 \\ 0.500 & -0.419 & -0.081 \end{bmatrix} \begin{bmatrix} R(x,y) \\ G(x,y) \\ B(x,y) \end{bmatrix} \tag{2.35}$$

$$\begin{bmatrix} R(x,y) \\ G(x,y) \\ B(x,y) \end{bmatrix} = \begin{bmatrix} 1.000 & 0.000 & 1.403 \\ 1.000 & -0.344 & -0.714 \\ 1.000 & 1.773 & 0.000 \end{bmatrix} \begin{bmatrix} Y(x,y) \\ C_b(x,y) \\ C_r(x,y) \end{bmatrix} \tag{2.36}$$

The UV, IQ, and C_bC_r planes, according to the transformations carried out, can contain both positive and negative values. For this reason, in the digital color coding conducted by the color model in the C_bC_r planes, an offset of 128 is added in the case that it is used as a data type to represent the 8-bit image.

Figure 2.18 shows the comparison of the three-color models YUV, YIQ, and C_bC_r. The values of the planes shown in Figure 2.18 incorporate a necessary value of 128 that allows their adequate display. Considering the above, a gray value would correspond to a real value close to zero, while a black to a negative one.

2.5 Useful Color Models for Printing Images

The CMY and CMYK color models are widely used in the color printing industry. Unlike additive plane models such as RGB, a subtractive color scheme is used for printing on paper, in which overlapping reduces the

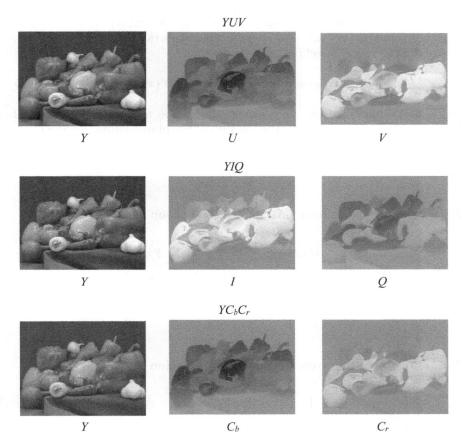

FIGURE 2.18
Comparison of the planes and chromatic components of the color spaces YUV, YIQ, and YC_bC_r.

intensity of the reflected light. In order to carry out this process, at least three basic colors are necessary, which are normally cyan (C), magenta (M), and yellow (Y).

Through the subtractive combination of the previous basic colors (C, M, and Y), when $C = M = Y = 0$, the color white is obtained, while if $C = M = Y = 1$, the color black is obtained. Cyan encompasses red (R), magenta encompasses green (G), and yellow encompasses blue (B). In its simplest form, the CMY model can be defined as follows:

$$C(x,y) = 1 - R(x,y)$$
$$M(x,y) = 1 - G(x,y) \qquad (2.37)$$
$$Y(x,y) = 1 - B(x,y)$$

For better coverage of the color space of the CMY model, in practice, it is usually complemented by incorporating the color black (K) as part of the scheme, where the value of K is defined as follows:

$$K(x,y) = \min(C(x,y), M(x,y), Y(x,y)) \qquad (2.38)$$

Using black as part of the color model allows you to reduce the values of the CMY planes by increasing the amount of the plane defined by the black value. In consideration of this incorporation, there are some variants of the model due to the way in which the black color plane contributes to the processing.

2.5.1 Transformation from CMY to CMYK (Version 1)

$$
\begin{bmatrix}
C'(x,y) \\
M'(x,y) \\
Y'(x,y) \\
K'(x,y)
\end{bmatrix}
=
\begin{bmatrix}
C(x,y - K(x,y)) \\
M(x,y) - K(x,y) \\
Y(x,y) - K(x,y) \\
K(x,y)
\end{bmatrix}
\qquad (2.39)
$$

2.5.2 Transformation from CMY to CMYK (Version 2)

$$
\begin{bmatrix}
C'(x,y) \\
M'(x,y) \\
Y'(x,y)
\end{bmatrix}
=
\begin{bmatrix}
C(x,y) - K(x,y) \\
M(x,y) - K(x,y) \\
Y(x,y) - K(x,y)
\end{bmatrix}
\cdot
\begin{cases}
\dfrac{1}{1-K} & \text{if } K < 1 \\
1 & \text{if not}
\end{cases}
\qquad (2.40)
$$

Since the values of all the planes that define this color model (CMYK) strongly depend on the printing process and the type of paper used, in practice, each plane is individually calibrated.

2.5.3 Transformation from CMY to CMYK (Version 3)

$$
\begin{bmatrix}
C'(x,y) \\
M'(x,y) \\
Y'(x,y) \\
K'(x,y)
\end{bmatrix}
=
\begin{bmatrix}
C(x,y) - f_1(K(x,y)) \\
M(x,y) - f_1(K(x,y)) \\
Y(x,y) - f_1(K(x,y)) \\
f_2(K(x,y))
\end{bmatrix}
\qquad (2.41)
$$

where the value of K is defined in Equation 2.38. The functions f_1 and f_2 are normally non-linear, and in the same way, the resulting values of C', M', Y', K' when using Equation 2.41 make them go outside the interval [0,1], so a restriction or clamping operation is necessary. The values of f_1 and f_2 can have different configurations. However, some of the most commonly used ones that correspond to those used by the commercial image processing program Adobe Photoshop are as follows:

$$f_1(K(x,y)) = const_k \cdot K(x,y)$$

$$f_2(K(x,y)) = \begin{cases} 0 & \text{if } K < K_0 \\ K\dfrac{K-K_0}{1-K_0} & \text{if } K \geq K_0 \end{cases}$$
(2.42)

where $const = 0.1$, $K_0 = 0.3$, and $K_{max} = 0.9$. As can be seen in this variant, the value of f_1 reduces the values of the CMY planes by 10% of the value of K.

2.6 Colorimetric Models

Calibrated color models are used to reproduce colors accurately, regardless of the display device. This need is found in virtually every stage of image processing, from rendering to printing. This problem cannot be considered trivial. It is difficult to print an image on a color printer and to obtain an exact resemblance to the pattern to be printed. All these problems are mostly due to the strong device dependency that occurs in the reproduction and handling of images.

All the color models discussed above are related to the physical measurements of the output devices used in displaying the images, such as the phosphor of television picture tubes or the configurable parameters of laser printers. To generate colors with different output modalities, which produce completely identical images regardless of the display device used, a color model is necessary that considers the independence of representation. These models are called colorimetric or calibrated.

2.6.1 The CIEXYZ Color Space

In 1920, the XYZ standardized model was developed by the "Commission Interbationale d'Éclairage," which is today the basis of most of the calibrated models used today.

The color model was developed from numerous measurements performed under strict conditions. The model consists of three virtual primary colors X, Y, and Z, which are chosen in such a way that all colors and combinations can be described by positive components. The colors defined by this scheme

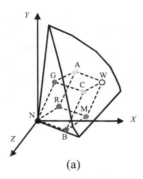

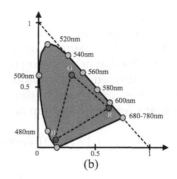

(a)   (b)

FIGURE 2.19
The CIEXY color model and the CIE color diagram. (a) The CIEXY color model is defined through three virtual colors X, Y, and Z. The Y coordinate defines the brightness, while the X and Z coordinates define the color. All visible colors are inside the irregular cube shown in the image. (b) The two-dimensional CIE color diagram corresponds to a horizontal plane of the three-dimensional CIEXYZ model. The CIE diagram represents all shades of visible colors regardless of brightness.

lie within a three-dimensional region, which, as Figure 2.19a shows, has the shape of a sugar crystal.

Most color models can be converted to the XYZ model by coordinate transformation or vice versa. In view of the above, the RGB model can be considered as an irregular cube (almost paralleliped) within the XYZ model, where, due to the linear transformation, the lines of the RGB model also form lines in the XYZ model. The CIEXYZ space is viewed from the point of view of a human observer as non-linear. That is, changes in distances made in the model do not correspond to linear changes in colors.

2.6.2 The CIE Color Diagram

In the XYZ color model, the brightness of the color, considering that the value of the black color is $= Y = Z = 0$, increases as the value of the Y axis increases. In order to clearly represent the color in two dimensions, the CIE color model defines the factors $x, y,$ and z as follows:

$$x = \frac{X}{X+Y+Z}$$

$$y = \frac{Y}{X+Y+Z} \tag{2.43}$$

$$z = \frac{Z}{X+Y+Z}$$

whereas it is evident $x + y + z = 1$, so the value of z is redundant. The x and y values form the space of the CIE diagram, which, as Figure 2.19b shows, has the form of a tongue. All visible colors of the CIE system can be represented

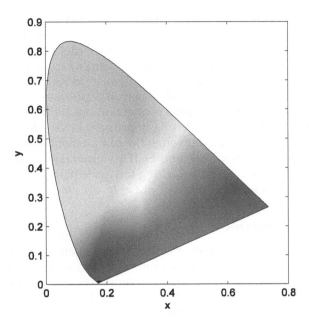

FIGURE 2.20
CIE two-dimensional color diagram, showing the respective colors that the xy pairs represent.

by the Y xy tuple, where Y represents the luminance component of the XYZ system. Figure 2.20 shows the CIE diagram with color mapping on its surface.

Although the mathematical relationship defined in Equation 2.43 seems trivial, it is not easy to understand and is by no means intuitive. Considering a constant Y value, a horizontal plane can be drawn from the CIE space, which represents a non-linear relationship between the variables x, y. In the case of $Y = 1$, the plane is defined as follows:

$$x = \frac{X}{X + 1 + Z}$$

$$y = \frac{1}{X + 1 + Z} \tag{2.44}$$

The opposite transformation that finds the values of the XYZ space, considering $Y = 1$ is produced by:

$$X = \frac{x}{y}$$

$$Y = 1 \tag{2.45}$$

$$Z = \frac{z}{y} = \frac{1 - x - y}{y}$$

The CIE diagram relates how the human eye is sensitive to colors. However, it simultaneously represents a mathematical construction that has some interesting features. The points (x, y) along the border of the CIE surface are the spectral colors that have the maximum saturation value, as well as different wavelengths ranging from 400 nm (violet) to 780 nm (red). With this, the position of each color can be calculated in relation to any primary color. The exception to this is the so-called connection line (or purple line) between 380 and 780 nm, which is outside of any primary color. The purple value of this color can only be obtained through the complement of the colors that are opposite to it. Toward the middle of the CIE diagram (Figure 2.20), the saturation of the colors increases until reaching the white point of the model, which is reached when $x = y = 1/3$, or $X = Y = Z = 1$.

2.6.3 Lighting Standards

A central objective of colorimetry is the measurement of the characteristics of colors in reality, and one of those important characteristics is lighting. For this reason, CIE defines a set of lighting standards, two of which are of special importance in the field of digital color models.

These two standards are as follows:

D50. It corresponds to a temperature of 5,000 K and imitates the lighting produced by a spotlight. D50 serves as a reference for reflection produced by images, mainly for printing applications.

D65. It corresponds to a temperature of 6,500 K and simulates the lighting present on a day in the morning. D65 is used as a reference device for image reproduction. Such is the case for monitors.

These standards have a dual purpose; on the one hand, they serve as a specification of ambient lighting for color observation, while on the other hand, they serve to determine the white point taken as a reference (Table 2.1) for the different color models emitted by the CIE diagram.

2.6.4 Chromatic Adaptation

The capture of a color that defines a space occurs in direct relation to the white point taken as a reference for the formation of the other colors. Consider that there are two different white points that form the reference of two different color spaces. These points are defined as follows:

$$W_1 = (X_{W1}, Y_{W1}, Z_{W1})$$
$$W_2 = (X_{W2}, Y_{W2}, Z_{W2})$$

(2.46)

Therefore, to find equivalencies between the two systems, it will be necessary to perform some transformations known as chromatic adaptation.

TABLE 2.1

Standards D50 and D65 of the Type of Lighting CIE

Norm	Temp (K)	X	Y	Z	x	Y
D50	5,000	0.96429	1.00000	0.82510	0.3457	0.3585
D65	6,500	0.95045	1.00000	1.08905	0.3127	0.3290
N	–	1.00000	1.00000	1.00000	1/3	1/3

N represents the absolute neutral point in the CIEXYZ color model.

The calculation carried out by this transformation converts the white point considered as a reference to the values to which it corresponds in another color space, where another reference white point is defined. In practice, this linear transformation is defined by the matrix M_{CAT}, which defines the following transformation:

$$
\begin{bmatrix} X_2 \\ Y_2 \\ Z_2 \end{bmatrix} = M_{CAT}^{-1} \begin{bmatrix} \dfrac{r_2}{r_1} & 0 & 0 \\ 0 & \dfrac{g_2}{g_1} & 0 \\ 0 & 0 & \dfrac{b_2}{b_1} \end{bmatrix} M_{CAT} \begin{bmatrix} X_1 \\ Y_1 \\ Z_1 \end{bmatrix} \tag{2.47}
$$

where (r_1, g_1, b_1) and (r_2, g_2, b_2) represent the values converted from the white reference points W_1 and W_2 by the linear transformation M_{CAT}. This process can be defined as follows:

$$
\begin{bmatrix} r_1 \\ g_1 \\ b_1 \end{bmatrix} = M_{CAT} \begin{bmatrix} X_{W1} \\ Y_{W1} \\ Z_{W1} \end{bmatrix} \quad \text{and} \quad \begin{bmatrix} r_2 \\ g_2 \\ b_2 \end{bmatrix} = M_{CAT} \begin{bmatrix} X_{W2} \\ Y_{W2} \\ Z_{W2} \end{bmatrix} \tag{2.48}
$$

The most commonly used transformation matrix in practice is the so-called "Bradford" model, which is defined by:

$$
M_{CAT} = \begin{bmatrix} 0.8951 & 0.2664 & -0.1614 \\ -0.7502 & 1.7135 & 0.0367 \\ 0.0389 & -0.0685 & 1.0296 \end{bmatrix} \tag{2.49}
$$

2.6.5 The Gamut

The entire set of colors that can be used for recording, playback, and display by a color model is called the Gamut. This set is related to a three-dimensional space region CIEXYZ, where the dimension is reduced by considering only

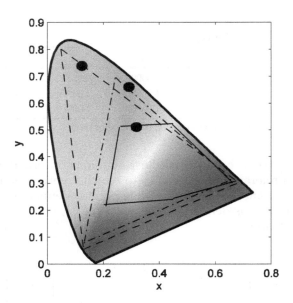

FIGURE 2.21
Gamut representation of different color spaces and display devices.

the tonality without taking into account the lighting, thus defining a two-dimensional region, like the one that has already been treated multiple times in previous subsections, with the name of CIE diagram.

Some examples of Gamut represented in the CIE diagram are shown in Figure 2.21. The Gamut of a display device essentially depends on the physical principle that it uses to represent the data. In this way, computer monitors (to cite an example) are not capable of displaying all the colors of the model that they use to represent colors. The opposite is also possible. That is, a monitor can display different colors that are not considered in the color model that the device uses for representation.

There are great differences between color spaces. This difference makes special sense in the case of the Gamut of the RGB space and that of the CMYK model. The same case can be extrapolated for display devices, where there are cases of laser printers that have a very wide Gamut (Figure 2.21).

2.7 Variants of the CIE Color Space

The CIEXYZ color model and the $x\ y$ system derived from it have a clear disadvantage when used as color models. This disadvantage represents the fact that small geometric distances considered within the color space result in an abrupt change in color perception. In this way, large changes in the magenta color region are produced by varying the position very little, while in the green field, large changes in position barely experience a small change in hue. Therefore, variants of the CIE system have been developed for different types of applications with the central objective of either better representing the way color is perceived by humans or better adapting to changes in position to the applications. These variants allow for improved presentation format and color perception without abandoning the quality of the CIE diagram. Examples of these variants are CIE YUV, YU'V, L*u*v*, and L*a*b*.

2.8 The CIE L*a*b* Model

The L*a*b* model was developed under the idea of linearizing the position change versus tonality change relationship, thus improving the way in which humans perceive these changes, making the model more intuitive. In this color model, the space is defined by three variables, L*, which represents brightness, and the hue components a* and b*. The value of a* defines the distance along the red-green axis, while the value of b* represents the distance along the blue-yellow axis, those axes specified in CIEXYZ space. The three components that define the space are relative to a white point defined as $C_{ref} = (X_{ref}, Y_{ref}, Z_{ref})$, where a non-linear correction (similar to the Gamma correction) is also used.

2.8.1 Transformation CIEXYZ → L*a*b*

The specification for the conversion of the CIEXYZ model to the L*a*b* space is defined according to ISO 13655:

$$L^* = (118 \cdot Y') - 16$$

$$a^* = 500 \cdot (X' - Y') \tag{2.50}$$

$$b^* = 200 \cdot (Y' - Z')$$

where

$$X' = f_1\left(\frac{X}{X_{ref}}\right)$$

$$Y' = f_1\left(\frac{Y}{Y_{ref}}\right) \tag{2.51}$$

$$Z' = f_1\left(\frac{Z}{Z_{ref}}\right)$$

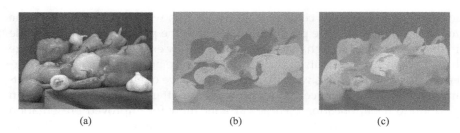

(a)   (b)   (c)

FIGURE 2.22
(a) $L*$, (b) $a*$, and (c) $b*$ components of the $L*a*b*$ color space.

And f_1 is defined as follows:

$$f_1(p) = \begin{cases} p^{1/3} & \text{if } p > 0.008856 \\ 7.787 \cdot p + \dfrac{16}{116} & \text{if } p \le 0.008856 \end{cases}$$ (2.52)

As the white reference point $C_{ref} = (X_{ref}, Y_{ref}, Z_{ref})$, defined as D65 (Table 2.1), is used, it specifies $X_{ref} = 0.95047$, $Y_{ref} = 1.0$ and $Z_{ref} = 1.08883$. The values of $L*$ are always positive and lie within the interval [0.100] (with the possibility of easily scaling to [0.255]). The values of $a*$ and $b*$ are within the interval [−127,127]. Figure 2.22 shows an example of the decomposition of an image into its different $L*a*b*$ components.

2.8.2 Transformation L*a*b* → CIEXYZ

The reverse transformation of converting from the L*a*b* model to the CIEXYZ is defined by the calculation of the following equations:

$$X = X_{ref} \cdot f_2\left(\frac{a*}{500} + Y' \right)$$

$$Y = Y_{ref} \cdot f_2(Y')$$ (2.53)

$$Z = Z_{ref} \cdot f_2\left(Y' - \frac{b*}{200} \right)$$

where

$$Y' = \frac{L* + 16}{116}$$

$$f_2(p) = \begin{cases} p^3 & \text{if } p^3 \le 0.008856 \\ \dfrac{p - (16/116)}{7.787} & \text{if } p^3 \le 0.008856 \end{cases}$$ (2.54)

2.8.3 Determination of Color Difference

The L*a*b* color model is designed to produce a consistent color change per position change. This high linearity allows, through the vector difference, to find a criterion that allows evaluating the difference in the color plane. The difference between two different colors Col_1 and Col_2 is, concretely, defined as the Euclidean distance between them. The Euclidean distance between both colors is defined as follows:

$$\text{Dist}(Col_1, Col_2) = Col_1 - Col_2$$
$$= \sqrt{(L_1^* - L_2^*)^2 + (a_1^* - a_2^*)^2 + (b_1^* - b_2^*)^2} \tag{2.55}$$

2.9 The sRGB Model

Color spaces based on the CIE model, such as L*a*b*, are display-independent and generally show a very wide gamut, thus allowing virtually all hues defined in the CIEXYZ space to be represented. The sRGB (standard RGB) model was developed precisely with the idea of having these advantages by being based on the CIEXYZ model. The sRGB model is composed not only of the color vector that defines the RGB primary colors but also implicitly includes the definition of the white point taken as a reference. Despite the above characteristics, the sRGB model has a much smaller Gamut compared to the L*a*b* model. Several formats for storing images are defined using this color model. Among them, we have EXIF or PNG.

The components of this model are obtained from the CIEXYZ model through a linear transformation determined by the matrix M_{RGB} and defined as follows:

$$\begin{bmatrix} R \\ G \\ B \end{bmatrix} = M_{RGB} \cdot \begin{bmatrix} X \\ Y \\ Z \end{bmatrix} \tag{2.56}$$

where

$$M_{RGB} = \begin{bmatrix} 3.2406 & -1.5372 & -0.4986 \\ -0.9689 & 1.8758 & 0.0415 \\ 0.0557 & -0.2040 & 1.0570 \end{bmatrix} \tag{2.57}$$

In the same way, the opposite conversion could be found:

$$\begin{bmatrix} X \\ Y \\ Z \end{bmatrix} = M_{RGB}^{-1} \cdot \begin{bmatrix} R \\ G \\ B \end{bmatrix} \tag{2.58}$$

where

$$M_{RGB}^{-1} = \begin{bmatrix} 0.4124 & 0.3576 & 0.1805 \\ 0.2126 & 0.7152 & 0.0722 \\ 0.0193 & 0.1192 & 0.9505 \end{bmatrix} \tag{2.59}$$

2.10 MATLAB Functions for Color Image Processing

This section describes the functions that MATLAB® has for color image processing. The functions described here allow you to manipulate, convert color spaces, and work interactively with color images.

2.10.1 Functions for Handling RGB and Indexed Images

An indexed image, as seen, is generated from two components: an index data array and an array that defines the colormap. The color map map is a matrix of dimension $m \times 3$. This matrix in MATLAB has the double data type. The length of m of the map specifies the number of colors it can represent, while dimension 3 specifies the value that corresponds to each RGB color plane that forms the combination of the indexed color. To display an indexed image, it is necessary to provide the information of the index data matrix and the color map in such a way that, using the imshow function, one would have:

```
imshow(index,map)
```

MATLAB has several predefined color maps. Table 2.2 shows the color maps available in MATLAB and their respective differences in displaying an image, as well as the color spectrum it represents.

TABLE 2.2

Color Maps Predefined by MATLAB®

Color Map	Description	Example Image and Color Spectrum
autumn	Performs a smooth variation from orange to yellow	

TABLE 2.2 (*Continued*)

Color Maps Predefined by MATLAB®

Color Map	Description	Example Image and Color Spectrum
bone	It is a grayscale color map, considering the high value of the blue plane	
colorcube	Contains a definition of colors sampled from the RGB model while maintaining more levels of gray, red, green, and blue	
cool	Defines a set of colors that varies smoothly from cyan to magenta	
copper	Varies slightly from black to copper in color	

(Continued)

TABLE 2.2 (*Continued*)

Color Maps Predefined by MATLAB®

Color Map	Description	Example Image and Color Spectrum
flag	Define colors as red, white, blue, and black. Your color definition changes completely (the transition is not smooth) from one index to another	
gray	Defines a grayscale pattern	
hot	Varies smoothly from black to red, orange, and yellow to white	

(*Continued*)

TABLE 2.2 (*Continued*)

Color Maps Predefined by MATLAB®

Color Map	Description	Example Image and Color Spectrum
hsv	Varies the hue component from maximum saturation to the minimum level. Its transition goes from red, yellow, green, cyan, blue, and magenta back again to red	
jet	Its color transition defines from blue to red, passing through the colors cyan, yellow, and orange	
pink	Defines a shade of pink. This map creates sepia images	

(*Continued*)

TABLE 2.2 (*Continued*)

Color Maps Predefined by MATLAB®

Color Map	Description	Example Image and Color Spectrum
prism	Defines a repetition of colors ranging from red, orange, yellow, green, blue, and violet	
spring	Defines colors that give a tint of magenta and yellow	
summer	Defines colors that give a shade of green and yellow	

(*Continued*)

TABLE 2.2 (*Continued*)

Color Maps Predefined by MATLAB®

Color Map	Description	Example Image and Color Spectrum
winter	Defines colors that give a tint of blue and green	

For clarity of explanation, this section uses the following convention: when dealing with RGB images, the image will be identified as rgb. When the image is grayscale, it will be identified as gray. If the image is indexed, it will be identified as index; if the image is binary, it will be identified as bw.

A common operation in image processing is to convert an RGB image to a grayscale image. The rgb2gray function allows this operation by applying one of the methods defined in Equation 2.7. The syntax of this function is described as follows:

```
gray=rgb2gray(rgb);
```

Dithering is a process used in the printing and advertising industries to give a grayscale visual impression by using marking points of different sizes with a different distribution density. In the case of grayscale images, applying dithering will form a binary image of black points on a white background or vice versa. The size of the pixels applied in the process varies from small dots in light areas to increasing their size in dark areas. Light areas could be obtained by tracing a white region contaminated by a distribution of black points, while a dark area is obtained by defining a black area and contaminating some white points. Evidently, the density of points has a determining effect on the dithering process. The main problem with an algorithm that implements dithering is the balance between the precision of visual perception and the complexity of the number and size of points. MATLAB implements the dither function to implement the dithering process. This algorithm is based on the scheme developed by Floyd and Steinberg. The general syntax of this function applied to grayscale images:

```
bw = dither(gray);
```

(a)   (b)

FIGURE 2.23
Result of applying the dithering process on a grayscale image using the dither function
implemented in MATLAB®. (a) Original image and (b) image resulting from having applied
the dither function to the image in (a).

Figure 2.23 shows the original image and the image obtained after applying
the dither function.

MATLAB uses the rgb2ind function to convert an RGB image to an
indexed image. The general syntax of this function is:

```
[index, map]=rgb2ind(rgb, n, ' option_for_dithering ')
```

where n determines the number of colors of the map used for the representation of the image, option _ for _ dithering, defines if the dithering process
will be applied to the image. This option admits two possible flags: dither for
the case that the dithering process is applied, or nodither, in case you do not
want to apply this process to the image conversion. The default option for these
two flags is dither. Index receives the data matrix that defines the indexed
image, while map is the color map that defines it. Figure 2.24 shows, as an
example, the indexed images produced by converting an RGB image and using
$n = 7$ as parameters for Figure 2.24a option _ for _ dithering= 'dither'
and for Figure 2.24b option _ for _ dithering= 'nodither'.

The ind2rgb function converts an indexed image to an RGB image. Its
syntax is defined as follows:

```
rgb = ind2rgb(index, map)
```

where index is the data array of the indexed image and map is the color map
that defines it. Table 2.3 lists the image processing toolbox functions used for
the conversion of RGB, indexed, and grayscale images.

2.10.2 Functions for Color Space Conversion

This section describes the functions contained in the MATLAB image processing toolbox to convert between the different color models. Most of the

(a) (b)

FIGURE 2.24
Indexed images produced by the function rgb2ind, using (a) dithering and (b) not using it.

TABLE 2.3

Image Processing Toolbox Functions Used for Converting RGB, Indexed, and Grayscale Images

MATLAB® Function	Objective
Dither	Create an indexed image from an RGB image using the dithering process
Grayslice	Create an indexed image from a grayscale image using a multithreshold technique
gray2ind	Create an indexed image from a grayscale image
ind2gray	Create a grayscale image from an indexed image
rgb2ind	Create an indexed image from an RGB image
ind2rgb	Create an RGB image from an indexed image
rgb2gray	Create a grayscale version from an RGB image

functions have a name that allows you to intuitively identify the type of conversion performed (there are some exceptions).

The rgb2ntsc function allows converting from an image defined in the RGB model to YIQ space (see Section 2.4). The name of the function represents the idea that this model is used in the American NTSC television system. The general syntax of this function is:

```
yiq = rgb2ntsc(rgb)
```

where rgb is an image defined in the RGB model. The yiq result is the image converted to the YIQ color space, corresponding to the rgb image. The data type of the image yiq is double. The components of the image yiq as seen in Section 2.4 are for luminance (Y) yiq(:,:,1), for hue (I) yiq(:,:,2), and for saturation (Q) yiq(:,:,3).

On the other hand, the ntsc2rgb function allows performing the opposite conversion, that is, from an image defined in the YIQ model to an RGB image. The syntax of this function is:

```
rgb = ntsc2rgb(yiq)
```

where both the yiq and rgb images are of type double; this is mainly important when generating the image display using the function imshow.

The rgb2ycbcr function allows converting from an image defined in the RGB
model to YCbCr space (see Section 2.4). The general syntax of this function is:

```
ycbcr = rgb2ycbcr(rgb)
```

where rgb is an image defined in the RGB model, the result ycbcr is the
image converted to the YCbCr color space, corresponding to the rgb image.
The data type of the image ycbcr is double.

In the opposite direction, the ycbcr2rgb function allows the opposite
conversion to be carried out, that is, from an image defined in the YCbCr
model to an RGB image. The syntax of this function is:

```
rgb = ycbcr2rgb(ycbcr)
```

where both the image ycbcr and rgb are of type double, the above is mainly
important when generating the image display using the function imshow.

The HSV model, as discussed in Section 2.3.4, is most widely used to select
colors from a predetermined palette. This color system can be considered
more intuitive than RGB since it better describes the way color is captured by
humans. The rgb2hsv function converts an image defined in the RGB model
to HSV space. The syntax of this function is:

```
hsv = rgb2hsv(rgb)
```

where the hsv image is of type double within the interval [0,1]. The hsv2rgb
function allows performing the inverse conversion, thus obtaining the image
defined in RGB space from one described in the HSV model. The syntax of
this function is defined as follows:

```
rgb = hsv2rgb(hsv)
```

where both hsv and rgb are of type double.

The colors cyan, magenta, and yellow are considered the secondary colors of
light in terms of pigmentation. Most devices used for pigmenting on paper, such
as printers and copiers, require as input data an image defined in the CMY format (see Section 2.5) and usually perform an RGB to CMY conversion internally.
The conversion can be performed as shown by a simple definite subtraction:

$$C(x,y) = 1 - R(x,y)$$

$$M(x,y) = 1 - G(x,y) \qquad (2.60)$$

$$Y(x,y) = 1 - B(x,y)$$

In this conversion, it is assumed that all values have already been normalized to the interval [0,1]. Several interesting observations can be derived from the model described in Equation 2.60, such as a color that contains only cyan will not contain red; similarly, the same thing happens in the magenta-green and yellow-blue relationships. Because, as seen in Equation 2.60, the CMY values correspond to the complement of the RGB contents, the conversion between these models can be done by applying the function complement `imcomple-ment` contained in the image processing toolbox. In such a way that to convert to CMY from an image described in the RGB model, we have:

```
cmy = imcomplement(rgb)
```

Similarly, the same function can be used to convert from CMY to an image defined in RGB, applying:

```
rgb = imcomplement(cmy)
```

2.11 Color Image Processing

This section studies the main image processing operations applicable to color images. In order to adequately discuss the techniques used in color image processing, operations will be classified into three groups: linear color transformations, spatial processing, and vector operations.

The category of linear transformations refers to operations carried out exclusively on the pixels of the image in each of the different planes that define its color. This type of processing is similar to the ones discussed in Chapter 1, with the difference that, in this case, the operations were applied to only one grayscale image. In the current context, these operations are applied to each of the color planes, so in theory, each of the operations seen in Chapter 1 can be used for color images, with the exception that they are performed separately for color images.

Spatial processing operations involve those operations that consider not only the pixel in question but also those that are in a certain neighborhood around it. This type of processing is closely related to that seen in Chapter 2, except that in the case of color images, the processing is performed on each of the color planes. Considering the above, most of the operations explained in Chapter 2, such as filtering, can be applied to this type of image.

While both pixel-level and spatial processing specify operations that are performed on each plane, in vector processing, each operation involves the participation of each of the color components simultaneously. To carry out vector processing, each pixel of the image is represented as a vector, which in the case of an image in the RGB model would be:

$$c(x,y) = \begin{bmatrix} c_R(x,y) \\ c_G(x,y) \\ c_B(x,y) \end{bmatrix} \tag{2.61}$$

Considering the above, an image of dimension $M \times N$ would have $M \cdot N$ vectors $c(x.y)$.

2.12 Linear Color Transformations

The techniques discussed in this section are based on individual pixel processing, performing this operation on each of the planes that define the image. This processing is similar to that discussed in Chapter 1 on grayscale images. The type of processing of these operations has the following model:

$$c_i = f_i(p_i) \quad i = 1, 2, 3. \tag{2.62}$$

where p is the value of the pixel plane i that will be processed by the function f_i, giving, as a result, the value of the pixel c for the same plane i.

The set of operations of this type that can be applied to color images includes most of those described in Chapter 1. For grayscale images, only in this case, the grayscale image will correspond to each plane of the image. Therefore, only those operations that, due to their importance, are considered in this section.

The linear transformation in an image can be defined as the relationship between the different intensity values present in the color planes of the image. The change in color intensity, on the other hand, is related to the way in which the intensity values are distributed in each plane in such a way that if they are concentrated more toward small intensity values, the image will be seen with less color content. On the contrary, if the intensity values are concentrated toward high-intensity values, the image will have a higher color content. The generic operator $f(\cdot)$ that is used to linearly transform color in an image can be defined as follows:

$$c_i = f_i(x,y) = o \cdot p_i + b \tag{2.63}$$

where o modifies the value of the contrast of the intensity values of the plane i while b modifies the value of the brightness or illumination. Figure 2.25 shows graphically the different modifications made by manipulating o and b.

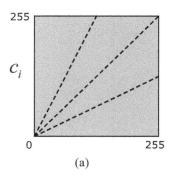
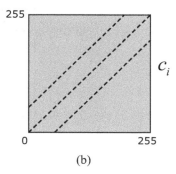

(a)   (b)

FIGURE 2.25
Graphic representation of the mapping that is generated in the resulting pixel of each plane when modifying the values of Equation 2.63 for (a) o and (b) b.

2.12.1 Linear Color Transformation Using MATLAB

The linear transformation operation that is performed on each plane of a color image can be performed by using the function imadjust contained in the image processing toolbox. The general syntax of this function is defined as follows:

```
newrgb = imadjust(rgb,[low_in; high_in],[low_out; high_out])
```

The imadjust function maps the intensity values of each rgb plane to new intensity values for each of the color planes in the new image newrgb. The operation is performed in such a way that the values low _ in and high _ in are linearly transformed to those specified by low _ out and high _ out. Those values below low _ in or above high _ in are simply redefined to those values. When you want to use the full range to specify the transformation, you use the empty array [] as a parameter, which would mean specifying [0,1]. All the values of the limits that define the transformation must be considered normalized in the interval of [0,1]. Figure 2.26 shows the mapping parameters and their relationship in the transformation of the output image.

In the context of color images, the parameters low _ in, high _ in, low _ out, and high _ out represent vectors of dimension three, where the values of each column define the limits of each color plane.

As an example of the application of this function, different linear transformations are considered, which are illustrated in Figure 2.27. All the transformations obtained are considered as the original image, the one shown in Figure 2.27a. In Figure 2.27b, low _ in=[0.2 0.3 0], high _ in=[0.6 0.7 1], low _ out=[0 0 0], and high _ out=[1 1 1] are considered as transformation parameters. In Figure 2.27c, low _ in=[0.2 0.2 0.2], high _ in=[0.5 0.5 0.5], low _ out=[0 0 0], and high _ out=[0.7 0.7 0.7] are considered as

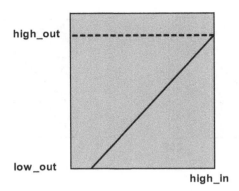

FIGURE 2.26
Relationship of the parameters considered in the transformation carried out on each plane of the color image.

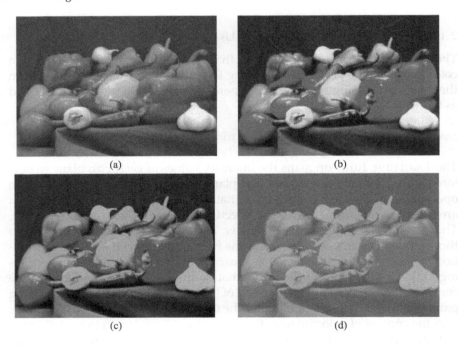

FIGURE 2.27
Examples of linearly transformed images obtained using the imadjust function, using different transformation parameters. (a) Original image; (b) parameters low_in=[0.2 0.3 0], high_in=[0.6 0.7 1], low_out=[0 0 0], and high_out=[1 1 1]; (c) parameters low_in=[0.2 0.2 0.2], high_in=[0.5 0.5 0.5], low_out=[0 0 0], and high_out=[0.7 0.7 0.7]; (d) parameters low_in=[0.2 0.2 0.2], high_in=[0.5 0.5 0.5], low_out=[0.3 0.3 0.3], and high_out=[0.7 0.7 0.7].

transformation parameters. Finally, in Figure 2.27d, the transformation parameters are considered low _ in=[0.2 0.2 0.2], high _ in=[0.5 0.5 0.5], low _ out=[0.3 0.3 0.3], and high _ out=[0.7 0.7 0.7].

2.13 Spatial Processing in Color Images

The essential feature of the linear transformation operations discussed in the previous section was that the new pixel value finally calculated depends exclusively on the original pixel value of each plane and is located in the same position in the planes of the new image. Although it is possible to perform many effects on images using pixel operations, there are conditions under which it is not possible to use them to generate certain effects, such as in the case of image smoothing or edge detection. Spatial processing of color images can be considered as an operation where the newly computed pixel depends not only on the original pixel but also on other pixels that are in a given neighborhood relative to it. Evidently, this processing considers that the operations are carried out independently on each color plane that defines the image. Figure 2.28 shows the process of a special operation on a color image.

This type of processing is closely related to the operations from Chapter 2, except that in the case of color images, the processing is performed on each color plane. Considering the above, most of the operations explained in Chapter 2, such as filtering, can be applied to this type of image. Therefore, only those operations that, due to their importance, are considered the most common will be discussed.

2.13.1 Color Image Smoothing

As has been discussed in Chapter 2, in an intensity image or a color image, regions or pixels can experiment with an abrupt change locally in the value

FIGURE 2.28
Spatial processing of a color image. The processing is performed using a coefficient matrix that defines a processing region that operates on each color plane.

of one plane. Conversely, there are also regions or pixels in each plane where the intensity of the image remains constant. One way of smoothing a color image is that each pixel in each plane is simply replaced by the average of its neighbors in a region around it.

Therefore, to calculate the pixel value of the smoothed plane $I(x,y)$, the pixel of the original plane $I'(x,y)$ is used plus its eight neighboring pixels $p_1, p_2, \ldots, p_8$ and the arithmetic average of these nine values is calculated:

$$I'(x,y) \leftarrow \frac{p_0 + p_1 + p_2 + p_3 + p_4 + p_5 + p_6 + p_7 + p_8}{9} \tag{2.64}$$

In coordinates relative to the plane, the above formulation could be expressed as follows:

$$I'(x,y) \leftarrow \frac{1}{9} \cdot \begin{bmatrix} I(x-1,y-1) & + & I(x,y-1) & + & I(x+1,y-1) & + \\ I(x-1,y) & + & I(x,y) & + & I(x+1,y) & + \\ I(x-1,y+1) & + & I(x,y+1) & + & I(x+1,y+1) \end{bmatrix} \tag{2.65}$$

which could be described in compact form as follows:

$$I'(x,y) \leftarrow \frac{1}{9} \cdot \sum_{j=-1}^{1} \sum_{i=-1}^{1} I(x+i, y+j) \tag{2.66}$$

This calculated local average refers to all the typical elements present in a filter. Actually, this filter is an example of one of the most used types of filters, the so-called linear filter. In the case of color images, this process must be executed for each plane of the image that defines it.

2.13.2 Smoothing Color Images with MATLAB

To smooth a color image using a spatial filter, the following process is performed:

1. Each plane of the color image is extracted.
2. Each color plane is individually filtered using the same filter structure.
3. The results of each plane are merged again to produce the new smoothed-out color image.

The function used in MATLAB to perform spatial filtering is `imfilter`; its syntax, parameters, and details are discussed in Volume 1, Chapter 2, Section 2.9.3. Under such conditions, it will only be used in this section.

Next, as an example, the series of commands used in MATLAB to smooth an RGB color image is exposed. In the example, a Box filter (Volume 1, Chapter 2) of dimension 7×7 is used. It is also considered that the image to smooth is stored in the variable RGB. Therefore, the commands that should be executed to smooth the image are the following:

```
1     >>R=RGB(:,:,1);
2     >>G=RGB(:,:,2);
3     >>B=RGB(:,:,3);
4     >>w=(ones(7,7)/49);
5     >>Rf=imfilter(R,w);
6     >>Gf=imfilter(G,w);
7     >>Bf=imfilter(B,w);
8     >>RGBf(:,:,1)=Rf;
9     >>RGBf(:,:,2)=Gf;
10    >>RGBf(:,:,3)=Bf;
```

Commands from 1 to 3 separate each of the planes and assign them to the variables R, G, and B. Command 4 generates the spatial filter coefficient matrix, which, as can be seen, is an average whose region of influence is of dimension 7×7 (for more details, see Volume 1, Chapter 2). Commands 5–7 conduct the spatial filtering on each plane using the filter defined in command 4. Finally, in commands from 8 to 10, the filtered planes are joined to form the new smoothed image. Figure 2.29 shows the results of these commands over a color image as an example.

2.13.3 Sharpness Enhancement in Color Images

If the Laplacian operator is applied to each plane of a color image, we will obtain the edges in the context of that plane. However, if what is desired

(a)   (b)

FIGURE 2.29
Color smoothed image that was obtained from executing the commands described above. (a) Original image, (b) smoothed image.

is to improve the sharpness of an image, then it is necessary to preserve the low-frequency information of the original plane and emphasize the details present in the plane through the Laplacian filter. To achieve this effect, it is required to subtract from the original plane a scaled version of the plane filtered by the Laplacian filter. Under such conditions, the plane with improved sharpness can be produced by the following equation:

$$I(x,y)_B = I(x,y) - w \cdot \nabla^2 I(x,y) \tag{2.67}$$

Figure 2.30 illustrates the idea that an image is sharpened by making the presence of its edges more apparent. To facilitate the explanation, the one-dimensional case is considered.

The effect of improving the sharpness of a plane can be carried out in a single process. Considering $w = 1$, the process can be modeled as follows:

$$I(x,y)_B = I(x,y) - (1) \cdot \nabla^2 I(x,y) \tag{2.68}$$

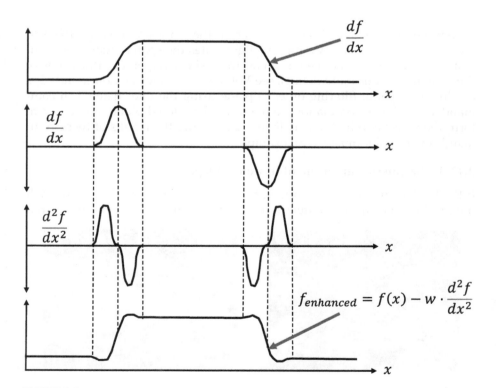

FIGURE 2.30
Sharpening by applying the second derivative. By subtracting a factor from the second derivative of the function, it allows you to maximize the presence of the contours in the image.

and considering that the Lapacian (see Section 1.5) has the structure defined as follows:

$$\nabla^2 I(x,y) = I(x+1,y) + I(x-1,y) + I(x,y+1) + I(x,y-1)$$
$$- 4I(x,y) \tag{2.69}$$

The final formulation can be defined as follows:

$$I(x,y)_B = 5I(x,y) - [I(x+1,y) + I(x-1,y) + I(x,y+1)$$
$$+ I(x,y-1)] \tag{2.70}$$

Or, expressed in a filter, the matrix of coefficients is defined by the following filter:

$$I(x,y)_{Bettered} = \begin{bmatrix} 0 & -1 & 0 \\ -1 & 5 & -1 \\ 0 & -1 & 0 \end{bmatrix} \tag{2.71}$$

2.13.4 Sharpening Color Images with MATLAB

To improve the sharpness of a color image by using a spatial filter, the same process previously described for smoothing color images is carried out, that is:

1. Each plane of the color image is extracted.
2. Each component is individually filtered using the filter defined in Equation 2.63.
3. The results of each plane are merged again to generate the new, sharper color image.

The function used in MATLAB to perform spatial filtering is imfilter; its syntax, parameters, and details were discussed in Volume 1, Chapter 2, Section 2.9.3, so it is only used in this section.

Next, as an example, the set of commands used in MATLAB to improve the sharpness of an RGB color image is exposed. In this process, the filter defined in Equation 2.69 is used. To carry out this example, it is considered that the input image is stored in the RGB variable. Therefore, the commands that need to be executed to improve the sharpness are the following:

```
1          >>R=RGB(:,:,1);
2          >>G=RGB(:,:,2);
3          >>B=RGB(:,:,3);
```

```
4      >>w=[0 -1 0;-1 5 -1;0 -1 0];
5      >>Rf=imfilter(R,w);
6      >>Gf=imfilter(G,w);
7      >>Bf=imfilter(B,w);
8      >>RGBf(:,:,1)=Rf;
9      >>RGBf(:,:,2)=Gf;
10     >>RGBf(:,:,3)=Bf;
```

Commands 1–3 separate each of the planes and assign them to the variables R, G, and B. Command 4 generates the matrix of coefficients of the spatial filter defined in Equation 2.70 (for more details, see Section 1.5). Commands 5–7 perform spatial filtering on each plane using the filter defined in command 4. Lastly, 8–10 of the filtered planes are integrated to produce the new color image with better sharpness. Figure 2.31 shows a sharpened color image obtained from executing the commands described above.

2.14 Vector Processing of Color Images

Until now, in the previous sections, the operations were carried out considering the planes independently. However, there are cases in which it is necessary to work with the entire vector of intensity values in all planes simultaneously.

There is an important set of operations that require direct processing of the data vector. In this section, only the case of edge detection in color images will be described since this application is considered one of the most common.

(a)   (b)

FIGURE 2.31
Color image whose sharpness has been enhanced by using a Laplacian filter. (a) Original image and (b) image with enhanced sharpness obtained after executing the set of MATLAB® commands described above.

2.14.1 Edge Detection in Color Images

The gradient can be considered as the derivative of a multidimensional function along a coordinate axis (with respect to one of the function variables), for example,

$$G_x = \frac{\partial I}{\partial x}(x,y), G_y = \frac{\partial I}{\partial y}(x,y) \qquad (2.72)$$

The formulations of Equation 2.72 represent the partial derivative of the image function with respect to the variable x or y. The vector

$$\nabla I(x,y) = \begin{bmatrix} \dfrac{\partial I}{\partial x}(x,y) \\ \dfrac{\partial I}{\partial y}(x,y) \end{bmatrix} \qquad (2.73)$$

$\nabla I(x,y)$ symbolizes the vector of the gradient of the function I at the point (x,y). The magnitude of the gradient is defined as follows:

$$|\nabla I| = \sqrt{\left(\frac{\partial I}{\partial x}\right)^2 + \left(\frac{\partial I}{\partial y}\right)^2} \qquad (2.74)$$

∇I is invariant to image rotations and thus also independent of the orientation of the structures contained in it. This property is important for locating the edge points of the image. Under such conditions, the value of $|\nabla I|$ is the practical value used in most of the algorithms for edge detection. $|\nabla I|$ is often approximated by using the following model:

$$|\nabla I| = \left|\frac{\partial I}{\partial x}\right| + \left|\frac{\partial I}{\partial x}\right| \qquad (2.75)$$

This approximation avoids the calculation of the power and the square root operations, which makes it computationally more economical.

An important characteristic of the gradient vector (Equation 2.73) is its direction, which expresses the angle where the maximum value of the gradient is presented. This direction can be calculated as follows:

$$\theta(x,y) = \tan^{-1}\left(\frac{\dfrac{\partial I}{\partial y}}{\dfrac{\partial I}{\partial x}}\right) = \tan^{-1}\left(\frac{G_y}{G_x}\right) \qquad (2.76)$$

The difference between pixels within small neighborhood regions approximates the value of the gradient in practice. Equation 2.77 shows the coefficient matrices of the Sobel filter, one of the most common for the calculation of the magnitude of the gradient. Chapter 3 provides a more detailed explanation of how these differences are established, as well as the most common filters used to calculate the magnitude of the gradient.

$$
G_x = \begin{bmatrix} -1 & -2 & -1 \\ 0 & 0 & 0 \\ 1 & 2 & 1 \end{bmatrix} \quad \text{and} \quad G_y = \begin{bmatrix} -1 & 0 & 1 \\ -2 & 0 & 2 \\ -1 & 0 & 1 \end{bmatrix} \tag{2.77}
$$

The gradient value computed under Equation 2.77 is the most common method for determining the edges in a grayscale image, as discussed in Chapter 3. However, this method is applied only to intensity images. Under such conditions, this process needs to be extended for color images such as RGB. One way to extend the process to color images is to find the gradient for each color plane and combine their results. This methodology is not a good solution since there will be color regions that cannot be detected by this method, and therefore their borders cannot be calculated.

The problem is to define both the magnitude of the gradient and its direction from the color vector defined in Equation 2.61. One of the most common ways to extend the gradient concept to vector functions is described below.

Consider the unit vectors *r*, *g*, and *b* as the unit vector that describes the RGB color space (see Figure 2.1), from which the following vector relationships are defined:

$$
\begin{aligned}
u &= \frac{\partial R}{\partial x} r + \frac{\partial G}{\partial x} g + \frac{\partial B}{\partial x} b \\[2mm]
v &= \frac{\partial R}{\partial y} r + \frac{\partial G}{\partial y} g + \frac{\partial B}{\partial y} b
\end{aligned} \tag{2.78}
$$

From these relations, the following vector products are defined:

$$
\begin{aligned}
g_{xx} &= u \cdot u = u^T \cdot u = \left(\frac{\partial R}{\partial x}\right)^2 + \left(\frac{\partial G}{\partial x}\right)^2 + \left(\frac{\partial B}{\partial x}\right)^2 \\[2mm]
g_{yy} &= v \cdot v = v^T \cdot v = \left(\frac{\partial R}{\partial y}\right)^2 + \left(\frac{\partial G}{\partial y}\right)^2 + \left(\frac{\partial B}{\partial y}\right)^2 \\[2mm]
g_{xy} &= u \cdot v = u^T \cdot v = \left(\frac{\partial R}{\partial x}\right)\left(\frac{\partial R}{\partial y}\right) + \left(\frac{\partial G}{\partial x}\right)\left(\frac{\partial G}{\partial y}\right) + \left(\frac{\partial B}{\partial x}\right)\left(\frac{\partial B}{\partial y}\right)
\end{aligned} \tag{2.79}
$$

An important observation results from the fact that both R, G, and B, as well as the values of g_{xx}, g_{yy} and g_{xy} are functions that depend on x and y. Considering the previous notation, Di Zenso showed that the direction where the maximum value of change of the color vector $c(x,y)$ is found as a function of (x,y) is defined as follows:

$$\theta(x,y) = \frac{1}{2} \tan^{-1}\left[\frac{2g_{xy}}{(g_{xx} - g_{yy})} \right] \qquad (2.80)$$

While the maximum value $M(x,y)$ of the gradient occurs in the $\theta(x,y)$ direction. $M(x,y)$ is calculated as follows:

$$M(x,y) = \left\{ \frac{1}{2}\left[(g_{xx} + g_{yy}) + (g_{xx} - g_{yy})\cos(2\theta) + 2g_{xy}\sin(2\theta) \right] \right\} \qquad (2.81)$$

It is important to note that both $\theta(x,y)$ and $M(x,y)$ produce matrices of the same dimension as the color image whose edges need to be found.

Because $\tan(\alpha) = \tan(\alpha \pm \pi)$, if θ is a solution of Equation 2.80, then $\theta_A + \pi/2$ is also a solution. Considering this, it is true that $M_\theta(x,y) = M_{\theta + \pi/2}(x,y)$. Assuming this property, $M(x,y)$ should be calculated only in the middle of the interval $[0,\pi]$. Therefore, the other values can be found by recalculating the values of $M(x,y)$, but this time considering $\theta + \pi/2$. If the calculation is carried out as described in the previous procedure, there will be two matrices with the values of the gradients $M_\theta(x,y)$ and $M_{\theta+\pi/2}(x,y)$. For the final calculation, the maximum of the two will be considered. Figure 2.32 shows the vector gradient magnitude and direction calculated from the algorithm described above.

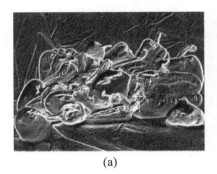
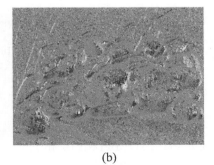

(a)　　　　　　　　　　　　(b)

FIGURE 2.32
(a) Vector gradient magnitude and (b) gradient direction.

2.14.2 Edge Detection in Color Images Using MATLAB

For the vectorial calculation of the gradient of a color image, there is no direct function implemented in the image processing toolbox. Therefore, the algorithm described in the previous section will have to be implemented.

In this subsection, the implementation of two functions is described. The first one is the algorithm for the vectorial calculation of the gradient of a color image, while the second one represents the calculation of the gradient of a color image, calculating it individually at each plan. This last program has been done in order to make a comparison of both methods and show that vector processing is more robust.

Program 2.2 shows the full implementation of the gradcol function that computes the vector color gradient $M(x,y)$, and its direction $\theta(x,y)$, from an RGB image.

PROGRAM 2.2   FUNCTION GRADCOL THAT CALCULATES THE MAGNITUDE OF THE VECTOR GRADIENT *M(X, Y)* AND ITS DIRECTION

```
%%%%%%%%%%%%%%%%%%%%%%%%%%%%%%%%%%%%%%%%%%%%%%%%%%%%%%%%%%%%%%%%
%Function that allows the vector gradient of a color
%image from an RGB (rgb) image, the function returns
%the vector gradient value Gv and its address D
%%%%%%%%%%%%%%%%%%%%%%%%%%%%%%%%%%%%%%%%%%%%%%%%%%%%%%%%%%%%%%%%
function [Gv, Di]=gradcol(rgb)
%Coefficient matrices for the calculation of the
%horizontal and vertical gradient (Equation 2.76)
hx=[1 2 1;0 0 0; -1 -2 -1];
hy=hx';
%RGB is decomposed into its different planes
R=rgb(:,:,1);
G=rgb(:,:,2);
B=rgb(:,:,3);
%The gradients of each of the planes are obtained,
%in the horizontal and vertical x y directions.
Rx=double(imfilter(R,hx));
Ry=double(imfilter(R,hy));
Gx=double(imfilter(G,hx));
Gy=double(imfilter(G,hy));
Bx=double(imfilter(B,hx));
By=double(imfilter(B,hy));
%The cross products defined in 2.79 are performed
gxx=Rx.^2+Gx.^2+Bx.^2;
gyy=Ry.^2+Gy.^2+By.^2;
gxy=Rx.*Ry+Gx.*Gy+Bx.*By;
```

```
%Get the address from 0 to pi/2 eps is used to avoid
%division by zero when gxx and gyy are equal
Di=0.5*(atan(2*gxy./(gxx-gyy+eps)));
%The magnitude of the gradient M(x,y) is obtained for
%the directions from 0 to pi/2
G1=0.5*((gxx+gyy)+(gxx-gyy).*cos(2*A)+2*gxy.*sin(2*A));
%Address solutions are extended up to pi
Di=Di+pi/2;
%The value of M(x,y) is calculated again for
%these directions.
G2=0.5*((gxx+gyy)+(gxx-gyy).*cos(2*A)+2*gxy.*sin(2*A));
%The square root is extracted from the gradients
G1=G1.^0.5;
G2=G2.^0.5;
%The maximum of the two gradients is obtained and by
%means of the mat2gray function it is scaled to the
%interval [0,1]
Gv=mat2gray(max(G1,G2));
%The address is also scaled from [0,1]
Di=mat2gray(Di);
```

Program 2.3 shows the complete implementation of the gradplan function that calculates the magnitude of the gradient of a color image. In this implementation, the gradient of each plane is independently computed.

PROGRAM 2.3 GRADPLAN FUNCTION THAT CALCULATES THE MAGNITUDE OF THE GRADIENT INDEPENDENTLY FOR EACH PLANE DEFINED IN THE COLOR IMAGE

```
%%%%%%%%%%%%%%%%%%%%%%%%%%%%%%%%%%%%%%%%%%%%%%%%%%%%%%%%%
%Function that allows the gradient computation of each
plane
% of an RGB (rgb) image. The function returns the
gradient value Gp
%%%%%%%%%%%%%%%%%%%%%%%%%%%%%%%%%%%%%%%%%%%%%%%%%%%%%%%%%
function [Gp]=gradplan(rgb)
% Coefficient matrices for calculating the horizontal
% and vertical gradient (Equation 2.69)
hx=[1 2 1;0 0 0; -1 -2 -1];
hy=hx';
%The image RGB is divided into different planes
R=rgb(:,:,1);
G=rgb(:,:,2);
B=rgb(:,:,3);
% The gradients of each plane are obtained.
```

```
Rx=double(imfilter(R,hx));
Ry=double(imfilter(R,hy));
Gx=double(imfilter(G,hx));
Gy=double(imfilter(G,hy));
Bx=double(imfilter(B,hx));
By=double(imfilter(B,hy));
% The magnitude of the gradient of each plane is obtained
RG=sqrt(Rx.^2+Ry.^2);
GG=sqrt(Gx.^2+Gy.^2);
BG=sqrt(Bx.^2+By.^2);

% All gradient results are merged
Gt=RG+GG+BG;
% The magnitude is also scaled from [0,1]
Gp=mat2gray(Gt);
```

In Program 2.3, it can be seen how, after obtaining the values of the gradients of each plane, the total gradient is calculated as the sum of each of the gradients obtained Gt=RG+GG+BG.

In order to compare the direct vector gradient method with the gradient calculated independently in each plane, the images obtained from locating the edges are shown in Figure 2.33. From both images, it is assumed a threshold of 0.3. The gradients calculated for this comparison have been obtained from the gradcol and gradplan functions implemented in Programs 2.2 and 2.3.

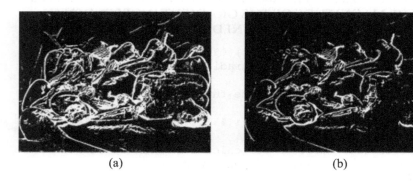

(a)   (b)

FIGURE 2.33
(a) Edge location using the vector gradient method and (b) edge location using the plane-by-plane gradient calculation method.

Note

1. card{...} represents cardinality, the number of elements.

References

[1] Woods, R. E. (2015). *Digital image processing* (4th ed.). Pearson.

[2] Jain, A. K. (1989). *Fundamentals of digital image processing*. Prentice Hall.

[3] Tirkel, A. Z., Osborne, C. F., & Van Schyndel, R. G. (1996). Image watermarking-a spread spectrum application. In Proceedings of ISSSTA'95 international symposium on spread spectrum techniques and applications (Vol. 2, pp. 785–789). IEEE.

[4] Burger, W., & Burge, M. J. (2016). *Digital image processing: An algorithmic introduction using Java*. Springer.

[5] Gonzalez, R. C., & Woods, R. E. (2008). *Digital image processing* (3rd ed.). Prentice Hall.

[6] Milanfar, P. (2013). *A tour of modern image processing: From fundamentals to applications*. CRC Press.

[7] Szeliski, R. (2010). *Computer vision: Algorithms and applications*. Springer.

[8] Gonzalez, R. C., Woods, R. E., & Eddins, S. L. (2004). *Digital image processing using MATLAB*. Prentice Hall.

3

Geometric Operations in Images

Geometric operations are widely used in practice, especially in current and modern graphical user interfaces and video games [1]. In fact, there are no graphic applications that do not have zoom capabilities to highlight small aspects of the images. Some examples of geometric operations such as displacement, rotation, scaling, and distortion are shown in Figure 3.1.

In the area of computer graphics, the topic of geometric operations is also important, whether for the representation of textures, 3-D environments, or simply for the representation of environments in real time [2]. However, although this type of operation seems trivial, to obtain a good result, it is necessary, even in modern computers, to consume a considerable amount of machine time.

Fundamentally, a geometric operation applied to an original image produces the following transformation in a target image:

$$I(x,y) \rightarrow I'(x',y') \tag{3.1}$$

where not only the value of the pixel is changed but also its position in the new image. To do this, a coordinate transformation is first needed in the form of a geometric transformation, such that:

$$T : \mathbb{R}^2 \rightarrow \mathbb{R}^2 \tag{3.2}$$

which, for each coordinate of the image $I(x,y)$ original image $x = (x,y)$, indicates in which new position $x' = (x',y')$ of the image $I'(x',y')$ must match. That is:

$$x \rightarrow x' = T(x) \tag{3.3}$$

As the previous expressions show, the coordinates that participate both in the original image and those calculated through the transformation $T(x)$ are considered as points on a surface of real numbers $\mathbb{R} \times \mathbb{R}$, as well as of the continuous type. However, the main problem with geometric transforms is that the coordinates in the images actually correspond to a discrete array of the type $\mathbb{Z} \times \mathbb{Z}$, so the computed transformation x' from x will not exactly

DOI: 10.1201/9781032662466-3

FIGURE 3.1
Examples of geometric transformations that will be treated in this chapter.

correspond to this array, that is, it will have a coordinate value that will be between two-pixel coordinates at best, so its value will be uncertain.

The solution to this problem consists in the calculation of the intermediate value of the coordinate transformed through interpolation, which corresponds to an important part in each geometric operation.

3.1 Coordinate Transformation

The transformation carried out by Equation 3.3 is fundamentally a function, which can be divided into two independent functions, such that:

$$x' = T_x(x, y) \quad \text{and} \quad y' = T_y(x, y) \tag{3.4}$$

3.1.1 Simple Transformations

Simple transformations include displacement, scaling, skewing, and rotation [3].

3.1.1.1 Displacement

Also known as a translation, it allows to shift an image by defining a displacement vector (d_x, d_y), such that:

$$T_x : x' = x + d_x$$

$$T_y : y' = y + d_y \tag{3.5}$$

$$\begin{bmatrix} x' \\ y' \end{bmatrix} = \begin{bmatrix} x \\ y \end{bmatrix} + \begin{bmatrix} d_x \\ d_y \end{bmatrix}$$

3.1.1.2 Scaling

Either in the direction x (s_x) or y (s_y) it allows to increase or contract the space occupied by the rectangular array of the image, such that:

$$T_x : x' = x \cdot s_x$$

$$T_y : y' = y \cdot s_y \tag{3.6}$$

$$\begin{bmatrix} x' \\ y' \end{bmatrix} = \begin{bmatrix} s_x & 0 \\ 0 & s_y \end{bmatrix} \begin{bmatrix} x \\ y \end{bmatrix}$$

3.1.1.3 Inclination

Either in the x (b_x) or y (b_y) direction, it allows tilting the space occupied by the rectangular array of the image (in tilting, only one direction should be considered while the other remains zero), such that:

$$T_x : x' = x + b_x \cdot y$$

$$T_y : y' = y + b_y \cdot x \tag{3.7}$$

$$\begin{bmatrix} x' \\ y' \end{bmatrix} = \begin{bmatrix} 1 & b_x \\ b_y & 1 \end{bmatrix} \begin{bmatrix} x \\ y \end{bmatrix}$$

3.1.1.4 Rotation

Allows the image rectangle to be rotated by a certain angle α, considering the center of the image as the center of rotation. That is:

$$T_x : x' = x \cdot \cos(\alpha) + y \cdot \text{sen}(\alpha)$$

$$T_y : y' = -x \cdot \text{sen}(\alpha) + y \cdot \cos(\alpha) \tag{3.8}$$

$$\begin{bmatrix} x' \\ y' \end{bmatrix} = \begin{bmatrix} \cos(\alpha) & \text{sen}(\alpha) \\ -\text{sen}(\alpha) & \cos(\alpha) \end{bmatrix} \begin{bmatrix} x \\ y \end{bmatrix}$$

Figure 3.2 shows the representation of the simple transformations discussed above.

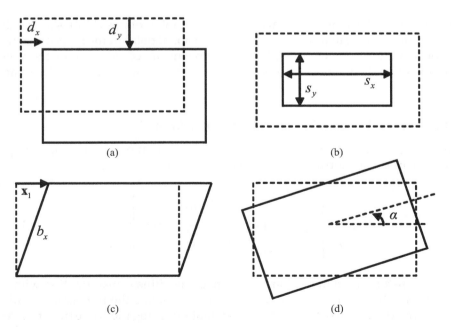

(a)

(b)

(c)

(d)

FIGURE 3.2
Simple geometric transformations. (a) Displacement, (b) scaling, (c) pitch, and (d) rotation.

3.1.2 Homogeneous Coordinates

The operations defined in Equations 3.5–3.8 represent an important class of transformations called the affine transforms (affine) [4]. For the concatenated application of these operations, it would be necessary to describe them in general matrix form. An elegant way to solve this is to use homogeneous coordinates.

In homogeneous coordinates, each vector is augmented with an additional component (h), that is:

$$
x = \begin{bmatrix} x \\ y \end{bmatrix} \rightarrow \hat{x} = \begin{bmatrix} \hat{x} \\ \hat{y} \\ h \end{bmatrix} = \begin{bmatrix} hx \\ hy \\ h \end{bmatrix} \tag{3.9}
$$

With this definition, each Cartesian coordinate $x = (x, y)$ is represented by a three-dimensional vector called the homogeneous coordinate vector $\hat{x} = (\hat{x}, \hat{y}, h)$. If the component h of this vector is not zero, the real coordinates can be obtained through:

$$
x = \frac{\hat{x}}{h} \quad \text{and} \quad y = \frac{\hat{y}}{h} \tag{3.10}
$$

Considering the above, there are an infinite number of possibilities (through different h values) to represent a two-dimensional point in the homogeneous coordinate format. For example, the homogeneous coordinates of the vectors $\hat{x}_1 = (2, 1, 1)$, $\hat{x}_1 = (4, 2, 2)$ and $\hat{x}_1 = (20, 10, 10)$ represent the same Cartesian point $(2, 1)$.

3.1.3 Affine Transformation (Triangle Transformation)

By using homogeneous coordinates, the combination of translation, scaling, and rotation transformations can be represented in the form:

$$
\begin{bmatrix} \hat{x}' \\ \hat{y}' \\ \hat{h}' \end{bmatrix} = \begin{bmatrix} x' \\ y' \\ 1 \end{bmatrix} = \begin{bmatrix} a_{11} & a_{12} & a_{13} \\ a_{21} & a_{22} & a_{23} \\ 0 & 0 & 1 \end{bmatrix} \begin{bmatrix} x \\ y \\ 1 \end{bmatrix} \tag{3.11}
$$

This transformation definition is known as the affine transformation with 6 degrees of freedom $a_{11}, \ldots, a_{23}$, where a_{13} and a_{23} define the translation, while a_{11}, a_{12}, a_{21} define the scaling, tilting, and rotation. Using the affine transformation, lines are transformed into lines, triangles into triangles, and rectangles

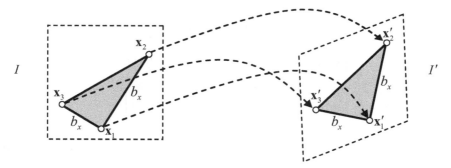

FIGURE 3.3
Affine transformation. By defining three points, the affine transformation is fully characterized. Through this transformation, the points that are on the lines maintain their relationships as far as distance is concerned.

into parallelograms (see Figure 3.3). Something characteristic of this type of transformation is that the relationship between the distances of the points contained in the lines of the converted image is maintained.

3.1.3.1 Determination of Transformation Parameters

The parameters of the transformation defined in Equation 3.11 are completely determined by the definition of three points with coordinates $\left(x_1, x_1' \right)$, $\left(x_2, x_2' \right)$ and $\left(x_3, x_3' \right)$, where $x_i = (x_i, y_i)$ corresponds to the points of the original image while $x_i' = \left(x_i', y_i' \right)$ corresponds to the transformed image. The parameters of the transform are obtained from the solution of the following system of equations:

$$x_1' = a_{11} \cdot x_1 + a_{12} \cdot y_1 + a_{13} \quad y_1' = a_{21} \cdot x_1 + a_{22} \cdot y_1 + a_{23}$$

$$x_2' = a_{11} \cdot x_2 + a_{12} \cdot y_2 + a_{13} \quad y_2' = a_{21} \cdot x_2 + a_{22} \cdot y_2 + a_{23} \qquad (3.12)$$

$$x_3' = a_{11} \cdot x_3 + a_{12} \cdot y_3 + a_{13} \quad y_3' = a_{21} \cdot x_3 + a_{22} \cdot y_3 + a_{23}$$

This system has a solution under the condition that the three points $\left(x_1, x_1' \right)$, $\left(x_2, x_2' \right)$ and $\left(x_3, x_3' \right)$ must be linearly independent, which means that they must not be located on the same line. Solving this system of equations, we get:

$$a_{11} = \frac{1}{F} \cdot \left[y_1 \left(x_2' - x_3' \right) + y_2 \left(x_3' - x_1' \right) + y_3 \left(x_1' - x_2' \right) \right]$$

$$a_{12} = \frac{1}{F} \cdot \left[x_1 \left(x_3' - x_2' \right) + x_2 \left(x_1' - x_3' \right) + x_3 \left(x_2' - x_1' \right) \right]$$

$$a_{21} = \frac{1}{F} \cdot \left[y_1 \left(y_2' - y_3' \right) + y_2 \left(y_3' - y_1' \right) + y_3 \left(y_1' - y_2' \right) \right]$$

$$a_{22} = \frac{1}{F} \cdot \left[x_1 \left(y_3' - y_2' \right) + x_2 \left(y_1' - y_3' \right) + x_3 \left(y_2' - y_1' \right) \right] \qquad (3.13)$$

$$a_{13} = \frac{1}{F} \cdot \left[x_1 \left(y_3 x_2' - y_2 x_3' \right) + x_2 \left(y_1 x_3' - y_3 x_1' \right) + x_3 \left(y_2 x_1' - y_1 x_2' \right) \right]$$

$$a_{23} = \frac{1}{F} \cdot \left[x_1 \left(y_3 y_2' - y_2 y_3' \right) + x_2 \left(y_1 y_3' - y_3 y_1' \right) + x_3 \left(y_2 y_1' - y_1 y_2' \right) \right]$$

$$F = x_1 \left(y_3 - y_2 \right) + x_2 \left(y_1 - y_3 \right) + x_3 \left(y_2 - y_1 \right)$$

3.1.3.2 The Inversion of the Affine Transformation

The inverse transformation T^{-1} of the affine transformation, which is widely used to find correspondences between geometric changes made to images, is obtained from the inversion of Equation 3.11. So, this would be:

$$\begin{bmatrix} x \\ y \\ 1 \end{bmatrix} = \begin{bmatrix} a_{11} & a_{12} & a_{13} \\ a_{21} & a_{22} & a_{23} \\ 0 & 0 & 1 \end{bmatrix}^{-1} \begin{bmatrix} x' \\ y' \\ 1 \end{bmatrix}$$

$$\qquad (3.14)$$

$$= \frac{1}{a_{11}a_{22} - a_{12}a_{21}} \begin{bmatrix} a_{22} & -a_{12} & a_{12}a_{23} - a_{13}a_{22} \\ -a_{21} & a_{11} & a_{12}a_{21} - a_{11}a_{23} \\ 0 & 0 & a_{11}a_{22} - a_{12}a_{21} \end{bmatrix} \cdot \begin{bmatrix} x' \\ y' \\ 1 \end{bmatrix}$$

Similarly, the parameters $a_{11}, \ldots, a_{23}$ are obtained by defining three points between the original and transformed images and calculated them from Equations 3.13. Figure 3.4 shows a geometrically transformed image from the affine transform. In the conversion, the definition of the following points were considered: $x_1 = (400, 300)$, $x_1' = (200, 280)$, $x_2 = (250, 20)$, $x_2' = (255, 18)$, $x_3 = (100, 100)$ and $x_3' = (120, 112)$.

3.1.3.3 Affine Transform in MATLAB

To show how to implement the geometric transformations that are treated in this chapter, the code and methodology to develop a test program, which in

(a)   (b)

FIGURE 3.4
Affine transformation. (a) Original image and (b) effect of the affine transform on an image considering the following transformation points $x_1 = (400, 300)$, $x_1' = (200, 280)$, $x_2 = (250, 20)$, $x_2' = (255, 18)$, $x_3 = (100, 100)$ and $x_3' = (120, 112)$.

this case implements the affine transform, are presented in this section. The program is based on the development of Equations 3.13 for the determination of the parameters $a_{11}, \ldots, a_{23}$ and on the implementation of Equation 3.3 to determine the values of the original image x_i that correspond to the points of the transformed image x_i'. This is since the implementation methodology starts with finding the correspondence of the transformed values with those of the original. Carrying out the transformation in this direction, each element of the transformed image will have a corresponding value to the original image, which would not happen if the correspondence was carried out in the other direction. However, despite this methodology, it may happen, due to the definition of the points used in the transformation, that there are values of the transformed image that correspond to undefined points of the original image. By undefined, it refers to the fact that they are not within the image space, which would imply that the indices were negative or of values greater than those of the image dimension. If a point in the transformed image does not have coordinates corresponding to the original image, then the pixel in the transformed image is assumed to be equal to zero. Figure 3.4 clearly illustrates the problem of non-correspondence between the transformed image and the original. Program 3.1 shows the code used to implement the affine transform of an image, considering the transformation points $x_1 = (400, 300)$, $x_1' = (200, 280)$, $x_2 = (250, 20)$, $x_2' = (255, 18)$, $x_3 = (100, 100)$ and $x_3' = (120, 112)$.

3.1.4 Projective Transformation

Although the affine transformation is especially suitable for the triangle transformation, a general distortion into a rectangular shape is sometimes necessary. To perform this rectangular geometric transformation of four points, 8 degrees of freedom are established, two more than in the

PROGRAM 3.1 IMPLEMENTATION OF THE AFFINE TRANSFORMATION IN MATLAB

```
%%%%%%%%%%%%%%%%%%%%%%%%%%%%%%%%%%%%%%%%%%%%%%%%%%%%%
%Program that implements the affine transform from
%a set of transformation points
%%%%%%%%%%%%%%%%%%%%%%%%%%%%%%%%%%%%%%%%%%%%%%%%%%%%%
%Transformation points cnl are defined
%where c indicates the x or y coordinate
%n the point number 1,2 or 3.
%1 if it corresponds to the original or
%1 if corresponds to the transform d
x1o=400;
y1o=300;
x1d=200;
y1d=280;
x2o=250;
y2o=18;
x2d=255;
y2d=20;
x3o=100;
y3o=100;
x3d=120;
y3d=112;

%Determination of the parameters of Equation 3.13
F=x1o*(y3o-y2o)+x2o*(y1o-y3o)+x3o*(y2o-y1o);

a11=(1/F)*(y1o*(x2d-x3d)+y2o*(x3d-x1d)+y3o*...
(x1d-x2d));
a12=(1/F)*(x1o*(x3d-x2d)+x2o*(x1d-x3d)+x3o*...
(x2d-x1d));
a21=(1/F)*(y1o*(y2d-y3d)+y2o*(y3d-y1d)+y3o*...
(y1d-y2d));
a22=(1/F)*(x1o*(y3d-y2d)+x2o*(y1d-y3d)+x3o*...
(y2d-y1d));

a13=(1/F)*(x1o*(y3o*x2d-y2o*x3d)+x2o*...
(y1o*x3d-y3o*x1d)+x3o*(y2o*x1d-y1o*x2d));
a23=(1/F)*(x1o*(y3o*y2d-y2o*y3d)+x2o*...
(y1o*y3d-y3o*y1d)+x3o*(y2o*y1d-y1o*y2d));

Den=1/(a11*a22-a12*a21);
Im = imread("fotos/paisaje.jpg");
Im = rgb2gray(Im);
imshow(Im)
figure
%The indices of the image are obtained
```

```
[m n]=size(Im);
%The transformed image of the same size is created
%as the original
I1=zeros(size(Im));
%The values of the transformed image are calculated
%by their correspondences with the original image
for re=1:m
    for co=1:n
        %Calculation of correspondences according to the
        %Ec. 3.14
        xf=round((a22*co-a12*re+...
                 (a12*a23-a13*a22))*Den);
yf=round((-a21*co+a11*re+...
                 (a13*a21-a11*a23))*Den);
        %If there is no correspondence the pixel=0
        if ((xf>n)||(xf<1)||(yf>m)||(yf<1))
        I1(re,co)=0;
        else
        I1(re,co)=Im(yf,xf);
        end
    end
end
imshow(uint8(I1))
```

affine transformation. This type of transformation is known as a projective transformation. And it is defined as follows:

$$
\begin{bmatrix} \hat{x}' \\ \hat{y}' \\ \hat{h}' \end{bmatrix} = \begin{bmatrix} h'x' \\ h'y' \\ h' \end{bmatrix} = \begin{bmatrix} a_{11} & a_{12} & a_{13} \\ a_{21} & a_{22} & a_{23} \\ a_{31} & a_{32} & 1 \end{bmatrix} \begin{bmatrix} x \\ y \\ 1 \end{bmatrix}
\tag{3.15}
$$

This operation corresponds to the following non-linear transformation of the coordinates of the image obtained:

$$
x' = \frac{1}{h'} \cdot (a_{11}x + a_{12}y + a_{13}) = \frac{a_{11}x + a_{12}y + a_{13}}{a_{31}x + a_{32}y + 1}
$$

$$
x' = \frac{1}{h'} \cdot (a_{21}x + a_{22}y + a_{23}) = \frac{a_{21}x + a_{22}y + a_{23}}{a_{31}x + a_{32}y + 1}
\tag{3.16}
$$

The lines, despite the non-linearity of the transformation, remain as lines, with a projection or perspective effect. This transformation can be said to,

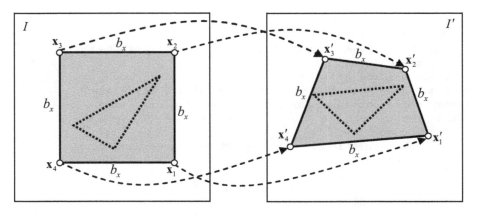

FIGURE 3.5
Projective transformation. In this transformation, lines are converted to lines, squares to polygons, parallel lines are transformed to non-parallel lines, and distance relationships between points on a line are lost.

in general, transform parallel lines into non-parallel lines, squares into polygons, and algebraic curves of order pi into algebraic curves of order pi. For example, circles or ellipses are, by this transformation, converted into second-order curves. In contrast to the affine transformation, the parallel lines are not converted in the resulting image into parallel lines; in the same way, the relation of distances between points that are on a line is not maintained. Figure 3.5 shows an illustration of the projective transformation.

3.1.4.1 Determination of Transformation Parameters

The parameters of the projective transformation are completely determined by the definition of 4 coordinate points $\left(x_1, x_1' \right), \left(x_2, x_2' \right), \left(x_3, x_3' \right)$ and $\left(x_4, x_4' \right)$, $x_i = \left(x_i, y_i \right)$ corresponds to the points of the original image while $x_i' = \left(x_i', y_i' \right)$ corresponds to the transformed image. The eight parameters of the transform are obtained from the resolution of the following system of equations:

$$x_i' = a_{11}x_i + a_{12}y_i + a_{13} - a_{31}x_ix_i' - a_{32}y_ix_i'$$

$$y_i' = a_{21}x_i + a_{22}y_i + a_{23} - a_{31}x_iy_i' - a_{32}y_iy_i'$$

(3.17)

where $i = 1,\ldots,4$. Developing the system defined in Equation 3.17 in matrix form for each parameter of the transform, we obtain:

$$
\begin{bmatrix} x_1' \\ y_1' \\ x_2' \\ y_2' \\ x_3' \\ y_3' \\ x_4' \\ y_4' \end{bmatrix}
=
\begin{bmatrix}
x_1 & y_1 & 1 & 0 & 0 & 0 & -x_1 x_1' & -y_1 x_1' \\
0 & 0 & 0 & x_1 & y_1 & 1 & -x_1 y_1' & -y_1 y_1' \\
x_2 & y_2 & 1 & 0 & 0 & 0 & -x_2 x_2' & -y_2 x_2' \\
0 & 0 & 0 & x_2 & y_2 & 1 & -x_2 y_2' & -y_2 y_2' \\
x_3 & y_3 & 1 & 0 & 0 & 0 & -x_3 x_3' & -y_3 x_3' \\
0 & 0 & 0 & x_3 & y_3 & 1 & -x_3 y_3' & -y_3 y_3' \\
x_4 & y_4 & 1 & 0 & 0 & 0 & -x_4 x_4' & -y_4 x_4' \\
0 & 0 & 0 & x_4 & y_4 & 1 & -x_4 y_4' & -y_4 y_4'
\end{bmatrix}
\begin{bmatrix} a_{11} \\ a_{12} \\ a_{13} \\ a_{21} \\ a_{22} \\ a_{23} \\ a_{31} \\ a_{32} \end{bmatrix}
\qquad (3.18)
$$

That expressed in compact form would be:

$$ x' = M * a \qquad (3.19) $$

The values of the parameters $a = (a_{11}, a_{12} \ldots, a_{32})$ can be determined by solving the system defined in Equation 3.18 using a standard numerical method (such as the Gaussian algorithm).

3.1.4.2 The Inversion of the Projective Transformation

A linear transformation of the form $x' = A \cdot x$ can in general be reformulated indirectly by inverting the matrix A, that is $x = A^{-1} \cdot x'$. A fundamental requirement for this reformulation is that the matrix A be non-singular ($\text{Det}(A) \neq 0$). The inverse of a 3×3 matrix can be calculated in a relatively simple way, through the relation:

$$ A = \frac{1}{\text{Det}(A)} A_{adj} \qquad (3.20) $$

where:

$$
A = \begin{bmatrix}
a_{11} & a_{12} & a_{13} \\
a_{21} & a_{22} & a_{23} \\
a_{31} & a_{32} & a_{33}
\end{bmatrix}
$$

$$ \text{Det}(A) = a_{11}a_{22}a_{33} + a_{12}a_{23}a_{31} + a_{13}a_{21}a_{32} - a_{11}a_{23}a_{32} - a_{12}a_{21}a_{33} - a_{13}a_{22}a_{31} \qquad (3.21) $$

$$
A_{adj} = \begin{bmatrix}
a_{22}a_{33} - a_{23}a_{32} & a_{13}a_{32} - a_{12}a_{33} & a_{12}a_{23} - a_{13}a_{22} \\
a_{23}a_{31} - a_{21}a_{33} & a_{11}a_{33} - a_{13}a_{31} & a_{13}a_{21} - a_{11}a_{23} \\
a_{21}a_{32} - a_{22}a_{31} & a_{12}a_{31} - a_{11}a_{32} & a_{11}a_{22} - a_{12}a_{21}
\end{bmatrix}
$$

 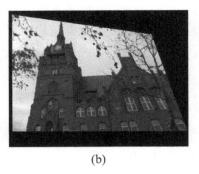

(a)   (b)

FIGURE 3.6
Projective transformation. (a) Original image and (b) effect of the projective transform on an image.

In the projective transformation, the parameter $a_{33}=1$, which simplifies the calculation of the previous equations. Since in homogeneous coordinates, multiplication by a scalar formulates the same equivalent point (see Section 3.1.2), the determination of the determinant of A is not necessary, so it would suffice to calculate the inverse of the projective transform, the homogeneous coordinates of the points, with the calculation of the adjoining matrix A_{adj}. Figure 3.6 shows a geometrically transformed image from the projective transform.

3.1.4.3 Projective Transformation on the Unit Square

An alternative to the solution by numerical methods to the set of equations defined in Equation 3.18 of eight unknown parameters is the transformation of the unit square C_1. In this transformation, as illustrated in Figure 3.7, the conversion of a square of unitary dimensions C_1 to a polygon P_1 of four points

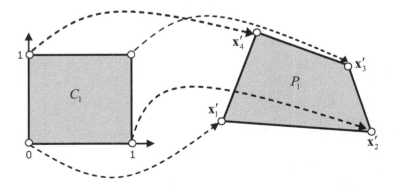

FIGURE 3.7
Projective transformation of the unit square C_1 to any polygon P_1.

with distorted characteristics is established. Such conversion considers the following transformation of points:

$$(0,0) \rightarrow x_1' \quad (1,1) \rightarrow x_3'$$

$$(1,0) \rightarrow x_2' \quad (0,1) \rightarrow x_4' \tag{3.22}$$

Due to the relationship between the transformation points, the set of equations defined in Equation 3.18 reduces to:

$$x_1' = a_{13}$$

$$y_1' = a_{23}$$

$$x_2' = a_{11} + a_{13} - a_{31} \cdot x_2'$$

$$y_2' = a_{21} + a_{23} - a_{31} \cdot y_2'$$

$$x_3' = a_{11} + a_{12} + a_{13} - a_{31} \cdot x_3' - a_{32} \cdot x_3' \tag{3.23}$$

$$y_3' = a_{21} + a_{22} + a_{23} - a_{31} \cdot y_3' - a_{32} \cdot y_3'$$

$$x_4' = a_{12} + a_{13} - a_{32} \cdot x_4'$$

$$y_4' = a_{22} + a_{23} - a_{33} \cdot y_4'$$

whose solution for the parameters $a_{11}, \ldots, a_{32}$ is obtained through the following relationships:

$$a_{31} = \frac{\left(x_1' - x_2' + x_3' - x_4'\right) \cdot \left(y_4' - y_3'\right) - \left(y_1' - y_2' + y_3' - y_4'\right) \cdot \left(x_4' - x_3'\right)}{\left(x_2' - x_3'\right) \cdot \left(y_4' - y_3'\right) - \left(x_4' - x_3'\right) \cdot \left(y_2' - y_3'\right)}$$

$$a_{32} = \frac{\left(y_1' - y_2' + y_3' - y_4'\right) \cdot \left(x_2' - x_3'\right) - \left(x_1' - x_2' + x_3' - x_4'\right) \cdot \left(y_2' - y_3'\right)}{\left(x_2' - x_3'\right) \cdot \left(y_4' - y_3'\right) - \left(x_4' - x_3'\right) \cdot \left(y_2' - y_3'\right)}$$

$$a_{11} = x_2' - x_1' + a_{31} \cdot x_2' \tag{3.24}$$

$$a_{21} = y_2' - y_1' + a_{31} \cdot y_2'$$

$$a_{12} = x_4' - x_1' + a_{32} \cdot x_4'$$

$$a_{22} = y_4' - y_1' + a_{32} \cdot y_4'$$

$$a_{13} = x_1'$$

$$a_{23} = y_1'$$

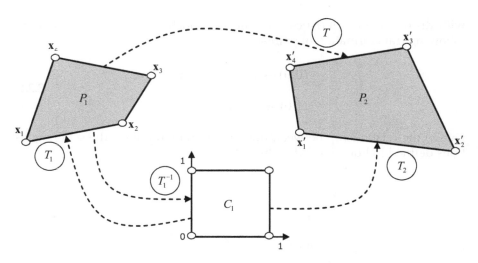

FIGURE 3.8
Projective transformation between any two polygons of four points. This type of transformation is performed using a two-step method; the first involves an inverse transformation A_1^{-1} from polygon P_1 to unit square C_1, while the second involves a direct transformation A_2 from unit square C_1 to polygon P_2, in such a way that the complete transformation is characterized by $A = A_2 \cdot A_1^{-1}$.

As already mentioned in this section, through the inversion of matrix A, the inverse transformation T^{-1} can be calculated, which in this case would mean obtaining the unit square from any polygon of four points.

As Figure 3.8 shows, the transformation from any four-point polygon P_1 to any other four-point polygon P_2 can be performed using a two-step transformation performed on the unit frame. This can be expressed as follows:

$$P_1 \stackrel{T_1^{-1}}{\rightarrow} C_1 \stackrel{T_2}{\rightarrow} P_2 \tag{3.25}$$

The operations T_1 and T_2 for the transformation from the unit square to each of the four-point polygons are obtained from the points that define them x_i and x_i' using the expressions defined in Equation 3.24, while the inverse transformation T_1^{-1} is obtained by calculating the matrix A_1. The complete transformation T is finally produced through the coupling of the transformations T_1^{-1} and T_2, in such a way that:

$$x' = T(x) = T_2\left(T_1^{-1}(x)\right) \tag{3.26}$$

Or in matrix form:

$$x' = A \cdot x = A_1 \cdot A_2 \cdot x \tag{3.27}$$

The transformation matrix $A = A_2 \cdot A_1^{-1}$ must be calculated only once for a certain transformation using the points that define the polygons P_1 and P_2.

Calculation example. Projective transformation of two polygons

It is desired to perform the geometric transformation of polygon P_1 to polygon P_2 where the coordinates that define both polygons correspond to:

$$P_1 \quad x_1 = (2,5) \quad x_2 = (4,6) \quad x_3 = (7,9) \quad x_4 = (5,9)$$

$$P_2 \quad x_1' = (4,3) \quad x_2' = (5,2) \quad x_3' = (9,3) \quad x_4' = (7,5) \tag{3.28}$$

Then the projective transformation matrices are produced in relation to the unit square C_1 where $A_1 : C_1 \rightarrow P_1$ and $A_2 : C_1 \rightarrow P_2$, in such a way that:

$$A_1 = \begin{bmatrix} 3.33 & 0.50 & 2 \\ 3.00 & -0.50 & 5 \\ 0.33 & -0.5 & 1 \end{bmatrix} \quad A_2 = \begin{bmatrix} 1 & -0.50 & 4 \\ -1 & -0.50 & 3 \\ 0 & -0.5 & 1 \end{bmatrix} \tag{3.29}$$

Through the coupling of the transformation matrix A_2 and A_1^{-1}, the general transformation matrix is obtained, which is defined as $A = A_2 \cdot A_1^{-1}$, where:

$$A_1^{-1} = \begin{bmatrix} 0.6 & -0.45 & 1.05 \\ -0.40 & 0.8 & -3.2 \\ -0.4 & 0.55 & -0.95 \end{bmatrix} \quad A = \begin{bmatrix} -0.8 & 1.35 & -1.12 \\ 1.6 & 1.7 & -2.3 \\ -0.2 & 0.15 & 0.65 \end{bmatrix} \tag{3.30}$$

3.1.5 Bilinear Transformation

The bilinear transformation is defined as:

$$\begin{aligned} T_x : x' &= a_1 x + a_2 y + a_3 xy + a_4 \\ T_y : y' &= b_1 x + b_2 y + b_3 xy + b_4 \end{aligned} \tag{3.31}$$

From this definition, there are eight parameters $(a_1, \ldots, a_4, b_1, \ldots, b_4)$ that fully characterize the transform, so to calculate them, it will be necessary to have at least four pairs of points. From the terms present in Equation 3.31 there are combinations where both variables xy are involved; therefore, this type of transformation performs a non-linear modification in the geometry of the resulting image [5]. In this type of transformation, unlike the projective transformation, the lines are converted into quadratic curves.

A bilinear transformation is fully specified by defining four pairs of coordinates $(x_1, x_1'), \ldots, (x_4, x_4')$. In general, the transformation can be formulated by defining four pairs of points that form the following system of equations:

$$\begin{bmatrix} x_1' \\ x_2' \\ x_3' \\ x_4' \end{bmatrix} = \begin{bmatrix} x_1 & y_1 & x_1y_1 & 1 \\ x_2 & y_2 & x_2y_2 & 1 \\ x_3 & y_3 & x_3y_3 & 1 \\ x_4 & y_4 & x_4y_4 & 1 \end{bmatrix} \begin{bmatrix} a_1 \\ a_2 \\ a_3 \\ a_4 \end{bmatrix}$$

$$\begin{bmatrix} y_1' \\ y_2' \\ y_3' \\ y_4' \end{bmatrix} = \begin{bmatrix} x_1 & y_1 & x_1y_1 & 1 \\ x_2 & y_2 & x_2y_2 & 1 \\ x_3 & y_3 & x_3y_3 & 1 \\ x_4 & y_4 & x_4y_4 & 1 \end{bmatrix} \begin{bmatrix} b_1 \\ b_2 \\ b_3 \\ b_4 \end{bmatrix}$$

(3.32)

For the special case in which the bilinear transformation is performed from the unit square C_1 to any polygon P_1, the calculation of the parameters $(a_1,\ldots,a_4,b_1,\ldots,b_4)$ is simplified, obtaining:

$$a_1 = x_2' - x_1'$$

$$a_2 = x_4' - x_1'$$

$$a_3 = x_1' - x_2' + x_3' - x_4'$$

$$a_4 = x_1'$$

(3.33)

$$b_1 = y_2' - y_1'$$

$$b_2 = y_4' - y_1'$$

$$b_3 = y_1' - y_2' + y_3' - y_4'$$

$$b_4 = y_1'$$

Figure 3.9 shows a series of images that represent the different effects of performing different geometric transformations on the same image.

3.1.5.1 Bilinear Transformation in MATLAB

This section presents how to implement the bilinear transformation in MATLAB®. Unlike Program 3.1 made for the affine transformation, in the case of the bilinear transformation, it is not trivial to find an inverse formulation, so the methodology will be based on the direct calculation of the pixel

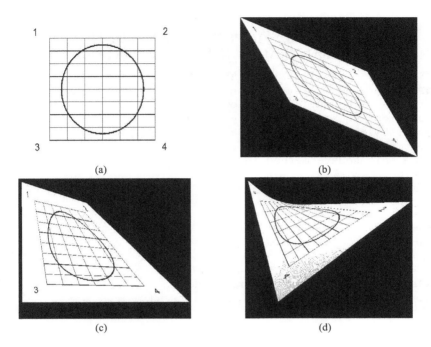

FIGURE 3.9
Comparison of geometric transformations. (a) Original image, (b) affine transformation, (c) projective transformation, and (d) bilinear transformation.

values of the transformed image. Although this way of calculating the values of the image gives a good result, sometimes it does not allow you to find the value of pixels whose non-linear transformation does not have a corresponding pixel in the original image. This effect is clearly visible because holes (black dots) usually appear at these points, as can be seen in Figure 3.9d. Program 3.2 shows the MATLAB code to implement the bilinear transformation. In this program, the transformation from the unit square to the four-point polygon was considered for ease of calculation, so the transformation points are defined as follows:

$$(0,0) \to x_1' \quad (1,1) \to x_3'$$
$$(1,0) \to x_2' \quad (0,1) \to x_4' \tag{3.34}$$

3.1.6 Other Nonlinear Geometric Transformations

The bilinear transformation is just one example of a nonlinear transformation that cannot be represented by simple matrix multiplication. However, there are a considerable number of non-linear transformations that allow you to

PROGRAM 3.2   IMPLEMENTATION OF THE BILINEAR TRANSFORMATION IN MATLAB

```
%%%%%%%%%%%%%%%%%%%%%%%%%%%%%%%%%%%%%%%%%%%%%%%%%%%%%%%%%%
%Program that implements the bilinear transformation
%from a set of transformation points
%considering the unit square
%%%%%%%%%%%%%%%%%%%%%%%%%%%%%%%%%%%%%%%%%%%%%%%%%%%%%%%%%%
%Definition of transformation points
%The unit square method is considered to be used.
x1=100;
y1=80;
x2=500;
y2=70;
x3=100;
y3=350;
x4=10;
y4=10;
%Determination of parameters a and b.
a1=x2-x1;
a2=x4-x1;
a3=x1-x2+x3-x4;
a4=x1;
b1=y2-y1;
b2=y4-y1;
b3=y1-y2+y3-y4;
b4=y1;
%Get the size of the image
Im = imread("fotos/paisaje.jpg");
Im = rgb2gray(Im);
[m n]=size(Im);
%Each of the points of the result image is set to black,
%this is because there will be values of the result image
% that do not have a corresponding value in the original
image.
I1=zeros(size(Im));
%All pixels of the transformed image are traversed
for re=1:m
    for co=1:n
%The coordinates of the original image
%correspond to points on the unit square so
%they are divided between m and n
        re1=re/m;
        co1=co/n;
%Get the values of the transformed image
        x=round(a1*co1+a2*re1+a3*re1*co1+a4);
        y=round(b1*co1+b2*re1+b3*re1*co1+b4);
%It is protected for pixel values that due to
```

```
%the transformation do not have a corresponding
    if ((x>=1)||(x<=n)||(y>=1)||(y<=m))
        I1(y,x)=Im(re,co);
    end

  end
end
%Convert the image to a data type
I1=uint8(I1);
%The image is displayed
imshow(I1)
```

add interesting effects and distortions to images. The following three examples make extensive use of the reverse formulation of the transformation:

$$x = T^{-1}(x')$$

(3.35)

Depending on the type of transformation in question, the inverse formulation is not always easy, although for practical purposes on many occasions (using the source-origin transformation technique) inversion is not necessary.

3.1.6.1 The Twirl Transformation

The Twirl transformation produces an α rotation of the image about the rotation point $x_c = (x_c, y_c)$, this rotation decreases as the distance of the image pixel from the rotation point increases. The geometric transformation produced on the image only has an effect within a certain radius r_{max} of distortion, so outside of it, the image remains unchanged [6]. The inverse formulation of this transformation is defined as follows:

$$T_x^{-1} : x = \begin{cases} x_c + r \cdot \cos(\beta) & \text{si } r \leq r_{max} \\ x' & \text{si } r > r_{max} \end{cases}$$

(3.36)

$$T_y^{-1} : y = \begin{cases} y_c + r \cdot \text{sen}(\beta) & \text{si } r \leq r_{max} \\ y' & \text{si } r > r_{max} \end{cases}$$

(3.37)

where:

$$dx = x' - x_c$$

$$dy = y' - y_c$$

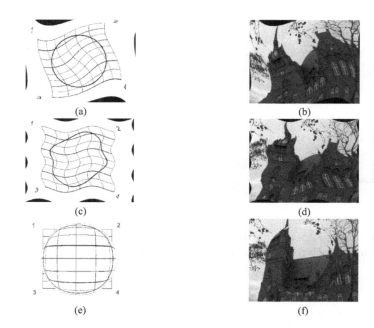

FIGURE 3.10
Different nonlinear transformations. (a) and (b) Twirl transformation, (c) and (d) Ripple transformation, and (e) and (f) spherical distortion.

$$r = \sqrt{d_x^2 + d_y^2}$$

$$\beta = a\tan 2\left(d_y, d_x\right) + \alpha \cdot \left(\frac{r_{max}}{r_{max}}\right) \tag{3.38}$$

Figure 3.10a and d show two examples of the Twirl transformation, considering the center of the image as the point of rotation x_c, r_{max} as half the main diagonal of the image, and the angle of rotation $\alpha = 28°$.

3.1.6.2 *The Twirl Transformation in MATLAB*

This section presents how to implement the Twirl transformation in MATLAB. The implementation methodology uses the inverse formulation of the transformation; that is, it starts by finding the correspondence of the transformed values with those of the original. This is convenient since the transformation itself, according to Equations 3.36 and 3.37, is expressed in terms of the inverse formulation. The code for this implementation is shown in Program 3.3, considering as the point of rotation x_c the center of the image, r_{max} as half the main diagonal of the image, and the angle of rotation $\alpha = 28°$.

PROGRAM 3.3   IMPLEMENTATION OF THE
TWIRL TRANSFORMATION IN MATLAB

```
%%%%%%%%%%%%%%%%%%%%%%%%%%%%%%%%%%%%%%%%%%%%%%%%%%%%%
%Program that implements the Twirl transformation
%%%%%%%%%%%%%%%%%%%%%%%%%%%%%%%%%%%%%%%%%%%%%%%%%%%%%
Im=imread("fotos\paisaje.jpg")
Im = rgb2gray(Im);
imshow(Im)
figure
%Get the size of the image
[m n]=size(Im);
%The center of rotation is defined
%as the center of the image
xc=n/2;
yc=m/2;
%The angle of rotation is defined approx. 28 degrees
%1 rad
alfa=1;
%rmax is defined
rmax=sqrt(xc*xc+yc*yc);
%Convert the image to double to avoid numerical problems
Imd=double(Im);
%The resulting image is filled with zeros in such a way
that
% where there are no geometric correspondences,
% the value of the pixels will be zero.
I1=zeros(size(Im));
%All pixels of the transformed image are traversed
for re=1:m
    for co=1:n
%The values defined in 3.34 are obtained
        dx=co-xc;
        dy=re-yc;
        r=sqrt(dx*dx+dy*dy);
%The transformations of
%Equations 3.33-3.343 are calculated
        if (r<=rmax)
            Beta=atan2(dy,dx)+alfa*...
                ((rmax-r)/rmax);
            xf=round(xc+r*cos(Beta));
            yf=round(yc+r*sin(Beta));
        else
            xf=co;
            yf=re;

        end
%It is protected for pixel values that due to
```

```
%the transformation do not have a corresponding
        if ((xf>=1)&&(xf<=n)&&(yf>=1)&&(yf<=m))
                I1(re,co)=Imd(yf,xf);
        end
    end
end
    I1=uint8(I1);
    imshow(I1)
```

3.1.6.3 The Ripple Transformation

The Ripple transform produces a local waveform distortion in the x or y direction. The parameters of this transformation are the periods of the wavelength τ_x and τ_y that are defined in each of the directions and the displacement amplitudes in each direction, defined by the parameters a_x and a_y [6]. The inverse formulation of this transformation is defined as follows:

$$T_x^{-1} : x = x' + a_x \cdot \text{sen}\left(\frac{2\pi y'}{\tau_x}\right)$$

$$T_y^{-1} : y = y' + a_y \cdot \text{sen}\left(\frac{2\pi x'}{\tau_y}\right)$$

(3.39)

Figure 3.10b and e shows two examples of the Ripple transformation, considering $\tau_x = 120$ and $\tau_y = 250$, as well as $a_x = 10$ and $a_y = 12$.

3.1.6.4 The Ripple Transformation in MATLAB

This section presents how to implement the Ripple transformation in MATLAB. The implementation methodology uses the inverse formulation of the transformation; that is, it starts by finding the correspondence of the transformed values with those of the original. This is convenient since the transformation itself, according to Equation 3.39, is expressed in terms of the inverse formulation. The code for this implementation is shown in Program 3.4, considering $\tau_x = 120$ and $\tau_y = 250$, also $a_x = 10$ and $a_x = 10$.

3.1.6.5 Spherical Distortion

Spherical distortion produces an effect similar to that of a sphere-shaped lens. The parameters for performing this transformation are the center of the lens $x_c = (x_c, y_c)$, the maximum distortion radius r_{max} and the lens index \rho [6]. The inverse formulation of this transformation is defined as follows:

PROGRAM 3.4   IMPLEMENTATION OF THE RIPPLE TRANSFORMATION IN MATLAB

```
%%%%%%%%%%%%%%%%%%%%%%%%%%%%%%%%%%%%%%%%%%%%%%%%%%%%%%%%%%%%%
%Program that implements the Ripple transformation
%%%%%%%%%%%%%%%%%%%%%%%%%%%%%%%%%%%%%%%%%%%%%%%%%%%%%%%%%%%%%
Im=imread("fotos\paisaje.jpg")
Im = rgb2gray(Im);
imshow(Im)
figure
%Get the size of the image
[m n]=size(Im);
%The periods of the wavelength are defined
tx=120;
ty=250;
%Displacements of each of the directions
ax=10;
ay=12;
%Convert the image to double to avoid
%numerical problems
Imd=double(Im);
%The resulting image is filled with zeros in such a way
% that where there are no geometric correspondences,
% the value of the pixels will be zero.
I1=zeros(size(Im));
%All pixels of the transformed image are traversed
for re=1:m
    for co=1:n
%The transformations of Eq. 3.36 are calculated
            Angulo1=sin((2*pi*re)/tx);
            Angulo2=sin((2*pi*co)/ty);
            xf=round(co+ax*Angulo1);
            yf=round(re+ay*Angulo2);
        %It is protected for pixel values that due to the
        %transformation do not have a corresponding
        if ((xf>=1)&&(xf<=n)&&(yf>=1)&&(yf<=m))
            I1(re,co)=Imd(yf,xf);
        end
    end
end
        I1=uint8(I1);
        imshow(I1);
```

$$T_x^{-1} : x = x' - \begin{cases} z \cdot \tan(\beta_x) \text{ si } r \leq r_{max} \\ 0 \qquad\qquad \text{ si } r > r_{max} \end{cases}$$

$$T_y^{-1} : y = y' - \begin{cases} z \cdot \tan(\beta_y) \text{ si } r \leq r_{max} \\ 0 \qquad\qquad \text{ si } r > r_{max} \end{cases}$$

(3.40)

where:

$$dx = x' - x_c$$

$$dy = y' - y_c$$

$$r = \sqrt{d_x^2 + d_y^2}$$

$$z = \sqrt{r_{max}^2}$$

$$\beta_x = \left(1 - \frac{1}{\rho}\right) \cdot \mathrm{sen}^{-1}\left(\frac{d_x}{\sqrt{d_x^2 + z^2}}\right)$$

$$\beta_y = \left(1 - \frac{1}{\rho}\right) \cdot \mathrm{sen}^{-1}\left(\frac{d_y}{\sqrt{d_y^2 + z^2}}\right)$$

(3.41)

Figure 3.10c and f shows two examples of spherical distortion, considering as the point of rotation x_c the center of the image, r_{max} as half of the main diagonal of the image, and the lens index $\rho = 1.8$.

3.1.6.6 Spherical Distortion in MATLAB

This section presents how to implement spherical distortion in MATLAB. The implementation methodology uses the inverse formulation of the transformation; that is, it starts by finding the correspondence of the transformed values with those of the original. This is convenient since the transformation itself, according to Equation 3.40, is expressed in terms of the inverse formulation. The code for this implementation is shown in Program 3.5, considering the rotation point x_c to be the center of the image, r_{max} to be half the main diagonal of the image, and the lens index $\rho = 1.8$.

PROGRAM 3.5   IMPLEMENTATION OF SPHERICAL DISTORTION IN MATLAB

```
%%%%%%%%%%%%%%%%%%%%%%%%%%%%%%%%%%%%%%%%%%%%%%%%%%%%%%
%Program that implements spherical distortion
%%%%%%%%%%%%%%%%%%%%%%%%%%%%%%%%%%%%%%%%%%%%%%%%%%%%%%
Im=imread("fotos\paisaje.jpg")
Im = rgb2gray(Im);
imshow(Im)
figure
%Get the size of the image
[m n]=size(Im);
%The center of the spherical lens is defined as
%the center of the image
xc=n/2;
yc=m/2;
%Define the lens index
ro=1.8;
%rmax is defined
rmax=sqrt(xc*xc+yc*yc);
%Convert the image to double to avoid numerical problems
Imd=double(Im);
%The resulting image is filled with zeros
%in such a way that where there are
%no geometric correspondences,
% the value of the pixels will be zero.
I1=zeros(size(Im));
%All pixels of the transformed image are traversed
for re=1:m
    for co=1:n
%The values defined in 3.37 are obtained
        dx=co-xc;
        dy=re-yc;
        r=sqrt(dx*dx+dy*dy);
        if (r<=rmax)
%The transformations of Eq. 3.37 are calculated
            z=sqrt(rmax*rmax-r*r);
            R1=dx/(sqrt(dx*dx+z*z));
            R2=dy/(sqrt(dy*dy+z*z));
            Bx=(1-(1/ro))*asin(R1);
            By=(1-(1/ro))*asin(R2);
            xf=round(co-z*tan(Bx));
            yf=round(re-z*tan(By));
        else
            xf=co;
            yf=re;

        end
```

```
%It is protected for pixel values that due
%to the transformation do not have a corresponding
        if ((xf>=1)&&(xf<=n)&&(yf>=1)&&(yf<=m))
            I1(re,co)=Imd(yf,xf);
        end
    end
end
        I1=uint8(I1);
        imshow(I1)
```

3.2 Reassignment of Coordinates

Until now, in the manipulation of geometric operations, it has been considered that the coordinates of the image are continuous, that is, of real value. However, the value of the elements of an image is indexed discreetly, using only integer values. Considering the above, a non-trivial problem of geometric transformations is to find the correspondence of coordinates between the original image and the transformed image (without loss of information produced by the assignment or rounding of the coordinates).

Based on a geometric transformation $T(x,y)$ that operates on a source image $I(x,y)$ to produce a result image $I'(x',y')$, and where all coordinates are discrete, $x,y \in \mathbb{Z}$ and $x',y' \in \mathbb{Z}$, it is possible to use two different methods which differ in the sense in which they perform the transformation. These methods are called Source-Destination Mapping and Destination-Source Mapping.

3.2.1 Source-Destination Mapping

In this first approach, for each pixel of the source image $I(x,y)$, its corresponding position in the transformed (destination) image $I'(x',y')$ is calculated. The computed coordinates x',y' normally do not correspond to integer or discrete values (see Figure 3.11), so it is necessary to decide which intensity value of the original image I will correspond to that of the transformed image I'. The solution to this problem is not trivial, so a method that allows finding the correct value from intermediate intensities (interpolation) could be required.

The main problem with this method is that, depending on the geometric transformation $T(x,y)$, there will be elements in the transformed image $I'(x',y')$ that do not have correspondence with those of the original image $I(x,y)$. For example, in the case of magnification of the original image, there will be gaps in the intensity function of the transformed image that

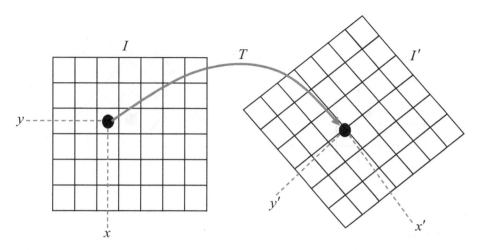

FIGURE 3.11

Source-destination mapping. For each discrete position of the source image $I(x,y)$, its corresponding pixel in the transformed image $I'(x',y')$ is calculated using the transformation operator $T(x,y)$.

must be filled. On the other hand, in the case of a reduction in the size of the original image, it must also be considered that there will be pixels in the original image that will no longer exist in the transformed image, so that a loss of information is evident.

3.2.2 Destination-Source Mapping

This method can be considered as the opposite of source-destination mapping, in which from a point in the transformed image (x',y') its corresponding point in the source image (x,y) is calculated. To do the above, it is necessary to express the transformation by means of its inverse formulation, such that:

$$(x,y) = T^{-1}(x',y') \tag{3.42}$$

In this method, as well as the source-destination mapping, depending on the inverse geometric transformation $T^{-1}(x,y)$, there will be elements in the original image $I(x,y)$ that do not have correspondence with those of the transformed image $I'(x',y')$. The solution to this problem requires finding from intermediate intensities the correct value (interpolation). Figure 3.12 illustrates the transformation process using the Destination-Source Mapping method.

The advantage of the destination-source mapping method is that the calculation for all the pixels in the new image and their corresponding points

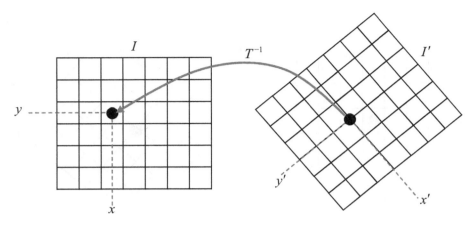

FIGURE 3.12
Destination-source mapping. For each discrete position of the destination image $I'(x',y')$, its corresponding pixel in the source image $I(x,y)$ is calculated from the inverse transformation operator $T^{-1}(x,y)$.

in the original image is guaranteed. By doing the above, the possibility of having gaps in the new image as a result of a lack of correspondence between the points is eliminated. Perhaps a disadvantage of this method is the need for the inverse formulation of the transformation, which in many cases is not easy to obtain. Notwithstanding the foregoing, its properties and calculation advantages make this method the most widely used for performing geometric transformations. Algorithm 3.1 shows the procedure for computing a generic geometric transform using this method.

ALGORITHM 3.1   GEOMETRIC TRANSFORMATION DESTINATION-SOURCE MAPPING. AS INPUT, WE HAVE THE ORIGINAL IMAGE AND THE GEOMETRIC TRANSFORM DEFINED ACCORDING TO ITS INVERSE FORMULATION

1: **Geometric Transformation Destination-Source Mapping (I, (x,y),T)**
2: $I(x,y) \rightarrow$ Source Image
3: $T \rightarrow$ Geometric coordinate transformation
4: The destination image is created with zeros
5: **for** all image coordinates (x',y') **do**

$$(x,y) \leftarrow T^{-1}(x',y')$$

$I(x,y) \leftarrow$ Interpolated value (I,x,y)
return $I'(x',y')$

3.3 Interpolation

Interpolation refers to the method by which the values of a function are calculated at those points where there are no exact relationships between the value of the function and the point that represents it [7]. In geometric transformations performed on images, it is necessary to use the interpolation process in the transformation $T(x,y)$. Through the transformation $T(x,y)$ (or $T^{-1}(x,y)$) values of the transformed image will be calculated, which will not have an exact correspondence with the original, so the use of an interpolation method makes it obvious.

3.3.1 Simple Interpolation Methods

To illustrate the interpolation methods, the one-dimensional case will be analyzed first for simplicity, so it will be considered that there is a discrete signal $g(u)$ like the one described in Figure 3.13a. To interpolate the values of the discrete function at any of the intermediate $x \in \mathbb{R}$ positions, different approaches can be used. The simplest approximation is to assign to the value of x, the value of the closest neighbor u_0 to its position in a discrete way if it is defined, that is:

$$\hat{g}(x) = g(u_0)$$

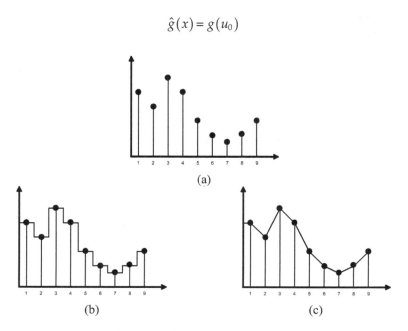

(a)

(b)   (c)

FIGURE 3.13
Interpolation of a discrete signal. (a) Discrete signal, (b) nearest neighbor interpolation, and (c) linear interpolation.

where

$$u_0 = \text{Round}(x) = (x + 0.5) \qquad (3.43)$$

This so-called Nearest-Neighbor interpolation method is illustrated in Figure 3.13b as a result of interpolating the values of the discrete signal described in Figure 3.13a. This interpolation method was used in all the geometric transformation algorithms discussed in previous sections.

Another simple interpolation method is linear interpolation, where the intermediate values of the domain of the variable are calculated as solid lines between points. Figure 3.13c shows the result of linearly interpolating the function defined in Figure 3.13a.

3.3.2 Ideal Interpolation

Obviously, the previously seen interpolation alternatives do not produce a good approximation of the function, so it will be necessary to establish others that allow the intermediate values of a discrete signal to be expressed in a better way.

The objective of this section is to analyze the counterpart of the previous simple interpolation methods, that is, to raise the possibility of modeling the best possible way to interpolate a discrete function.

A discrete function, as seen in Chapter 13, has a limited bandwidth whose maximum value is characterized by half the sampling frequency $\omega_s / 2$ with which it was obtained. In the same way, it was investigated in Chapter 13 how these signals, both in the space domain and in the frequency domain, present periodicity. In view of the above, if you only want to take one version of the frequency spectrum $\overline{F}(\omega)$, it will suffice to multiply the spectrum (which is periodic) by a rectangular function $H(\omega)$ of width $\pm\omega_s / 2$ or $\pm\pi$. Figure 3.14 illustrates this process of obtaining the spectrum.

All of the above was considered from the point of view of the frequency domain; as it was seen in Chapter 13, a multiplication in the frequency domain corresponds to a convolution in the space domain. So, a multiplication in the frequency domain by a rectangular function would mean convolving by the transform of the rectangle function, which in this case would be by the function $Sync(x)$, which is defined by:

$$Sync(x) = \left(\frac{\text{sen}(\pi x)}{\pi x} \right) \qquad (3.44)$$

Theoretically, the function $Sinc(x)$ is the ideal interpolation function for the reconstruction of continuous functions. To interpolate a value of the function $g(u)$ at any position x_0, the $Sync(x)$ function moves in such a way that its origin is the point x_0, then the point-to-point convolution between $g(u)$ and

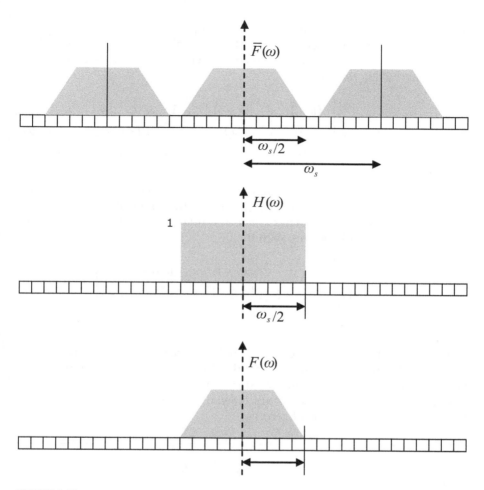

FIGURE 3.14
Isolating a frequency spectrum by multiplying the rectangular function.

the $Sync(x)$ function. Considering these operations, the interpolated function will have the following expression:

$$\hat{g}(x_0) = \sum_{u=-\infty}^{\infty} Sync(x_0 - u) \cdot g(u) \tag{3.45}$$

3.3.3 Cubic Interpolation

Due to the infinite size of the interpolation kernels necessary for the $Sinc(x)$ function during the convolution, this method is not feasible in practice. For this reason, we try to reproduce the effects of the ideal interpolation by means of the $Sinc(x)$ function. but using compact kernels that approximate their results. A widely used approach for the realization of these kernels is the so-called cubic interpolation, which uses cubic polynomials to make the approximation [8], that is:

$$w_{cubic}(x,a) = \begin{cases} (a+2)\cdot|x|^3 - (a+3)\cdot|x|^2 + 1 & \text{si } 0 \le |x| < 1 \\ a\cdot|x|^3 - 5a\cdot|x|^2 + 8a\cdot|x| - 4a & \text{si } 1 \le |x| < 2 \\ 0 & \text{si } |x| \ge 2 \end{cases} \quad (3.46)$$

where a is a control parameter that defines how steep the cubic approximation falls. Figure 3.15 shows different kernels of the cubic interpolation using different values of the parameter a. For a standard value of $a = -1$ a simplification of Equation 3.46 occurs, such that:

$$w_{cubic}(x) = \begin{bmatrix} |x|^3 - 2\cdot|x|^2 + 1 & \text{if } 0 \le |x| < 1 \\ -|x|^3 + 5\cdot|x|^2 - 8\cdot|x| + 4 & \text{if } 1 \le |x| < 2 \\ 0 & \text{if } |x| \ge 2 \end{bmatrix} \quad (3.47)$$

From the comparison between the function $Sync(x)$ and the cubic kernel $w_{cubic}(x)$ in Figure 3.16, it is shown that the difference between both functions is negligible when $|x| \le 1$, while the differences become more evident when $|x| > 1$. The most critical case occurs when $||x| > 2$, which is when the cubic kernel returns only a value of zero.

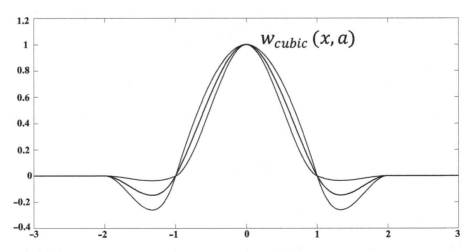

FIGURE 3.15
Different cubic kernels used for interpolation. The graph considers three different values of the control parameter a, considering $a = -0.25$, $a = -1$, and $a = -1.75$.

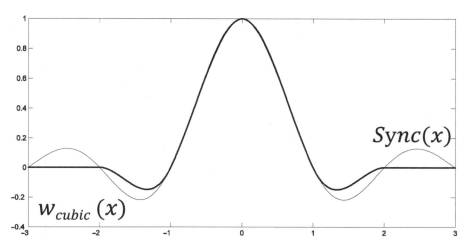

FIGURE 3.16
Comparison between the function $Sync(x)$ and $w_{cubic}(x)$.

Considering the above, the cubic interpolation of a function $g(u)$ at a certain point x_0 is reduced to the calculation of the following equation:

$$\hat{g}(x_0) = \sum_{u=x_0-1}^{x_0+2} w_{cúbica}(x_0 - u) \cdot g(u) \tag{3.48}$$

Figure 3.17 shows the two-dimensional function $Sync(x,y)$.

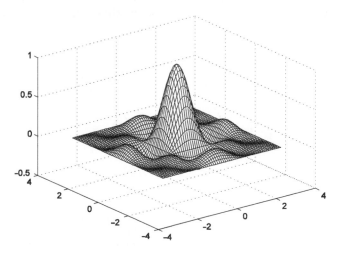

FIGURE 3.17
Representation of the two-dimensional function $Sync(x,y)$.

However, as in the one-dimensional case, the kernels required for this ideal interpolation mean that in practice they cannot be carried out, so other alternatives must be considered. These alternatives include some of the interpolation approaches discussed in the one-dimensional case and include the following methods: nearest neighbors, bilinear, and bicubic interpolation [8].

3.3.3.1 Nearest Neighbor Interpolation Method

For the interpolation of a certain point (x_0, y_0), the coordinates of the pixel (u_0, v_0) that is closest to it are assigned; in many cases, to carry out this method, it is enough to apply a rounding to the coordinates obtained by the geometric transformation.

This is:

$$I(x_0, y_0) = I(u_0, v_0)$$

where

$$u{\cdot}_0 = \text{round}(x_0)$$
$$v{\cdot}_0 = \text{round}(y_0)$$

(3.49)

3.3.3.2 Bilinear Interpolation

What linear interpolation represents for the one-dimensional case, bilinear interpolation represents for the two-dimensional or image case. To explain the operation of this type of interpolation, the illustration shown in Figure 3.18 will be used. Where each of the neighboring pixels to (x_0, y_0) are defined as:

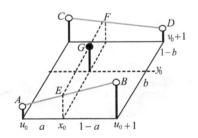

FIGURE 3.18
Bilinear interpolation. The interpolation of point G at position (x_0, y_0) is produced in two steps considering the neighboring pixels defined at points $A, B, C,$ and D. First through linear interpolation, points E and F are obtained considering the distance between the point to be interpolated and the adjoining pixel $a = (x_0 - u_0)$, then the vertical interpolation is performed, obtaining the intermediate points between E and F by means of the distance $b = (y_0 - v_0)$.

$$A = I(u_0, v_0) \qquad B = I(u_0 + 1, v_0)$$
$$C = I(u_0, v_0 + 1) \quad C = I(u_0 + 1, v_0 + 1)$$

(3.50)

To obtain the value (x_0, y_0), two different linear interpolations are obtained that are established on the points E and F from the distance $a = (x_0 - u_0)$ that is established between the point and the nearest neighbor. These values, when calculated from a linear interpolation, are defined as:

$$E = A + (x_0 - u_0) \cdot (B - A) = A + a \cdot (B - A)$$
$$F = C + (x_0 - u_0) \cdot (D - C) = C + a \cdot (D - C)$$

(3.51)

From the previous values, the interpolation for point G is obtained considering the vertical distance $b = (y_0 - v_0)$, such that:

$$\hat{I}(x_0, y_0) = G = E + (y_0 - u_0) \cdot (F - E) = E + b \cdot (F - E)$$
$$= (a - 1)(b - 1)A + a(b - 1)B + (1 - a)bC + abD$$

(3.52)

Just as the linear convolution kernel was formulated, the two-dimensional bilinear interpolation kernel $W_{bilinear}(x, y)$ can also be defined. This will be the product of two one-dimensional kernels $w_{bilinear}(x)$ and $w_{bilinear}(y)$. Performing this multiplication is obtained as follows:

$$W_{bilinear}(x, y) = w_{bilinear}(x) \cdot w_{bilinear}(y)$$

$$W_{bilinear}(x, y) = \begin{cases} 1 - x - y - xy & \text{si } 0 \leq |x|, |y| < 1 \\ 0 & \text{if not} \end{cases}$$

(3.53)

3.3.3.3 Bicubic Interpolation

As in the previous section, the bicubic interpolation kernel $W_{bicubic}(x, y)$ can be obtained from the multiplication of the one-dimensional kernels $W_{bicubic}(x)$ and $w_{bicubic}(y)$, that is:

$$W_{bicubic}(x, y) = w_{bicubic}(x) \cdot w_{bicubic}(y)$$

(3.54)

The one-dimensional cubic kernels used in multiplication (3.51) are defined in Equation 3.47. The bicubic kernel of Equation 3.54 is shown in Figure 3.19a, while Figure 3.19b shows the arithmetic difference between the bicubic kernel and that of the $Sync(x, y)$ function.

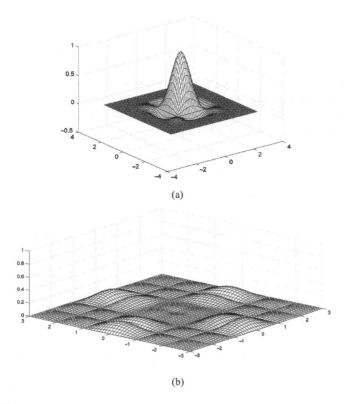

(a)

(b)

FIGURE 3.19
(a) Kernel of cubic interpolation and (b) difference between cubic kernel and $Sync(x,y)$ in the form of $\left|Sync(x,y) - W_{cubic}(x,y)\right|$.

3.4 Aliases

As discussed throughout this chapter, a geometric transformation is essentially performed in three steps:

1. For each one of the coordinates of the transformed image (x',y'), its corresponding coordinates in the original image (x,y) are obtained by means of the inverse of the transformed $T^{-1}(x,y)$.

2. From the transformed image, the values are interpolated by using one of the previously seen kernels, with the aim of reconstructing the image.

3. When a geometric transformation demands the creation or elimination of pixels, it will be necessary to have a criterion that allows for establishing the way in which these pixels will be treated in such a way that artifacts do not appear.

When an image is reduced in size, obviously some of the original pixels will be lost as a result of the geometric transformation. This problem can cause aliases. The aliasing effect can be considered as a problem caused by image reduction, which has the consequence of adding artifacts to the transformed image that are not present in the original image.

There are some methods that reduce this effect; one of the best, according to its speed and effectiveness ratio, is adding a low-pass filter to the image processing chain. The effect of the filter will attenuate the problem of artifacts without causing excessive computation weight; this is especially important when it comes to an artificial vision system that performs real-time processing.

3.5 Functions for Geometric Transformation in MATLAB

This section describes the functions for implementing geometric transformations contained in the MATLAB image processing toolbox. A geometric transformation (as seen throughout this chapter) modifies the spatial relationships between pixels in an image by using operators that map pixel coordinates in an input image to new coordinates in the resulting image.

To change the size of an image in MATLAB, the `imresize` function is implemented. The general syntax of this function is:

```
B = imresize(A, [mre ncol],method
```

This function computes a new image B from the original image A, whose size is specified by the vector [mre ncol]. The interpolation method to be used is configured in the method variable and can be one of those specified in Table 3.1.

TABLE 3.1

Interpolation Methods Used by Most MATLAB® Functions That Implement Geometric Transformations

Syntax	Method
`'nearest'`	Interpolation by nearest neighbors (this is the default option). See Section 3.3.4
`'bilinear'`	Bilinear interpolation. See Section 3.3.4
`'bicubic'`	Bicubic interpolation. See Section 3.3.4

To rotate an image, use the `imrotate` function. The general syntax of this function is:

```
B = imrotate(A,angle,method)
```

This function performs a rotation of image A, considering its center as the axis of rotation. The angle by which the image is rotated is defined in the Angle variable, while the interpolation method used is described by the method variable and corresponds to one of those defined in Table 3.1.

MATLAB allows the implementation of spatial transformations such as the **affine or projective transformation**, the effects of which are in any case more interesting and elaborate than `imresize` or `imrotate`. Considering the above, the way to carry out this type of transformation in MATLAB is a little more complicated, for which the following procedure is developed:

1. The parameters of the geometric transformation are defined, which could consist of a series of parameters that define the mapping performed by the operator $T(x,y)$.
2. A transformation structure is created, called TFORM, which can be considered as the coupling in matrix form of the parameters defined in step 2.
3. The spatial operation is performed by using the `imtransform` function.

As a first step, the transformation to be performed must be defined. In many types of geometric transformations, the parameters can be characterized by a transformation matrix MT of size 3 × 3. Table 3.2 shows the relationship between some simple transformations and the transformation matrix that models them.

For the creation of the TFORM structure that absorbs the important characteristics of the transformation, the `maketform` function is used. The general syntax of this function is:

```
TFORM = maketform(type, MT)
```

This function creates the TFORM structure from the definition of the MT transformation matrix and the type of geometric operation to be performed. The type of geometric operation can be either 'affine' or 'projective'.

The 'affine' transformation includes rotation, translation, scaling, and distortion. In this type of geometric operation, as seen in this chapter, the lines remain as lines, with the special property that parallel lines remain as such. Considering this property, the rectangles become parallelograms.

In the 'projective' transformation, the lines are also preserved as lines, with the difference that if they are parallel, they do not remain as such in the resulting image. This transform takes its name precisely from the fact that

TABLE 3.2

Geometric Transformations and the Transformation Matrix That Model Them

Transformation	Example	MT Transformation Matrix	
Translation		$\begin{bmatrix} 1 & 0 & 0 \\ 0 & 1 & 0 \\ t_x & t_y & 1 \end{bmatrix}$	t_x specifies the offset along the x axis t_y specifies the offset along the y axis
Scaling		$\begin{bmatrix} s_x & 0 & 0 \\ 0 & s_y & 0 \\ 0 & 0 & 1 \end{bmatrix}$	s_x specifies the scaling along the x axis s_y specifies the scaling along the y axis
Inclination		$\begin{bmatrix} 1 & i_y & 0 \\ i_x & 1 & 0 \\ 0 & 0 & 1 \end{bmatrix}$	s_x specifies the slope about the x-axis s_y specifies the slope about the y-axis
Rotation		$\begin{bmatrix} \cos(\alpha) & \text{sen}(\alpha) & 0 \\ -\text{sen}(\alpha) & \cos(\alpha) & 0 \\ 0 & 0 & 1 \end{bmatrix}$	α specifies the angle of rotation of the image that considers the center, as the axis of rotation

the lines are transformed, generating a perspective effect where the lines are projected to points at infinity.

Finally, the geometric operation is performed by using the `imtransform` function. The general syntax of this function is:

```
B = imtransform(A,TFORM,method)
```

This function returns the geometric transformation B modeled by means of the `TFORM` structure on the image A. The interpolation method to be used is configured in the `method` variable and can be one of those specified in Table 3.1.

3.5.1 Application Example

As an example, the geometric transformation of an image will be performed in such a way that a double tilt is applied along the x-axis. Considering the above, first the transformation matrix is established, which according to Table 3.2 would be:

$$\mathbf{MT} = \begin{bmatrix} 1 & 0 & 0 \\ 2 & 1 & 0 \\ 0 & 0 & 1 \end{bmatrix} \qquad (3.55)$$

Subsequently, the TFORM structure is generated, for which it is established in the command line:

```
MT = [1 0 0; 2 1 0; 0 0 1];
TFORM = maketform('affine', MT);
```

Assuming that the image shown in Figure 3.20a is stored in variable A, the geometric operation is performed by using the imtransform function and writing on the command line:

```
B = imtransform(A,TFORM,'bilinear');
        Imshow(B)
```

As can be seen in Figure 3.20, while the original image has a lower dimension (600 × 800), the resulting image has a higher dimension (600 × 1600). To leave the resulting image the same size as the original, the imresize function is used, for which we write:

```
C=imresize(B,[600 800]);
imshow(C)
```

(a)

(b)

FIGURE 3.20
Result of the tilt geometry operation. (a) Original image and (b) result obtained.

References

[1] González-Campos, J. S., Arnedo-Moreno, J., & Sánchez-Navarro, J. (2021). GTCards: A video game for learning geometric transformations: A cards-based video game for learning geometric transformations in higher education. In *Ninth international conference on technological ecosystems for enhancing multiculturality (TEEM'21)* (pp. 205–209).

[2] Freeman, W. T., Anderson, D. B., Beardsley, P., Dodge, C. N., Roth, M., Weissman, C. D., ... & Tanaka, K. I. (1998). Computer vision for interactive computer graphics. *IEEE Computer Graphics and Applications, 18(3)*, 42–53.

[3] Solomon, C., & Breckon, T. (2010). *Fundamentals of digital image processing: A practical approach with examples in MATLAB*. Wiley.

[4] Bebis, G., Georgiopoulos, M., da Vitoria Lobo, N., & Shah, M. (1999). Learning affine transformations. *Pattern Recognition, 32(10)*, 1783–1799.

[5] Jain, A. K. (1989). *Fundamentals of digital image processing*. Prentice-Hall, Inc.

[6] Petrou, M. M., & Petrou, C. (2010). *Image processing: The fundamentals*. John Wiley & Sons.

[7] Annadurai, S. (2007). *Fundamentals of digital image processing*. Pearson Education India.

[8] Han, D. (2013). Comparison of commonly used image interpolation methods. In *Conference of the 2nd international conference on computer science and electronics engineering (ICCSEE 2013)* (pp. 1556–1559). Atlantis Press.

4

Comparison and Recognition of Images

When it is necessary to compare one image with another or to identify if a certain pattern is contained in an image, the question is: How can the similarity between two certain images be evaluated? Evidently, it can be defined in a simple way that two images I_1 and I_2 are equal, if the difference between both images $I_1 - I_2$ is zero.

The difference between two images can be useful for detecting changes in consecutive images that have constant illumination. However, this very simple way of defining the comparison is far from being reliable in determining an index of similarity between images [1]. This is due to the fact that a simple change in the global illumination of the image, a displacement of the contained object, or a small rotation can cause the difference $I_1 - I_2$ to present a considerable value [2]. Despite this high difference, both images, in the opinion of a human observer, are the same. The comparison between images, therefore, cannot be considered a simple problem and formulates one of the most interesting research topics in image processing and computer vision [3].

The chapter describes the different similarity measures used for image comparison.

4.1 Comparison in Grayscale Images

First, the problem of finding a reference image $R(i, j)$ (Pattern) in a grayscale image $I(x, y)$ will be addressed. The task is to find the pixel (u, v) of the image $I(x, y)$ in which there is an optimal match between the contents of the segment of $I(x, y)$ and the reference image $R(i, j)$. If $R_{r,s}(i, j) = R(i - r, j - s)$ is defined as a displacement (r, s) in the horizontal and vertical directions, then the problem of comparing images in grayscale can be stated as follows:

Defining $I(x, y)$ as the image that probably contains a given pattern $R(i, j)$. We must find the displacement (r, s) where the evaluation of similarity between the pattern $R(i, j)$ and the image segment that covers $R(i, j)$ is maximum (see Figure 4.1).

In order to design an algorithm that solves the previous problem, it is necessary to consider three important situations: First, an appropriate definition of a measure of similarity between the two images is needed. Second,

DOI: 10.1201/9781032662466-4

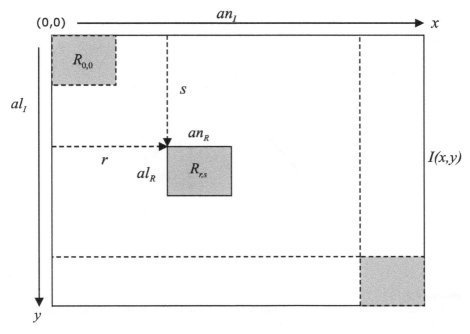

FIGURE 4.1

Image recognition problem. The reference image $R(i,j)$ is shifted through the image $I(x,y)$, where the image origin (0,0) serves as the reference point. The size of the image and the pattern determine the search field for performing the comparison.

a search strategy where the optimal displacement (r,s) is found as quickly as possible. Finally, it must be decided what the minimum value of similarity that ensures a reliable match between both images is. Each of these points will be discussed in the following sections.

4.1.1 Distance between Patterns

To determine the point where there is the maximum coincidence between $I(x,y)$ and $R(i,j)$, it is necessary to identify the distance between the displaced reference $R_{r,s}$ and the corresponding section of the image for each position (r,s) (see Figure 4.2). To measure the distance between two two-dimensional elements, there are different indexes. Only the most important ones will be described below.

The sum of the differences:

$$d_A(r,s) = \sum_{(i,j)\in R} \left| I(r+i,s+j) - R(i,j) \right| \tag{4.1}$$

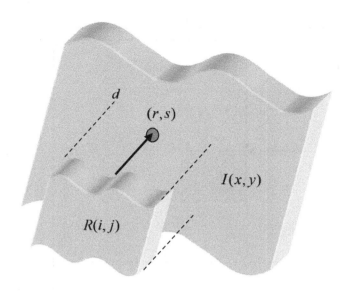

FIGURE 4.2
Evaluating the distance between two-dimensional features. The reference image is positioned on the pixel $I(r,s)$.

The maximum of the differences:

$$d_M(r,s) = \max_{(i,j)\in R}\left|I(r+i,s+j) - R(i,j)\right| \tag{4.2}$$

The sum of the squared distances:

$$d_E(r,s) = \sqrt{\sum_{(i,j)\in R}\left((I(r+i,s+j) - R(i,j))^2\right)} \tag{4.3}$$

In order to illustrate the effects of each index on images, we test each of them when they are used to determine the best matching points. For this experiment, the image $I(x,y)$ and pattern $R(i,j)$ are considered as shown in Figure 4.3.

4.1.1.1 Sum of Differences

For each index, a MATLAB® program is implemented. The implementation vmethodology of these indexes exemplifies the way to develop more complex algorithms to identify patterns using techniques that use distance measures as similarity criteria. Program 4.1 shows how to calculate the sum of differences between an image and a reference pattern.

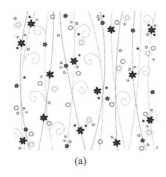

(a)

(b)

FIGURE 4.3
Images used to show the effect of different distance measurements for the comparison of an image $I(x,y)$ and a reference image $R(i,j)$. (a) Image $I(x,y)$ and (b) reference image $R(i,j)$.

PROGRAM 4.1 COMPUTATION OF THE DISTANCE OF THE SUM OF DIFFERENCES BETWEEN AN IMAGE $I(x,y)$ AND A PATTERN $R(i,j)$

```
%%%%%%%%%%%%%%%%%%%%%%%%%%%%%%%%%%%%%%%%%%%%%%%%%%%
% Program that allows calculating the distance of
% the sum of differences between I(x,y) and R(i,j)
%%%%%%%%%%%%%%%%%%%%%%%%%%%%%%%%%%%%%%%%%%%%%%%%%%%
% Erik Cuevas, Alma Rodríguez
%%%%%%%%%%%%%%%%%%%%%%%%%%%%%%%%%%%%%%%%%%%%%%%%%%%
% Get the dimension of the image
[m n]=size(Im);
% Convert to double to avoid numerical problems
Imd=double(Im);
Td=double(T);
% Get the size of the reference image
[mt nt]=size(T);
% Variable sum is initialized to zero
suma=0;
% The distances between I(x,y) and R(i,j)
%are obtained according to 4.1
for re=1:m-mt
for co=1:n-nt
indice=0;
for re1=0:mt-1
for co1=0:nt-1
suma=abs(Imd(re+re1,co+co1)-Td(re1+1,co1+1))+suma;
end
end
```

```
da(re,co)=suma;
suma=0;
end
end
```

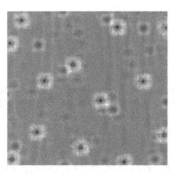

FIGURE 4.4
Result of the calculation of the distance of the sum of differences, considering Figure 4.3a as the image and Figure 4.3b as the reference image.

Figure 4.4 shows the result of the determination of the distance of the sum of differences, considering Figure 4.3a as the image $I(x,y)$ and Figure 4.3b as the reference image $R(i,j)$.

In Figure 4.4, the dark locations show the pixels of the image where a small distance is obtained, which means that there is a high similarity between those regions of the image and the reference image.

4.1.1.2 Maximum of the Differences

Program 4.2 shows how to calculate the distance of the maximum of the differences between an image and a reference pattern.

**PROGRAM 4.2   CALCULATION OF THE DISTANCE
OF THE MAXIMUM OF THE DIFFERENCES BETWEEN
AN IMAGE AND A REFERENCE PATTERN**

```
%%%%%%%%%%%%%%%%%%%%%%%%%%%%%%%%%%%%%%%%%%%%%%%%%%
% Program for calculating the distance of the
% maximum differences between I(x,y) and R(i,j)
%%%%%%%%%%%%%%%%%%%%%%%%%%%%%%%%%%%%%%%%%%%%%%%%%%
% Erik Cuevas, Alma Rodríguez
%%%%%%%%%%%%%%%%%%%%%%%%%%%%%%%%%%%%%%%%%%%%%%%%%%
```

```
% Get the dimension of the image
[m n]=size(Im);
% Convert to double to avoid numerical problems
Imd=double(Im);
Td=double(T);
% Get the size of the reference image
[mt nt]=size(T);
% A matrix is defined that collects the results of the
% differences
Itemp=zeros(size(T));
% The distances between I(x,y) and R(i,j)
%are obtained according to 4.2
for re=1:m-mt
    for co=1:n-nt
        indice=0;
        for re1=0:mt-1
            for co1=0:nt-1
 Itemp(re1+1,co1+1)=abs(Imd(re+re1,co
+co1)-Td(re1+1,co1+1));
            end
        end
        dm(re,co)=max(max(Itemp));
    end
end
```

Figure 4.5a shows the result of the determination of the distance of the maximum of the differences between an image and a reference pattern (Figure 4.3a and b, respectively). As can be seen, this image does not suggest that this type of measurement can be used as a similarity index.

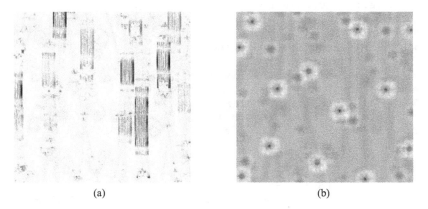

(a)   (b)

FIGURE 4.5
Results of distance calculations between an image and a reference pattern. (a) Distance of the maximum of the differences and (b) distance of the sum of the squared distances.

4.1.1.3 Sum of Squared Distances

Program 4.3 shows how to calculate the sum of the squared distances between an image and a reference pattern.

In Figure 4.5b, the dark points show the pixels where a small distance between an image and a reference has been obtained (Figure 4.3a and b, respectively), which means that there is a high resemblance between those regions of the image and the reference pattern.

4.1.2 Distance and Correlation

The Euclidean distance defined in Equation 4.3 is especially important because of its statistical properties. To find the maximum coincidence between the reference image $R(i, j)$ and the image $I(x, y)$, it is enough to minimize the square of d_E^2, which is defined as positive. d_E^2 can be described as follows:

**PROGRAM 4.3   CALCULATION OF THE DISTANCE
OF THE SUM OF THE QUADRATIC DISTANCES
BETWEEN AN IMAGE AND A REFERENCE PATTERN**

```
%%%%%%%%%%%%%%%%%%%%%%%%%%%%%%%%%%%%%%%%%%%%%%%%%%%%%%%%
% Program to calculate the distance of the sum
% of squared distances between I(x,y) and R(i,j)
%%%%%%%%%%%%%%%%%%%%%%%%%%%%%%%%%%%%%%%%%%%%%%%%%%%%%%%%
% Erik Cuevas, Alma Rodríguez
%%%%%%%%%%%%%%%%%%%%%%%%%%%%%%%%%%%%%%%%%%%%%%%%%%%%%%%%
% Get the dimension of the image
[m n]=size(Im);
% Convert to double to avoid numerical problems
Imd=double(Im);
Td=double(T);
%Get the size of the reference image
[mt nt]=size(T);
% Variable sum is initialized to zero
suma=0;
% The distances between I(x,y) and R(i,j)
%are obtained according to 4.3
for re=1:m-mt
    for co=1:n-nt
        indice=0;
        for re1=0:mt-1
            for co1=0:nt-1
        suma=(Imd(re+re1,co+co1)-Td(re1+1,co1+1))^2+suma;
            end
        end
```

```
        de(re,co)=sqrt(suma);
        suma=0;
    end
end
```

$$d_E^2(r,s) = \sum_{(i,j)\in R} \left(I(r+i,s+j)-R(i,j)\right)^2$$

$$= \underbrace{\sum_{(i,j)\in R}(I(r+i,s+j))^2}_{A(r,s)} + \underbrace{\sum_{(i,j)\in R}(R(i,j))^2}_{B} \underbrace{-2\sum_{(i,j)\in R}I(r+i,s+j)\cdot R(i,j)}_{C(r,s)} \qquad (4.4)$$

The part B in Equation 4.4 represents the sum squared of all values of the reference image $R(i,j)$. Since these values do not depend on the offset (r,s), this factor is constant throughout the processing of Equation 4.4. Therefore, B could be ignored for the evaluation. The expression $A(r,s)$ represents the sum of the values of the image pixels corresponding to the squared $R(i,j)$. The value $A(r,s)$ clearly depends on the offset (r,s). $C(r,s)$ corresponds to the so-called cross-correlation $(I \otimes R)$ between $I(x,y)$ and $R(i,j)$. This cross-correlation is defined as follows:

$$(I \otimes R)(r,s) = \sum_{i=-\infty}^{\infty}\sum_{j=\infty}^{\infty} I(r+i,s+j)\cdot R(i,j) \qquad (4.5)$$

Since the elements outside the dimensions of images $I(x,y)$ and $R(i,j)$ are considered zero, Equation 4.5 can be rewritten as follows:

$$\sum_{i=0}^{an_R-1}\sum_{j=0}^{al_R-1} I(r+i,s+j)\cdot R(i,j) = \sum_{(i,j)\in R} I(r+i,s+j)\cdot R(i,j) \qquad (4.6)$$

Correlation is fundamentally the same operation as convolution, except that in convolution, the kernel of the operation is inverted on itself.

If the factor $A(r,s)$ in Equation 4.4 remains approximately constant throughout the image $I(x,y)$, it would mean that the energy in the image is uniformly distributed. Thus, the maximum value of the correlation $C(r,s)$ corresponds to the point of the image $I(x,y)$ where the reference image $R(i,j)$ has the maximum coincidence. In this case, the minimum value of $d_E^2(r,s)$ can only be calculated by means of the maximum value of the $I \otimes R$ correlation.

This fact is very important since, using the Fourier transform, it is highly efficient to calculate the correlation in the frequency domain.

4.1.2.1 Implementation of General Correlation

This section shows how to implement the general correlation defined in Equation 4.6 between an image and a reference pattern. The code is shown in Program 4.4.

PROGRAM 4.4   CALCULATION OF THE GENERAL CORRELATION DEFINED IN EQUATION 4.6 BETWEEN AN IMAGE AND A REFERENCE PATTERN

```
%%%%%%%%%%%%%%%%%%%%%%%%%%%%%%%%%%%%%%%%%%%%%%%%%%%%%%%%%%%%%%%
% Program that allows calculating the general correlation
% between I(x,y) and R(i,j)
%%%%%%%%%%%%%%%%%%%%%%%%%%%%%%%%%%%%%%%%%%%%%%%%%%%%%%%%%%%%%%%
% Erik Cuevas, Alma Rodríguez
%%%%%%%%%%%%%%%%%%%%%%%%%%%%%%%%%%%%%%%%%%%%%%%%%%%%%%%%%%%%%%%
% Get the dimension of the image
[m n]=size(Im);
% Convert to double to avoid numerical problems
Imd=double(Im);
Td=double(T);
%Get the size of the reference image
[mt nt]=size(T);
%Variable sum is initialized to zero
suma=0;
% The distances between I(x,y) and R(i,j)
%are obtained according to 4.6
for re=1:m-mt
    for co=1:n-nt
        indice=0;
        for re1=0:mt-1
            for co1=0:nt-1

suma=Imd(re+re1,co+co1)*Td(re1+1,co1+1)+suma;
            end
        end
        de(re,co)=suma;
        suma=0;

    end
end
%The elements of de are transformed within the interval [0,1]

C=mat2gray(de);
imshow(C)
```

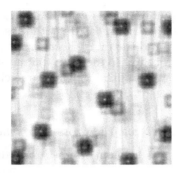

FIGURE 4.6
Result of the calculation of the global correlation, considering the image shown in Figure 4.3a as the image and the one shown in Figure 4.3b as the reference image.

Figure 4.6 shows the result of the correlation between image 4.3a and reference pattern 4.3b. In Figure 4.6, the dark points show the pixels of the image where small values were obtained, which means, according to Equation 4.6, that there is a great similarity between those locations of the image and the reference pattern.

4.1.3 The Normalized Cross-Correlation

In practice, the assumption that A (r, s) remains approximately constant in the image is not fulfilled. Therefore, the result of the correlation is highly dependent on the intensity changes of the image I (x, y) [4]. The normalized cross-correlation C_N (r, s) compensates for this dependence through the consideration of the total energy of the image. The normalized cross-correlation is defined as follows:

$$C_N(r,s) = \frac{C(r,s)}{\sqrt{A(r,s) \cdot B}} = \frac{C(r,s)}{\sqrt{A(r,s)} \cdot \sqrt{B}}$$

$$= \frac{\sum_{(i,j) \in R} I(r+i, s+j) \cdot R(i,j)}{\left[\sum_{(i,j) \in R} (I(r+i, s+j))^2\right]^{1/2} \cdot \left[\sum_{(i,j) \in R} (R(i,j))^2\right]^{1/2}} \tag{4.7}$$

Since the values of both the image I (x, y) and the reference R (i, j) are positive, the resulting values of $C_N(r,s)$ are within the interval [0,1]. A value of $C_N(r,s) = 1$ represents a maximum index of similarity between $R(i,j)$ and the section of the image $I(x,y)$ with which it corresponds. The value produced by the normalized cross-correlation has the advantage that it can be used as a standard similarity index.

The formulation of Equation 4.7, as opposed to Equation 4.5, shows the characterization of a local distance measure of the absolute distance between the reference image $R(i,j)$ and the image section $I(x,y)$ with which it corresponds. However, it is important to mention that an increase in the general illumination of the image would produce very large changes in the values of $C_N(r,s)$.

4.1.3.1 Implementation of Normalized Cross-Correlation

This section shows how to implement the normalized cross-correlation defined in Equation 4.7 between an image and a reference image. Program 4.5 shows how to compute the generic normalized cross-correlation.

PROGRAM 4.5   DETERMINATION OF THE NORMALIZED CROSS–CORRELATION DEFINED IN EQUATION 4.7 BETWEEN AN IMAGE AND A REFERENCE PATTERN

```
%%%%%%%%%%%%%%%%%%%%%%%%%%%%%%%%%%%%%%%%%%%%%%%%%%%%%%%%%%%%%%%
% Program that allows calculating the normalized
% cross-correlation between I(x,y) and R(i,j)
%%%%%%%%%%%%%%%%%%%%%%%%%%%%%%%%%%%%%%%%%%%%%%%%%%%%%%%%%%%%%%%
% Erik Cuevas, Alma Rodríguez
%%%%%%%%%%%%%%%%%%%%%%%%%%%%%%%%%%%%%%%%%%%%%%%%%%%%%%%%%%%%%%%
% Get the dimension of the image
[m n]=size(Im);
% Convert to double to avoid numerical problems
Imd=double(Im);
Td=double(T);
%Get the size of the reference image
[mt nt]=size(T);
%Variable sum is initialized to zero
suma=0;
suma1=0;
%The matrixes C(r,s) y A(r,s) of Eq. 4.4 are obtained
for re=1:m-mt
    for co=1:n-nt
        indice=0;
        for re1=0:mt-1
            for co1=0:nt-1

    suma=Imd(re+re1,co+co1)*Td(re1+1,co1+1)+suma;

    suma1=Imd(re+re1,co+co1)*Imd(re+re1,co+co1)+suma1;
            end
        end
        C(re,co)=2*suma;
        A(re,co)=suma1;
        suma=0;
```

```
            suma1=0;
        end
end
sum=0;
% The matrix B of Eq. 4.4 is obtained
for re1=0:mt-1
            for co1=0:nt-1

sum=Td(re1+1,co1+1)*Td(re1+1,co1+1)+sum;
            end
end
% The normalized cross-correlation is obtained
%according to the Eq. 4.7
for re=1:m-mt
    for co=1:n-nt

 Cn(re,co)=C(re,co)/((sqrt(A(re,co)))*sqrt(sum));
    end
end
imshow(Cn)
```

Figure 4.7 shows the result of the normalized cross-correlation between image 4.3a and the reference standard 4.3b. In Figure 4.7, the bright points show the pixels of the image where the maximum correlation has been obtained (value of 1), which means that there is a great similarity between those locations of the image and the reference pattern, while the other pixels (less than 1) have little or no correlation (similarity).

4.1.4 Correlation Coefficient

The lighting problem is a typical problem that affects the normalized cross-correlation. This problem represents the situation where pixels (less than 1)

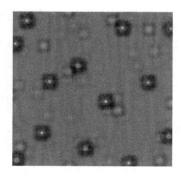

FIGURE 4.7
Result of the normalized cross-correlation calculation, considering the one shown in Figure 4.3a as the image and the one shown in Figure 4.3b as the reference image.

have little or no correlation or similarity due to the lighting conditions. A possibility to avoid this problem consists of considering the local differences of these pixel values in relation to their averages instead of only the intensity values of the pixels [5]. Therefore, Equation 4.7 is reformulated as follows:

$$C_L(r,s) = \frac{\sum_{(i,j)\in R}\left(I(r+i,s+j)-\bar{I}(r,s)\right)\cdot\left(R(i,j)-\bar{R}\right)}{\left[\sum_{(i,j)\in R}(I(r+i,s+j)-\bar{I}(r,s))^2\right]^{1/2}\cdot\underbrace{\left[\sum_{(i,j)\in R}(R(i,j)-\bar{R})^2\right]^{1/2}}_{\sigma_R^2}} \tag{4.8}$$

where $\bar{I}(r,s)$ and $\bar{R}$ are defined as follows:

$$\bar{I}(r,s) = \frac{1}{N}\sum_{(i,j)\in R}I(r+i,s+j) \quad \bar{R} = \frac{1}{N}\sum_{(i,j)\in R}R(i,j) \tag{4.9}$$

where N corresponds to the number of elements in the reference image $R(i,j)$. Equation 4.8 is known in the field of statistics as the correlation coefficient. The correlation coefficient cannot be considered as a global correlation index that evaluates the general data set but rather a local factor that considers only sections explicitly determined by the size of the reference image. The range of values in which the correlation coefficient fluctuates is $[-1,1]$, where the value of 1 represents the highest similarity index, while -1 represents that $I(x,y)$ and $R(i,j)$ are totally different.

The denominator of Equation 4.8 contains the expression:

$$\sigma_R^2 = \sum_{(i,j)\in R}(R(i,j)-\bar{R})^2 = \sum_{(i,j)\in R}(R(i,j))^2 - N\cdot\bar{R}^2 \tag{4.10}$$

Equation 4.10 corresponds to the variance of the pattern $R(i,j)$. This value is constant in the processing of the values of $C_L(r,s)$, so it should only be calculated once. Through the substitution of this factor in Equation 4.8, the expression would be reformulated as follows:

$$C_L(r,s) = \frac{\sum_{(i,j)\in R}\left(I(r+i,s+j)\cdot R(i,j)\right)-N\cdot\bar{I}(r,s)\cdot\bar{R}}{\left[\sum_{(i,j)\in R}(I(r+i,s+j))^2 - N\cdot(\bar{I}(r,s))^2\right]^{1/2}\cdot\sigma_R} \tag{4.11}$$

The previous expression corresponds to the most efficient way to calculate the local correlation coefficient. The efficiency is due to the fact that $\bar{R}$ and σ_R

only have to be calculated once, while the value of $\bar{I}(r,s)$ no longer partici-pates in the processing for each pixel of the image section but is now consid-ered only once.

The correlation coefficient calculated from Equation 4.11 corresponds to a local measurement index of the image as opposed to the linear correla-tion shown in Equation 4.5. Due to the fact that it is a local index, it is not possible to establish a method in the frequency domain that calculates the same index since the spectral techniques formulate the calculation of global characteristics.

4.1.4.1 Implementation of the Correlation Coefficient

This section shows how to implement the correlation coefficient defined in Equation 4.11 between an image and a reference pattern. Program 4.6 shows how to calculate the correlation coefficient.

PROGRAM 4.6   CALCULATION OF THE CORRELATION COEFFICIENT DEFINED IN EQUATION 4.8 BETWEEN AN IMAGE AND A REFERENCE PATTERN

```
%%%%%%%%%%%%%%%%%%%%%%%%%%%%%%%%%%%%%%%%%%%%%%%%%%%%%%%
% Program that allows calculating the coefficient of
%correlation between I(x,y) and R(i,j)
%%%%%%%%%%%%%%%%%%%%%%%%%%%%%%%%%%%%%%%%%%%%%%%%%%%%%%%
% Erik Cuevas, Alma Rodríguez
%%%%%%%%%%%%%%%%%%%%%%%%%%%%%%%%%%%%%%%%%%%%%%%%%%%%%%%
% Get the dimension of the image
[m n]=size(Im);
% Convert to double to avoid numerical problems
Imd=double(Im);
Td=double(T);
%Get the size of the reference image
[mt nt]=size(T);
%Variables sum are initialized to zero
suma1=0;
suma2=0;
suma3=0;
% The mean of the reference image is calculated
MT=mean(mean(Td));

for re=1:m-mt
    for co=1:n-nt

        for re1=0:mt-1
            for co1=0:nt-1
```

```
% The corresponding matrix of the image of
%reference
                Itemp(re1+1,co1+1)=Imd(re+re1,co+co1);
            end
        end
        % The average of the corresponding image is
calculated
        MI=mean(mean(Itemp));
        for re1=0:mt-1
            for co1=0:nt-1

    suma1=(Itemp(re1+1,co1+1)-MI)*(Td(re1+1,co1+1)-
MT)+suma1;
                suma2=((Itemp(re1+1,co1+1)-MI)^2)+suma2;
                suma3=((Td(re1+1,co1+1)-MT)^2)+suma3;
            end
        end
        % The correlation coefficient is calculated
according to 4.8
        CL(re,co)=suma1/((sqrt(suma2)*sqrt(suma3))+eps);
            % Accumulation variables are reset
            suma1=0;
            suma2=0;
            suma3=0;
        end
end
%The elements of CL are transformed within the interval
[0,1]
CLN=mat2gray(CL);
imshow(CLN)
```

Figure 4.8 shows the result of the normalized cross-correlation between image 4.3a and the reference pattern 4.3b. In Figure 4.8, the bright points show the pixels of the image where the maximum correlation was obtained (value of 1), which means that there is a great similarity between those regions of the image and the reference pattern, while the dark pixels (with values close to −1) have little or no correlation or similarity.

Figure 4.9 shows the surfaces of each of the previously discussed models used to measure the similarity between an image and a reference pattern contained in it. On surfaces, the peaks represent points or regions where the image and pattern are very similar.

Some important conclusions can be drawn from the surfaces shown in Figure 4.9. In Figure 4.9a, which illustrates the surface obtained as a product of the global correlation, it is shown how, although the point where the image and the pattern have a maximum similarity is clearly identifiable, it has a

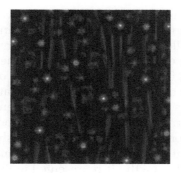

FIGURE 4.8
Result of the calculation of the correlation coefficient, considering the image shown in Figure 4.3a as the image and the one shown in Figure 4.3b as the reference image.

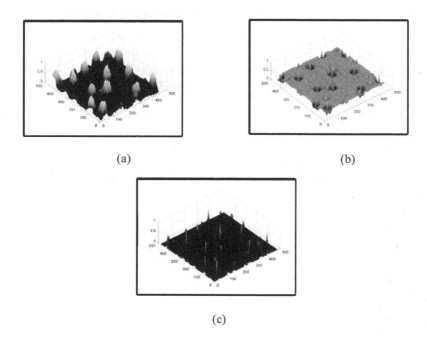

(a)   (b)

(c)

FIGURE 4.9
Surfaces obtained from the methods. (a) Global correlation, (b) normalized cross-correlation, and (c) correlation coefficient used as a measure of similarity between image 4.3a and the reference pattern 4.3b.

large extension. Under such conditions, this method requires additional methods that allow the analysis of the region to identify the exact point of maximum similarity. Figure 4.9b shows the area obtained as a product of the normalized cross-correlation. In this figure, it is evident how the point of maximum similarity is more clearly defined. However, the amplitudes of these points are barely greater than the rest. Something characteristic of this method is the small valley that occurs around the maximum peak. Figure 4.9c illustrates the surface obtained as a product of the calculation of the correlation coefficient. This figure shows how the points of maximum similarity between the image and the reference pattern are clearly defined (maximum peaks). It also maintains a good relationship between their amplitudes and the points where the correlation is not significant. Another interesting situation is that the correlation coefficient method establishes a higher number of peaks, which means that it is able to find a larger number of patterns and is more robust than the other methods represented in Figure 4.9a and b.

4.2 Pattern Recognition Using the Correlation Coefficient

This section describes how to implement a pattern recognition system using the correlation coefficient $C_L(x,y)$. As seen in the previous section, the way of calculating the correlation coefficient and the results in relation to the object to be identified make this method robust enough to be used as a criterion in pattern recognition [6].

The recognition algorithm is practically based on the calculation of the correlation coefficient using Equations 4.8 and 4.11. From these equations, an image will be obtained whose pixels will have a value between –1 and 1, where the value of 1 implies the highest index of similarity, while –1 indicates that the pattern has not been found [7]. Considering the example used in the previous section, Figure 4.10 is obtained as a result of calculating the correlation coefficient $C_L(x,y)$.

In image 4.10, it is clearly visible that the regions that present a considerable correlation coefficient are displaced from the pattern with which they are related. This is because the calculation method involves a shift regarding the upper left corner of the pattern $R(i,j)$ with the image section $I(x,y)$. Therefore, the maximum values correspond to the position of the window, whose dimensions are equal to those of the reference pattern $R(i,j)$. Figure 4.11 illustrates the relationship between the calculated correlation coefficient and the section of the image.

Of the regions obtained by calculating the correlation coefficients, a single point must be found that identifies the section of the image that presents the best similarity with the pattern to be detected. A point of the image $C_L(x,y)$ is considered a potential point of maximum correlation if the condition of Equation 4.12 is fulfilled.

$$C_L(x,y) > t_h \tag{4.12}$$

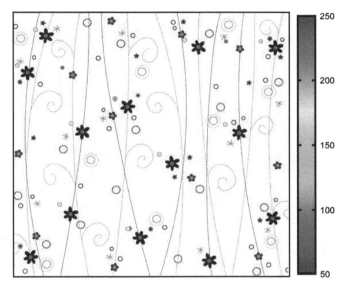

FIGURE 4.10
Contours of the maximum values of the correlation coefficient, considering Figure 4.3a as the image and Figure 4.3b as the pattern. The color scale used in the image is shown on the right.

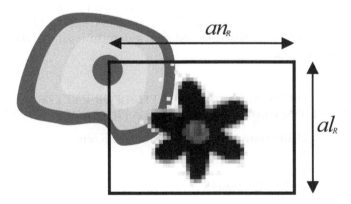

FIGURE 4.11
Relationship between the calculated correlation coefficient and the involved section of the image, which has the same dimensions as $R(i, j)$.

where t_h is a threshold whose typical value is within the range of 0.3–0.7, depending on the content of the image. Therefore, from the application of Equation 4.12, a binary matrix will be obtained containing ones (true) where the condition has been fulfilled and zeros (false) where it is not valid.

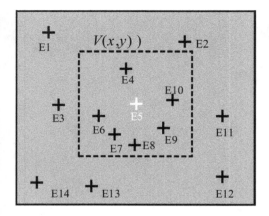

FIGURE 4.12

Process of obtaining a point of maximum correlation. Starting from $C_L(x,y)$, by applying the threshold t_h, the point whose value $C_L(x,y)$ is the maximum in a defined neighborhood $V(x,y)$ is selected. In this case, the value of pixel E5 has the maximum value of $C_L(x,y)$ compared to the other values E4, E6, E7, E8, E9, and E10 that are within the neighborhood region defined by $V(x,y)$.

For the location of the points that maintain the maximum correlation, only those pixels whose value of $C_L(x,y)$ is the highest within a given neighborhood are selected. Figure 4.12 shows an illustration of this process. In Algorithm 4.1, the detection of a pattern is described in a general way using the correlation coefficient $C_L(x,y)$. This technique is completely based on the computation of Equation 4.8 or 4.11 and on the determination of the points of maximum correlation.

ALGORITHM 4.1   ALGORITHM FOR PATTERN DETECTION USING THE CORRELATION COEFFICIENT

Pattern recognition using the correlation coefficient
$(I(x,y), R(i,j))$

1:   It is processed all the points of $I(x,y)$

     for $x \leftarrow 1,2,...,al_I - al_R$ **do**

     for $y \leftarrow 1,2,...,an_I - an_R$ **do**

     The value of x is calculated $\bar{I}(x,y) = \dfrac{1}{N}\sum_{(i,j)\in R} I(x+i,y+j)$

        end

     end

2:   $\bar{R} = \dfrac{1}{N}\sum_{(i,j)\in R} R(i,j)$. Is calculated

3: It is processed all the points of $I(x,y)$

    for $x \leftarrow 1,2,...,al_I - al_R$ **do**

        for $y \leftarrow 1,2,...,an_I - an_R$ **do**

    The value of $C_L(x,y)$ is calculated

    for $i \leftarrow 1,2,...,al_R$ **do**

        for $j \leftarrow 1,2,...,an_R$ **do**

$$C_L(x,y) = \frac{\sum_{(i,j)\in R}\left(I(x+i,y+j)-\bar{I}(x,y)\right)\cdot\left(R(i,j)-\bar{R}\right)}{\left[\sum_{(i,j)\in R}(I(x+i,y+j)-\bar{I}(x,y))^2\right]^{1/2} \cdot \underbrace{\left[\sum_{(i,j)\in R}(R(i,j)-\bar{R})^2\right]^{1/2}}_{\sigma_R^2}}$$

        end

      end

    end

  end

4: A binary matrix is obtained by applying the threshold t_h.

    $U(x,y) = C_L(x,y) > t_h$

5: The points with the maximum value are located. For this process, a binary matrix $S(x, y)$ is constructed, which contain values of one in those pixels whose correlation values are significant and zeros where the similarity is unlikely.

6: A neighborhood region $V(x, y)$ is defined.

7: $S(x, y)$ is initialized with all its elements in zero.

8: **for** all coordinates of the image $I(x, y)$ **do**

9: **if** $(U(x,y) == 1)$ **then**

10: **if** $(V(x, y) \geq$ each of the values of $R(x, y))$ **then**

11: $S(x, y) = 1$

12: end **for**

Lines 1–3 of Algorithm 4.1 formulate the process of calculating the matrix of the correlation coefficients $C_L(x,y)$. This process has already been explained in detail in Section 4.1.4. Considering an appropriate value of t_h, the binary matrix $U(x,y)$ is obtained according to line 4. At this point, we have the elements of the matrix $U(x,y)$. It contains information on those points that maintain significant correlation $C_L(x,y)$ values. To find the points of maximum correlation of the regions obtained from $C_L(x,y)$, the processes described in lines 5–12 are implemented. In this part, using the information contained in the matrix $U(x,y)$, they look for the "true correlation points," which are those that experiment with a maximum value of $C_L(x,y)$ compared to the other points contained in a neighborhood region $V(x,y)$ centered around the test point.

4.2.1 Implementation of the Pattern Recognition System by the Correlation Coefficient

This section shows how to implement the correlation coefficient to recognize objects considering Algorithm 4.1. Program 4.7 illustrates how to locate a reference pattern in an image using Algorithm 4.1.

Figure 4.13 shows the result obtained when executing the algorithm described in Program 4.7. Figure 4.13 shows the effectiveness of the method, being able to recognize rotated and scaled versions of the pattern to be detected. The white+symbol on the pattern defines the identified elements. The calculation of coordinates of the+symbols corresponds to the values of the points of maximum correlation plus half of the dimensions of the reference pattern. This offset allows centering the point of maximum correlation to the pattern of the image with which it corresponds.

PROGRAM 4.7   PROGRAM FOR PATTERN RECOGNITION BASED ON THE CALCULATION OF THE CORRELATION COEFFICIENT $C_L(x,y)$

```
%%%%%%%%%%%%%%%%%%%%%%%%%%%%%%%%%%%%%%%%%%%%%%%%%%%%%%%%%%%%%%%%
% Program that allows recognizing patterns through the
% correlation coefficient between I(x,y) and R(i,j)
%%%%%%%%%%%%%%%%%%%%%%%%%%%%%%%%%%%%%%%%%%%%%%%%%%%%%%%%%%%%%%%%
% Erik Cuevas, Alma Rodríguez
%%%%%%%%%%%%%%%%%%%%%%%%%%%%%%%%%%%%%%%%%%%%%%%%%%%%%%%%%%%%%%%%
% All the code described in Program 4.6 is used.
%The threshold value is set
th=0.5;
% The binary matrix U is obtained
U=CLN>0.5;
```

```
% The value of the neighborhood is set
pixel=10;
% Obtain the largest value of CLN from a neighborhood
% defined by the pixel variable
for r=1:m-mt
    for c=1:n-nt
        if(U(r,c))
        % Define the left boundary of the neighborhood
            I1=[r-pixel 1];
        % The right limit of the neighborhood is defined
            I2=[r+pixel m-mt];
        % Define the upper limit of the neighborhood
            I3=[c-pixel 1];
    % Define the lower bound of an of the neighborhood
            I4=[c+pixel n-nt];
        % Positions are defined taking into account that
            % its value is relative to r and c.
            datxi=max(I1);
            datxs=min(I2);
            datyi=max(I3);
            datys=min(I4);
            % The block is extracted from the CLN matrix
Bloc=CLN(datxi:1:datxs,datyi:1:datys);
            % Get the maximum value of the neighborhood
            MaxB=max(max(Bloc));
            % If the current pixel value is the maximum
            % then in that position, a one is placed in
            %the matrix S
            if(CLN(r,c)==MaxB)
                S(r,c)=1;
            end
        end
    end
end
%The original image is shown
imshow(Im)
% The graphic object is kept so that the others
% graphic commands have an effect on the image Im
hold on
% Half of the defined window is determined
% by the reference pattern.
y=round(mt/2);
x=round(nt/2);
% Half of the window defined by the reference
% pattern is added to each value of the maximum
correlation
% in S, in order to exactly identify the object.
```

```
for r=1:m-mt
    for c=1:n-nt
        if(S(r,c))
        Resultado(r+y,c+x)=1;
        end
    end
end
% The points of maximum correlation are defined in
% Resultado are plotted on the image Im.
for r=1:m-mt
    for c=1:n-nt
        if(Resultado(r,c))
        plot(c,r,'+g');
        end
    end
end
```

FIGURE 4.13
Image obtained from the recognition algorithm described in Program 4.7, using Figure 4.3a as the image and Figure 4.3b as the pattern.

4.3 Comparison of Binary Images

As it was already analyzed in the previous sections, the comparison between grayscale images can be solved by using the correlation. Although this approach does not offer an optimal solution, it can be used under certain circumstances to obtain reliable results as long as efficient computing equipment is available. However, if two binary images are compared directly, the difference found between them is irregular despite the complete similarity or complete difference between the image and the pattern to be detected [8].

The problem with the direct comparison of binary images is that even small differences between the two images, due to shifts, rotations, or distortions, produce strong differences [8]. Therefore, the question is how binary images can be compared in such a way that the comparison is tolerant to small deviations. The objective is then not to consider the number of pixels belonging to the object of the image that does not coincide with the reference image but to use a geometric measure that allows knowing how far or how close two patterns are similar.

4.3.1 The Transformation of Distance

A possible solution to this problem consists of determining in each pixel how far it is geometrically from the nearest pixel whose value is one. Under such conditions, a measure of the minimum displacement can be found. This value is necessary to determine when a pixel can overlap with another [9]. Considering a binary image $I_b(x,y)$, the following data sets are described:

$$FG(I) = \left\{ p \mid I(p) = 1 \right\} \tag{4.13}$$

$$BG(I) = \left\{ p \mid I(p) = 0 \right\} \tag{4.14}$$

where $FG(I)$ considers all the pixels of the image whose value is one, while $BG(I)$ considers the pixels whose value is zero. The distance transformation $D(p)$ of $I_b(x,y)$ is defined as follows:

$$D(p) = \min_{p' \in FG(I)} \ \text{dist}(p, p') \tag{4.15}$$

For all points $p = (x,y)$, where $x = 0,\ldots,N-1$ and $y = 0,\ldots,M-1$ (if considered as dimensions of the image $M \times N$). If a pixel p has a value of one, then $D(p) = 0$. This is because no displacement is necessary for that pixel to overlap a nearby pixel of value 1.

The function $\text{dist}(p, p')$ defined in Equation 4.14 evaluates the geometric distance between two coordinates $p = (x,y)$ and $p' = (x',y')$. Examples of appropriate distance functions are the Euclidean distance:

$$d_E(p, p') = p - p' = \sqrt{(x - x')^2 + (y - y')^2} \tag{4.16}$$

Or the Manhattan distance:

$$d_M(p, p') = |x - x'| + |y - y'| \tag{4.17}$$

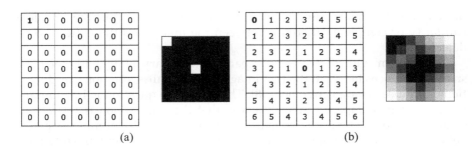

1	0	0	0	0	0	0
0	0	0	0	0	0	0
0	0	0	0	0	0	0
0	0	0	1	0	0	0
0	0	0	0	0	0	0
0	0	0	0	0	0	0
0	0	0	0	0	0	0

0	1	2	3	4	5	6
1	2	3	2	3	4	5
2	3	2	1	2	3	4
3	2	1	0	1	2	3
4	3	2	1	2	3	4
5	4	3	2	3	4	5
6	5	4	3	4	5	6

(a)   (b)

FIGURE 4.14
Example of the distance transformation of a binary image using the Manhattan distance as a function. (a) Binary image and (b) the resulting distance transform.

Figure 4.14 shows a simple example of the distance transformation using the Manhattan distance d_M.

The direct calculation of the distance transformation from definition (4.15) demands a high computational cost since for each pixel $p = (x, y)$, the closest pixel $p' = (x', y')$ must be found. This process requires generating a distance matrix for each pixel of the image, from which the minimum value will always be detected.

4.3.2 Chamfer Algorithm

The Chamfer algorithm is an efficient method for calculating distance transformations [10] and uses two processing loops that operate sequentially, in which the distance calculation propagates through the image in different directions. In the first loop, the calculation of the distance is made from the upper left corner downwards, while in the second, the calculation of the distance is propagated from the lower right corner upwards (in the opposite direction to the first). In calculating the distances for each of the loops, two different masks are used, where each of them corresponds to each of the loops:

$$M^I = \begin{bmatrix} m_2^I & m_3^I & m_4^I \\ m_1^I & \times & \cdot \\ \cdot & \cdot & \cdot \end{bmatrix} \quad M^D = \begin{bmatrix} \cdot & \cdot & \cdot \\ \cdot & \times & m_1^D \\ m_4^D & m_3^D & m_2^D \end{bmatrix} \quad (4.18)$$

The values of the masks M^I and M^D correspond to the geometric distances between the current point $\times$ and its relevant neighbors. The values of M^I and M^D depend on the selected distance function $\text{dist}(p, p')$. Algorithm 4.2 describes the computation of the distance transform $D(x, y)$ from a binary image $I_b(x, y)$ using Chamfer method.

ALGORITHM 4.2   CHAMFER ALGORITHM FOR CALCULATING DISTANCE TRANSFORMATION

Distance Transformation $(I_b(x, y))$
Binary image $I_b(x, y)$ of dimensions $M \times N$

1:   Step 1. It initializes.

for all coordinates of the image $I_b(x, y)$ **do**

if $(I_b(x, y) == 1)$ **then**

$D(x, y) = 0$

else

$D(x, y) =$ a big value.

2:   Step 2. The image with the mask M^I is processed from left to right and from top to bottom.

for $y \leftarrow 1, 2, ..., M$ **do**

   for $x \leftarrow 1, 2, ..., N$ **do**

if $(I_b(x, y) > 0)$ **then**

$d_1 = m_1^I + D(x - 1, y)$

$d_2 = m_2^I + D(x - 1, y - 1)$

$d_3 = m_3^I + D(x, y - 1)$

$d_4 = m_4^I + D(x + 1, y - 1)$

$D(x, y) = \min(d_1, d_2, d_3, d_4)$

   end

End

3:   Step 3. The image with the mask M^D is processed from right to left and from bottom to top.

for $y \leftarrow M - 1, ..., 1$ **do**

   for $x \leftarrow N - 1, ..., 1$ **do**

if $(I_b(x, y) > 0)$ **then**

$d_1 = m_1^R + D(x + 1, y)$

$d_2 = m_2^R + D(x + 1, y + 1)$

$$d_3 = m_3^R + D(x, y+1)$$
$$d_4 = m_4^R + D(x-1, y+1)$$
$$D(x,y) = \min(d_1, d_2, d_3, d_4, D(x,y))$$

    end

  end

4: Return the value of D.

The Chamfer algorithm using the Manhattan distance uses the masks defined as follows:

$$M_M^I = \begin{bmatrix} 2 & 1 & 2 \\ 1 & \times & \cdot \\ \cdot & \cdot & \cdot \end{bmatrix} \quad M_M^D = \begin{bmatrix} \cdot & \cdot & \cdot \\ \cdot & \times & 1 \\ 2 & 1 & 2 \end{bmatrix} \quad (4.19)$$

In the same way, if the Euclidean distance is used, the masks are defined as follows:

$$M_E^I = \begin{bmatrix} \sqrt{2} & 1 & \sqrt{2} \\ 1 & \times & \cdot \\ \cdot & \cdot & \cdot \end{bmatrix} \quad M_E^D = \begin{bmatrix} \cdot & \cdot & \cdot \\ \cdot & \times & 1 \\ \sqrt{2} & 1 & \sqrt{2} \end{bmatrix} \quad (4.20)$$

With these masks, an approximation of the true distance obtained by means of the point-to-point Euclidean distance is evidently reached. However, with the masks corresponding to the Euclidean distance, a more accurate estimation is obtained than those defined for the Manhattan distance. Figure 4.15 shows the results of using each of the masks.

4.3.2.1 Implementation of the Distance Transformation

This section shows how to implement the distance transformation using the Chamfer method defined in Algorithm 4.2. Program 4.8 shows the implementation of the algorithm in MATLAB.

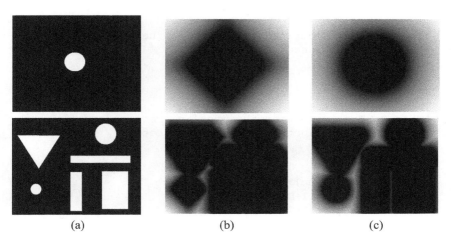

(a)   (b)   (c)

FIGURE 4.15
The distance transformation using the Chamfer algorithm. (a) Original images, (b) distance transformations using Manhattan distance masks, and (c) distance transformations using Euclidean distance masks.

PROGRAM 4.8   MATLAB PROGRAM TO CALCULATE THE DISTANCE TRANSFORMATION USING THE CHAMFER ALGORITHM. IN THE ALGORITHM, THE MANHATTAN APPROACH IS CONSIDERED A FUNCTION OF DISTANCE

```
%%%%%%%%%%%%%%%%%%%%%%%%%%%%%%%%%%%%%%%%%%%%%%%%%%%%%%%%%%%%
% Program to calculate the distance transformation
% of a binary image using the algorithm
%Chamfer
%%%%%%%%%%%%%%%%%%%%%%%%%%%%%%%%%%%%%%%%%%%%%
% Erik Cuevas, Alma Rodríguez
%%%%%%%%%%%%%%%%%%%%%%%%%%%%%%%%%%%%%%%%%%%%%
% Gets the size of the binary image
[m n]=size(Ib);
% The distance matrix D is defined
D=zeros(size(Ib));
%Step 1. Initialization
for re=1:m
    for co=1:n
        if(Ib(re,co))
            D(re,co)=0;
        else
            D(re,co)=300;
        end
    end
end
```

```
%The mask MI is defined, considering the
%Manhattan  distance
mI1=1;
mI2=2;
mI3=1;
mI4=2;
%Step 2. The image with the mask is processed
% from left to right and from top to bottom.
for re=2:m
    for co=2:n-1

        if(D(re,co)>0)
            d1=mI1+D(re,co-1);
            d2=mI2+D(re-1,co-1);
            d3=mI3+D(re-1,co);
            d4=mI4+D(re-1,co+1);
            Dis= [d1 d2 d3 d4];
        D(re,co)=min(Dis);
        end
    end
end
%The MD mask is defined, considering the
%Manhattan distance
mD1=1;
mD2=2;
mD3=1;
mD4=2;
%Step 3. The image with the mask is processed
% right to left and bottom to top.
for re=m-1:-1:1
    for co=n-1:-1:2
        if(D(re,co)>0)
            d1=mD1+D(re,co+1);
            d2=mD2+D(re+1,co+1);
            d3=mD3+D(re+1,co);
            d4=mD4+D(re+1,co-1);
            Dis=[d1 d2 d3 d4 D(re,co)];
        D(re,co)=min(Dis);
        end

    end
end
% The results are displayed
F=mat2gray(D);
imshow(F)
```

4.4 Chamfer Index Relationship

Once the distance transformation is explained through the Chamfer, it is possible to use it as a comparison index between binary images. The Chamfer ratio index $Q(r,s)$ uses the distance transformation to locate the point where a binary image and a binary reference pattern have the maximum similarity.

The similarity criterion in the Chamfer relation index method is based on the sum of the distance values of each pixel of the image segment that is compared in relation to the reference pattern. With this, the total distance necessary to move a segment of the image is computed in order to find a maximum similarity.

In the method, the binary reference pattern $R_b(i,j)$ is displaced on the image $I_b(r,s)$. Then, in each pixel within the neighborhood of $R_b(i,j)$, the sum of the distances of the pixels in the image $I_b(r,s)$ is calculated. This formulation can be defined as follows:

$$Q(x,y) = \frac{1}{K} \sum_{(i,j) \in FG(R)} D(r+i, s+j) \tag{4.21}$$

where $K = |FG(R)|$ corresponds to the number of pixels of the value of one contained in the pattern $R_b(i,j)$.

The complete process of calculating the Chamfer ratio index $Q(r,s)$ is summarized in Algorithm 4.3. If at a certain position of $I_b(r,s)$, all the pixels of the pattern $R_b(i,j)$ whose value is one, coincide with those of the covered section of the image $I_b(r,s)$, the sum of the distances will be zero, which represents a perfect similarity between both elements. The more pixels of value one of the pattern $R_b(i,j)$ do not have correspondence with those of the image $I_b(r,s)$, the sum of the distances will have a considerable value, which would imply a greater difference between the contents of information between $I_b(r,s)$ and $R_b(i,j)$. The best similarity index is reached at the point where $Q(r,s)$ has its minimum value. This can be formulated as follows:

$$p_{opt} = (r_{opt}, s_{opt}) = \min(Q(r,s)) \tag{4.22}$$

If the binary image shown in Figure 4.16a is considered as an example and Figure 4.16b as a reference pattern, the calculation of the Chamfer ratio index $Q(r,s)$ would be represented by Figure 4.16c, while Figure 4.16d represents the surface of $Q(r,s)$.

In Figure 4.16c and d, it can be observed how the calculation of the value of the Chamfer relation index gives a similarity indicator that varies smoothly. The red points show the locations where there is a better similarity between

ALGORITHM 4.3   ALGORITHM FOR CALCULATING THE CHAMFER RATIO INDEX

Chamfer ratio index $(I_b(r,s), R_b(i,j))$

$I_b(r,s)$ binary image of dimension $an_I \times al_I$

$R_b(i,j)$ binary reference pattern of dimension $an_R \times al_R$

1:   Step 1. The distance transformation $D(r,s)$ is obtained from the image $I_b(r,s)$ (see Algorithm 4.2)

2:   The number of pixels K of the pattern $R_b(i,j)$ whose value is equal to one is obtained.

3:   Step 2. Values of the Chamfer ratio index $Q(r,s)$ are calculated.

4:   **for** $r \leftarrow 1,2,...,al_I - al_R$ **do**

  for $s \leftarrow 1,2,...,an_I - an_R$ **do**

  The value of $Q(r,s)$ is calculated.

  sumadis=0

  for $i \leftarrow 1,2,...,al_R$ **do**

  for $j \leftarrow 1,2,...,an_R$ **do**

  if$(R_b(i,j) =1)$ **do**

  sumadis=sumadis+$D(r+i,s+j)$

  end

  end

  end

  $Q(r,s) = $ sumadis$/K$

  end

  end

5:   Return the value of Q.

the image $I_b(r,s)$ and the reference pattern $R_b(i,j)$. An obvious problem with this index is that it varies very smoothly, which at least visibly prevents the identification of global minima. However, if only those points with the smallest level were considered, as shown in Figure 4.17, these would correspond to those figures that show a better similarity with the reference pattern.

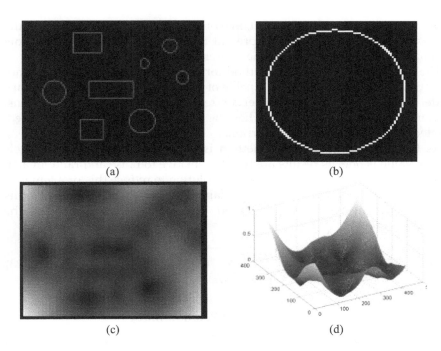

(a) (b)

(c) (d)

FIGURE 4.16
Calculation of the Chamfer ratio index. (a) Binary image, (b) reference pattern, (c) value of the Chamfer ratio index $Q(r,s)$, and (d) the surface of $Q(r,s)$.

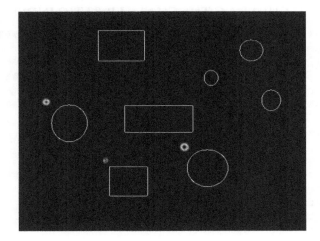

FIGURE 4.17
Representation of the Chamfer ratio index as contours of the smallest values.

In Figure 4.17, it can be seen that, like other algorithms in this chapter, the points of maximum similarity represent the upper left corner of a window that has the same dimension as the reference pattern.

The Chamfer relation index method for binary image comparison cannot be considered a magic method, capable of identifying practically any binary pattern, but it works well under certain restrictions on specific applications. This method presents problems when the pattern to be recognized is scaled, rotated, or has some type of distortion.

As the Chamfer ratio index method is based on the distance of pixels whose value is one, its results are highly sensitive to noise and random artifacts contained in the image. A possible solution to reduce this problem is to use, instead of the linear sum of the distances (Equation 4.21), the root means square of the distance values produced. This model can be defined by the following equation:

$$Q_{rms}(r,s) = \sqrt{\frac{1}{K} \sum_{(i,j)\in FG(R)} (D(r+i,s+j))^2} \qquad (4.23)$$

4.4.1 Implementation of the Chamfer Relation Index

This section shows how to implement the Chamfer relation index defined in Algorithm 4.3. Program 4.9 shows how to implement Algorithm 4.3 in MATLAB.

PROGRAM 4.9   MATLAB PROGRAM FOR CALCULATING THE CHAMFER RATIO INDEX

```
%%%%%%%%%%%%%%%%%%%%%%%%%%%%%%%%%%%%%%%%%%%%%%%%%%%%%%%%%%%%%%%
% Program to calculate the Chamfer ratio index
% Q(r,s) from a binary image and a pattern.
%%%%%%%%%%%%%%%%%%%%%%%%%%%%%%%%%%%%%%%%%%%%%%%%%%%%%%%%%%%%%%%
% Erik Cuevas, Alma Rodríguez
%%%%%%%%%%%%%%%%%%%%%%%%%%%%%%%%%%%%%%%%%%%%%%%%%%%%%%%%%%%%%%%
%Get the size of the binary image
[m n]=size(BW);
% The size of the reference pattern is obtained
[mt nt]=size(T);
%It is obtained the number of ones within
%the reference pattern
[dx dy]=find(T);
[K l]=size(dx);
%Se inicializan variables
suma=0;
Q=zeros(m-mt,n-nt);
```

```
% The entire binary image is processed to calculate
% the Chamfer ratio index Q(r,s)
for re=1:m-mt
    for co=1:n-nt
        for re1=0:mt-1
            for co1=0:nt-1
        if(T(1+re1,1+co1))
% D is the distance transformation of BW
        suma=D(re+re1,co+co1)+suma;
        end
        end
        end
        Q(re,co)=suma/K;
%The accumulator value is reset
        suma=0;

    end
end
% The results are displayed
QR=mat2gray(Q);
imshow(QR)
```

References

[1] Gose, E., Johnsonbaugh, R., & Jost, S. (2017). *Pattern recognition and image analysis*. CRC Press.

[2] Jahne, B. (2005). *Digital image processing: Concepts, algorithms, and scientific applications* (4th ed.). Springer.

[3] Burger, W., & Burge, M. J. (2010). *Principles of digital image processing: Advanced methods*. Springer.

[4] Shih, F. Y. (2010). *Image processing and pattern recognition: Fundamentals and techniques*. John Wiley & Sons.

[5] Fu, K. S. (1976). Pattern recognition and image processing. *IEEE Transactions on Computers, 100*(12), 1336–1346.

[6] Ślęzak, D., Pal, S. K., Kang, B.-H., Gu, J., Kuroda, H., & Kim, T.-H. (Eds.). (2009). Signal processing, image processing and pattern recognition: International conference, SIP 2009, held as part of the future generation information technology conference, FGIT 2009, Jeju island, Korea, December 10-12, 2009. Proceedings. Springer Berlin Heidelberg.

[7] Gose, E., Johnsonbaugh, R., & Jost, S. (1996). *Pattern recognition and image analysis*. Prentice-Hall, Inc.

[8] Chen, C. H. (Ed.). (2015). *Handbook of pattern recognition and computer vision*. World Scientific.

[9] Jähne, B. (2013). *Digital image processing: Concepts, algorithms, and scientific applications*. Springer.

[10] Burger, W., & Burge, M. J. (2016). *Digital image processing*. Springer.

5

Mean-Shift Algorithm for Segmentation

5.1 Introduction

Segmentation represents one of the main steps in computer vision for dividing an image into distinct, non-overlapping regions, considering a certain criterion of similarity. The efficiency of several image processing methods, such as content-based retrieval, object recognition, and semantic classification, is determined by the quality of the used segmentation method. However, the appropriate segmentation of a region or objects from a complex image is considered a complicated task. Recently, many interesting segmentation schemes have been proposed in the literature. These approaches can be divided into methods such as graph-based [1–3], histogram-based [4,5], contour detection-based [6], Markov random field-based [7], fuzzy-based [8,9], thresholding-based [10,11], texture-based [12], clustering-based [13,14], and principal component analysis (PCA)-based [15]. Among such schemes, histogram-based and thresholding-based segmentation methods correspond to the most widely used techniques in computer vision. Thresholding-based approaches include methods such as bi-level and multi-level segmentation. The operation of such algorithms depends on the number of regions to be segmented. Multi-level techniques are generally required when images contain more than two areas to be discriminated against. Depending on their operation mechanism, multi-level thresholding techniques can be classified into six groups [9] such as clustering-based methods, object attribute-based methods, histogram-based methods, object attribute-based methods, local methods and spatial methods, and entropy-based methods.

In histogram-based schemes, pixels are segmented through an analysis of several aspects of one-dimensional histograms, such as peaks, curvatures, valleys, etc. Nevertheless, since histograms with only one dimension do not relate local information among pixels, these schemes present in general an inadequate performance. To enhance the effects generated by one-dimensional histograms, several pixel features have been integrated to provide more information. One example includes techniques based on histograms of two dimensions for image thresholding segmentation introduced by Abutaleb [16]. Under this approach, each intensity pixel value is related

DOI: 10.1201/9781032662466-5

to its location to generate a two-dimensional histogram. From its results, it is evident that such a scheme gives better results in comparison to one-dimensional histogram-based methods. Once the concept of integrating several pixel characteristics has been introduced, many methods have included this concept for producing new segmentation approaches [17–21].

Multi-feature approaches such as two-dimensional histograms operate on information that combines intensity pixel values with their local pixel positions [16,22]. Therefore, each data piece integrates two elements: pixel intensity and its position. Under these schemes, the information of the diagonal in a two-dimensional histogram maintains important information about homogeneous regions to discriminate objects from the background. Differently, elements outside the diagonal represent heterogeneous sections in the image, corresponding to edges, texturized regions, or noise. The integration of pixel characteristics for segmentation purposes has also considered the combination of pixel intensity and its gradient information, as proposed in Ref. [23]. In spite of its good results, it has been demonstrated [24] that in different contexts, this scheme produces unsatisfactory results in comparison to gray-position schemes. Another interesting multi-feature approach is reported in Ref. [25], where a two-dimensional map is considered. In the scheme, the grayscale values and the results obtained by the application of a non-local means filter are integrated. Although all these techniques present competitive results, they also present an adverse characteristic associated with their high computational cost (CC) [25]. This problem is a consequence of the complexity of the search spaces in which the thresholding values must be found.

Metaheuristic computation schemes have been extensively employed as a way to face classical optimization formulations [19,21]. They are computational tools based on natural or social principles which are used to optimize formulations [26], as outlined by their high complexity. Metaheuristic approaches have already been employed for segmentation purposes, considering several mechanisms [17,19–21,27]. Likewise, these methods have also been proposed for multi-feature segmentation considering the approach based on histograms in two dimensions. Some examples involve methods such as Differential Evolution (DE) [28], Genetic Algorithms (GA) [29], Particle Swarm Optimization (PSO) [30,31], Artificial Bee Colony (ABC) [32], Simulated Annealing (SA) [33], Swallow Swarm Optimization (SSO) [34], Ant Colony Optimization (ACO) [35], Electromagnetics-like (EM) optimization [36], Stochastic Fractal Search (SFS) [37], and Cuckoo Search (CS) [38]. All of these approaches maintain one critical difficulty: the number of regions has to be established before their operation [25,39]. This flaw severely restricts their utilization when the type and main elements of the image are unknown. Segmentation schemes that consider metaheuristic algorithms produce excellent results with regard to the values of the optimization function that associates the segmentation task with a cost function. However, such results are not always reflected in the visual quality [25]. Another conflicting aspect of these methods is their high computational overload.

Histograms correspond to the most straightforward approach for producing feature maps in two-dimensional segmentation schemes. They are especially helpful when standard parametric models are inadequate. In their construction, the available data elements are spatially divided into disjoint sections or bins, while their concentration is determined by counting how many data objects fall into each region. Although histograms are easy to operate, they present critical disadvantages such as low precision and density discontinuity [40].

The nonparametric kernel density estimator (KDE) is an interesting approach to building an unknown feature map. KDE presents many attractive characteristics, such as differentiability properties, asymptotic regularity, and continuity and well-known mathematical foundations [41,42]. KDE methods, different from histograms, generate feature maps with better capacities, such as accuracy and smoother properties. Under the operation of KDE, the spatial concentration of each feature is calculated by using symmetric functions (kernel functions) that estimate the weighted accumulation of local elements. Many kernel functions have been introduced for their operation in KDE methods. In general, Gaussian functions are the models most widely used in KDE approaches. On the other hand, the Epanechnikov function [43] represents another interesting alternative for KDE. This kernel produces the best accuracy in the computation of the density map when the number of available elements is very limited [43].

Mean-shift (MS) represents an iterative method used generally for clustering applications [44]. In its operation, MS uses two stages [45]. In the first step, the density map of the feature distribution is produced. This process is performed with the application of a KDE method. Then, through a search strategy, the MS detects the locations with the highest concentration. Such points represent the local maximal elements of the density map.

The reliable and robust performance of MS has promoted its application in different scenarios, such as image segmentation [46] and image filtering [47]. For segmentation purposes, MS identifies similar sections joining pixels that are related to similar local maximal values of the density map. Many segmentation methods based on the MS scheme have been proposed in the literature. Any examples involve the method introduced in [48], where it incorporates a tree-based method with a MS scheme for the effective segmentation of boats in infrared images. Another interesting proposal has been introduced by Park et al. [49]. In this approach, a segmentation technique is produced through the combination of MS and a Gaussian mixture formulation.

Disregarding its good results, MS presents a critical flaw: its computational overload [43,50]. Through its operation, MS estimates the feature map at each point by using the contributions of all the available elements. Furthermore, the cluster assignment process is achieved with the iteration of a scheme based on the gradient method for each point contained in the feature map. These limitations make the use of MS prohibited in segmentation applications where the feature map is integrated by multiple characteristics, such as those described by histograms of two dimensions. For this reason, the MS segmentation algorithms consider only the use of grayscale values (one-dimensional data) with other computational techniques [43].

Under techniques based on one-dimensional and two-dimensional schemes, important details in images cannot be correctly segmented. In such conditions, the use of more pixel characteristics allows the classification of fine image details, since the possibilities of associating pixel characteristics increase. However, the employment of more characteristics (dimensions) in the density map expands the computational overload of the MS approach significantly. For this reason, the diminution of computational time in the MS technique permits it to expand its segmentation capabilities through the handling of multi-dimensional feature maps.

One widely used technique to diminish the investment cost of a computational approach is the consideration of only a random subgroup of elements from all available data. The idea behind it is to examine the operation of the process by using a very small, representative number of data instead of the whole information. After that, the partially produced results are extrapolated to involve information not used with the approach. Under such conditions, the reduction of the CC is determined by the portion of elements used in the operation of the approach in comparison with the total available data. Therefore, to obtain lower CCs, the number of used elements needs to be reduced until the approach presents a bad performance in terms as it has been operated with the complete dataset. This methodology has been considered in several schemes, such as the random sample consensus (RANSAC) [51] or the random hough transform (RHT) [52], among others.

In this chapter, a segmentation method for intensity images based on the MS (MS) method [44] is explained. In this chapter, it is considered a three-dimensional density map that involves the information of the intensity value, the non-local mean [53], and the local variance of each pixel from the image. In the process of MS, it first generates a density map. This map is produced through the use of an Epanechnikov kernel function [43], which allows us to model a density map accurately, even with a few data. Then, considering as an initial point the location of each feature position, a gradient ascent technique is employed to detect the local maxima, which corresponds to its cluster center. To reduce the CC provoked by the use of a three-dimensional map, by using schemes that have been successfully employed to avoid expensive computations [51,52], the MS scheme is operated considering only a representative group of elements randomly sampled from the complete image data [50]. For this purpose, two sets of data are produced: operative elements (the reduced data employed in the MS operation) and inactive elements (the remainder of the available data). Therefore, the results obtained with the operative set of elements are generalized to include the not-used data [54]. With this mechanism, the MS method is able to segment complex regions, such as texturized elements and objects, under different illumination conditions.

5.2 Kernel Density Estimation (KDE) and the Mean-Shift Method

There is a complete association between KDE and clustering. The objective of KDE is to build the probability function of data distribution by analyzing its point concentration, which could also be employed for classification purposes. KDE represents a set of nonparametric schemes that do not consider any particular probability approach to modeling the probability density function. Instead, KDE computes the probability density directly for every element in the dataset.

MS [44] is a computational method that has generally been considered for clustering. In its operation, each element x contained in the feature space, it is designed as a cluster C_i, whose central point x_i^* represents the local maximum of the density map. Accordingly, beginning at location x, a new position is determined following the orientation of the highest increment of the feature map until the nearest local maximal concentration x_i^* has been reached. The computation process of the MS consists of two stages. As a first step, the construction of a density map is achieved. This process is carried out through the use of a KDE scheme. Then, a search process that considers the gradient ascent as a basis is applied to detect the high local concentration points (local maxima) over the density map [55].

5.2.1 Concentration Map Generation

The nonparametric KDE is the most useful approach to generating an unknown density feature map. In the operation of a KDE scheme, the concentration in every location is estimated by using kernel functions that consider the collection of weighted near elements. A kernel model K is characterized as an asymmetric, non-negative kernel element K, such as it is defined in Equation 5.1.

$$K(\mathbf{x}) \geq 0; \quad K(-\mathbf{x}) = K(\mathbf{x}); \quad \int K(\mathbf{x})dx = 1 \tag{5.1}$$

Considering a group of n characteristics $\{\mathbf{x}_1, \mathbf{x}_2, \ldots, \mathbf{x}_n\}$, the density function $\hat{f}(\mathbf{x})$, can be determined in terms of K, as shown in Equation 5.2.

$$\hat{f}(\mathbf{x}) = \frac{1}{nh} \sum_{i=1}^{n} K\left(\frac{\mathbf{x} - \mathbf{x}_i}{h}\right), \tag{5.2}$$

where h corresponds to the support region of K.

The simplest kernel model is the discrete kernel function K_D, which calculates the respective concentration in a specific location by counting the number of data elements within a window of size h. K_D is defined in Equation 5.3.

$$K_D \left(\frac{x - x_i}{h} \right) = \begin{cases} 1 & \text{if } \left(\frac{x - x_i}{h} \right) \le h \\ 0 & \text{Otherwise} \end{cases} \tag{5.3}$$

Figure 5.1 presents the KDE considering the discrete kernel K_D for several magnitudes of the value h over a one-dimensional dataset. In the figure, the stack height represents the frequency at which the data are concentrated. As it is indicated in Figure 5.1a, if h presents a small value, the resulting probability density shows several local maximal points. Nevertheless, as the value of h increases from 0.25 to 2, the number of modes is reduced until h gets high enough to produce a distribution with only one mode (unimodal).

Even though different kernel models have been used in KDE methods, the Gaussian function $K_G(x)$ represents the most popular kernel scheme in KDE approaches. The Gaussian or normal function is characterized by Equation 5.4, whereas its representation is illustrated in Figure 5.2.

$$K_G(x) = \left(\frac{1}{\sqrt{2\pi}} \right) e^{\left(\frac{-x^2}{2h} \right)} \tag{5.4}$$

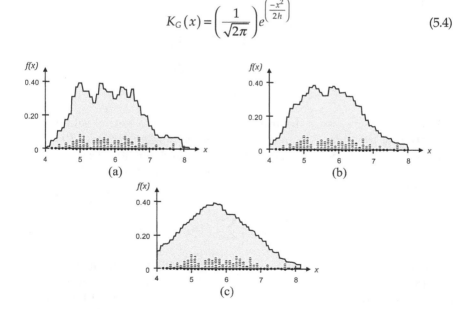

(a)

(b)

(c)

FIGURE 5.1
Probability density estimation by using the discrete kernel K_D by using different values of h.
(a) $h = 0.5$, (b) $h = 1.0$, and (c) $h = 2.0$.

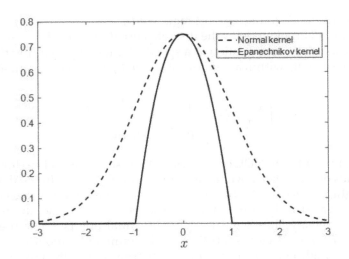

FIGURE 5.2
Distinct kernel functions: Normal kernel $K_G(x)$ and Epanechnikov kernel $K_E(x)$.

On the other hand, the Epanechnikov kernel $K_E(x)$ (see Figure 5.2) [43] is an alternative for KDE due to its interesting properties. $K_E(x)$ is defined in Equation 5.5.

$$K_E(x) = \begin{cases} \left(\dfrac{3}{4}\right)(1-x^2) & \text{if } |x| \le 1 \\ 0 & \text{otherwise} \end{cases} \tag{5.5}$$

$$x_2$$

A generic form to assess the modeling accuracy of a kernel scheme is the evaluation of the mean-squared error (*MSE*) generated between the density feature map $f(\mathbf{x})$ to be modeled and the estimated density $\hat{f}(\mathbf{x})$ obtained for a determined kernel formulation. This modeling precision can be computed using Equation 5.6.

$$MSE\left(\hat{f}(\mathbf{x})\right) = \frac{1}{n}\sum_{i=1}^{n}\left(\hat{f}(\mathbf{x}_i) - f(\mathbf{x}_i)\right)^2 \tag{5.6}$$

Under such conditions, the Epanechnikov kernel $K_E(x)$ exhibits the best representation accuracy with regard to the *MSE* index since its model $K_E(x)$, according to a different analysis reported in the literature [40,42], it delivers the functional solution that produces the minimal *MSE* value corresponding to Equation 5.6. This behavior persists even when there is a very limited amount of data available for computing the density of the feature map [40].

In general terms, this fact is a consequence of the modeling properties of the Epanechnikov kernel $K_E(x)$ function in which the density value at a specific point is computed considering only the data elements inside the influence distance h. Different form $K_E(x)$, other kernels, such as the Gaussian function $K_G(x)$, lost local accuracy since their estimated density values were influenced by data points located far from h.

The Epanechnikov function $K_E(x)$ produces the best estimation accuracy, but the number of elements needed to compute the concentration of the map of characteristics is quite limited. To illustrate the properties of the Epanechnikov function $K_E(x)$, a data modeling example is presented. Consider the initial probability density function (PDF), which is generated by a Gaussian mixture $M(x_1, x_2)$ of two dimensions. The mixture $M(x_1, x_2)$ integrates three Gaussian kernels $(j = 1, 2, 3)$, assuming the model $N_j(\mu_j, \Sigma_j)$, where μ represents its averaged point while Σ corresponds to its respective covariance. Figure 5.3a exhibits the Gaussian mixture modeled as

$$(x_1, x_2) = \left(\frac{2}{3}\right)N_1 + \left(\frac{1}{6}\right)N_2 + \left(\frac{1}{6}\right)N_3.$$ From such a PDF, a small subset of 120

elements is sampled (see Figure 5.3b). Assuming the only existence of these 120 data, the kernels $K_G(x)$ and $K_E(x)$ have been considered to determine the

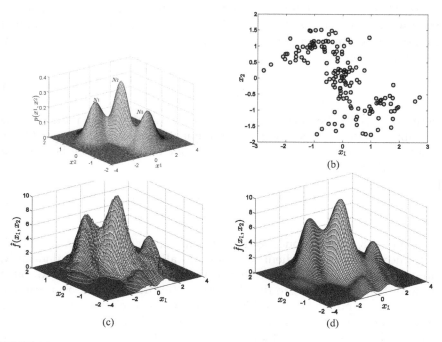

FIGURE 5.3
Modeling properties of the Normal $K_G(x)$ and Epanechnikov $K_E(x)$ functions in case of the group of available elements are reduced. (a) Two-dimensional PDF, (b) 120 characteristics drawn from the PDF, (c) calculated density map $\hat{f}(x_1, x_2)$, considering the Normal function $K_G(x)$, and (d) the Epanechnikov function $K_E(x)$.

density map $\hat{f}(x_1, x_2)$ producing Figure 5.2c and d, reciprocally. Figure 5.2c and d demonstrates that the Epanechnikov kernel $K_E(x)$ obtains a better estimation result than the normal function $K_G(x)$. From the figures, it is clear that the Gaussian function produces many false local maxima and a noisy surface in $\hat{f}(x_1, x_2)$ as a result of its difficulties in adequately representing the density map when the set of data is drastically small.

5.3 Density Attractors Points

The objective in the determination of a feature map $\hat{f}(\mathbf{x})$ corresponding to a certain data set is to detect the points $\mathbf{x}_i^*$, which corresponds to the central cluster points that better represent the probability distribution for the modeled data of $\hat{f}(\mathbf{x})$. The elements $\mathbf{x}_i^*$ model the local maxima points existent in the computed feature map $\hat{f}(\mathbf{x})$. These points can be identified by using an optimization approach based on gradient techniques. Assuming a group $\mathbf{X}$ of d points $(\mathbf{X} = \{\mathbf{x}_1, \ldots, \mathbf{x}_d\})$, a random element $\mathbf{x}_j$ is sampled $(j \in 1, \ldots, d)$. Afterward, a new position $\mathbf{x}_j^{t+1}$ is estimated in the direction to the gradient $\nabla \hat{f}(\mathbf{x}_j)$ with regard to the density. This process is executed as the maximal local position $\mathbf{x}_i^*$ has been obtained. This procedure can be modeled as indicated by Equation 5.7.

$$\mathbf{x}_j^{t+1} = \mathbf{x}^t + \delta \cdot \nabla \hat{f}(\mathbf{x}_j^t), \tag{5.7}$$

where t represents the iteration number currently in operation and δ is the step length. In the MS operation, the gradient at any data $\mathbf{x}$ with regard to its density is estimated by calculating the derivate of the PDF as it is modeled by Equation 5.8.

$$\nabla \hat{f}(\mathbf{x}) = \frac{\partial}{\partial x} \hat{f}(\mathbf{x}) = \frac{1}{nh} \sum_{i=1}^{n} \frac{\partial}{\partial x} K\left(\frac{x - x_i}{h}\right) \tag{5.8}$$

In Equation 5.8, n corresponds to the data dimension for $\mathbf{x} = (x_1, \ldots, x_n)$. With the application of the gradient technique to all d points in the dataset $\mathbf{X}$, many elements will be concentrated at the same local maximum $\mathbf{x}_i^*$. Such data will then be assigned to the cluster C_i. After this process, as a result, a list of c attractor points $\{\mathbf{x}_1^*, \ldots, \mathbf{x}_c^*\}$ is obtained, where each point $\mathbf{x}_i^*$ represents a group of elements $\mathbf{X}_i = (\mathbf{x}_a, \ldots, \mathbf{x}_g)$ that are drawn by $\mathbf{x}_i^* (\mathbf{x}_a, \mathbf{x}_g \in C_i)$.

Figure 5.4 shows a representation of the gradient method to detect the local optima. In this figure, the contour illustration of $\hat{f}(x_1, x_2)$ is shown. Therefore, beginning at locations $\mathbf{x}_p, \mathbf{x}_q$, and $\mathbf{x}_r$, new points are estimated considering orientation as the largest increment of the density map $\hat{f}(x_1, x_2)$. This process is repeated until the local optima of $\mathbf{x}_1^*, \mathbf{x}_2^*$, and $\mathbf{x}_3^*$ have been obtained.

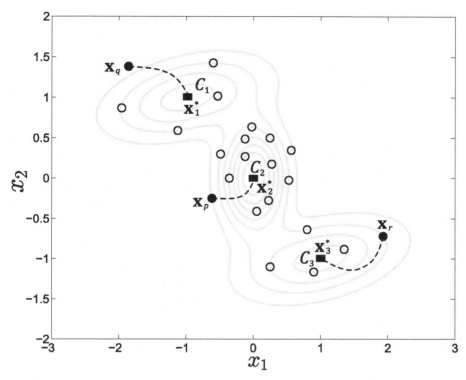

FIGURE 5.4
Representation of the gradient procedure to detect the local optima values.

Therefore, in the process of MS, it first generates a density map. This map is produced through the use of a KDE scheme, which provokes the emergence of several local peaks according to the data distribution. Then, considering as an initial point the location of each data position, a gradient ascent technique is employed to detect the local maxima, which corresponds to its cluster center (prototype) [56]. Due to the properties of kernel functions, the density map presents a notable smoothness with modes clearly separated [56]. Under such conditions, the correct convergence of the gradient ascended to the local maximum is guaranteed [56,57].

5.4 Segmentation with Camshift

In the MS method, called MULTI-SEGM, the segmentation is carried out by an analysis of the feature map defined in three dimensions. It involves the information of the intensity value, the non-local mean, and the local variance of each pixel from the image. The classification process of each pixel element in terms of its intrinsic features of the three-dimensional map is achieved by means of the MS method.

To diminish the computation of the process, the MS method is executed by using a subset of pixel characteristics, which include only a quite reduced number of elements from all available information. Therefore, two groups of data are defined: operative elements (the amount of data considered in the MS execution) and inactive elements (the rest of the data). In this chapter, instead of Gaussian functions, Epanechnikov kernel elements are employed to compute the density values of the feature map. With the results of the MS method, the obtained information is generalized to include inactive data. Under this process, each inactive pixel is designed to be in the same group as the nearest operative pixel. Finally, clusters that contain the fewest number of elements are merged with other neighboring clusters.

5.4.1 Feature Definition

Consider that $\mathbf{I}(x,y)$ represents a $M \times N$ image whose gray levels are ranged from 0 to 255 for each spatial coordinate (x, y). The MS method operates in the feature space. Therefore, each pixel of the image maintains three different characteristics $\mathbf{F}(x,y)$, such as the intensity value $\mathbf{I}(x,y)$, the non-local mean $\mathbf{NL}(x,y)$, and the local variance $\mathbf{V}(x,y)$.

The non-local means [53] characteristic for a certain pixel (x,y) estimates the weighted average amount of all the pixels within the image in relation to their local means values. Consider $\mathbf{I}(x,y)$ and $\mathbf{I}(p,q)$ the corresponding gray-scale values of the pixel positions (x,y) and (p,q), respectively. Therefore, the non-local means $\mathbf{NL}(x,y)$ in position (x,y) can be calculated as defined in Equation 5.9.

$$\mathbf{NL}(x,y) = \frac{\sum_{p=1}^{M} \sum_{q=1}^{N} \mathbf{I}(p,q) \cdot w\big((p,q),(x,y)\big)}{\sum_{p=1}^{M} \sum_{q=1}^{N} w\big((p,q),(x,y)\big)} \tag{5.9}$$

where $w\big((p,q),(x,y)\big)$ is a weighting value that corresponds to the result of a Gaussian function defined by Equation 5.8.

$$w\big((p,q),(x,y)\big) = e^{-\frac{|\mu(p,q)-\mu(x,y)|^2}{\sigma}} \tag{5.10}$$

where σ corresponds to the standard deviation. $\mu(p,q)$ and $\mu(x,y)$ represents the local mean values at pixels positions (p,q) and (x,y), considering a neighborhood NE of $m \times m$. Such values are estimated according to Equation 5.11.

$$\mu(p,q) = \frac{1}{m \times m} \sum_{(i,j) \in NE} \mathbf{I}(i,j) \quad \mu(x,y) = \frac{1}{m \times m} \sum_{(i,j) \in NE} \mathbf{I}(i,j) \tag{5.11}$$

On the other hand, $\mathbf{V}(x,y)$ is the variance magnitude at position (x, y), produced by considering a window of size $h \times h$. Therefore, the feature vector $\mathbf{F}(x,y)$ at the location (x, y) is represented by a three-dimensional structure defined by Equation 5.12.

$$\mathbf{F}(x,y) = \left[\mathbf{I}(x,y) \quad \mathbf{V}(x,y) \quad \mathbf{NL}(x,y)\right] \tag{5.12}$$

In $\mathbf{F}(x,y)$, all the values of grayscale $\mathbf{I}(x,y)$, variance $\mathbf{V}(x,y)$, and non-local mean $\mathbf{NL}(x,y)$ are normalized within the values [0,1].

The variance $\mathbf{V}(x,y)$ of contiguous pixels represents one of the simplest methods to evaluate the data dispersion. A low value corresponds to a homogeneous region, while a high magnitude could represent texturized objects. The non-local means $\mathbf{NL}(x,y)$ feature considers the mean of similar pixels in terms of their grayscale value. Under this characteristic, the resemblance among pixels presents better robustness in the presence of noise by assuming the comparison with regions and not with only pixels. With the use of $\mathbf{NL}(x,y)$, it is possible to identify if a pixel belongs to a homogeneous region with a specific intensity. Since this feature reduces the possible noise content within a region, its use presents high robustness. Therefore, with the integration of these three characteristics $\mathbf{I}(x,y)$, $\mathbf{NL}(x,y)$, and $\mathbf{V}(x,y)$ is possible to find pixel associations that allow for segmenting complex elements such as texturized regions or poorly illuminated components, etc.

5.4.2 Operative Data Set

The cost of processing the $M \times N$ features from the image through MS is prohibitive in cases where there are several characteristics per pixel. To diminish the computational overload of the process, MS is executed by considering only a subset of random elements, which represent a very reduced number of data extracted from all available elements from $\mathbf{F}(x,y)$. The objective is to obtain a small amount of similar data results, as the MS has been operated with the complete dataset. For this purpose, the whole set of characteristics $\mathbf{F}$ is classified into two sets: operative elements $\mathbf{O}$ and inactive elements $\tilde{\mathbf{O}}$. The set of operative data $\mathbf{O}$ includes the elements considered for the execution of MS, while the group of inactive data $\tilde{\mathbf{O}}$ corresponds to the remainder of the available data information. As they are defined, it is evident that $\tilde{\mathbf{O}}$ represents the complement group of $\mathbf{O}$ in $\mathbf{F}$.

The size s of $\mathbf{O}$ (number of random elements) has determinant importance in the resulting performance of the segmentation process. Therefore, the number s of used elements needs to be reduced until the approach presents a performance degradation in terms as it has been operated with the complete dataset. In order to analyze the effect of this parameter on the performance of the MS segmentation scheme, a sensitivity test has been considered. In the experiment, different values of s are experimented with, while the rest of the MULTI-SEGM parameters are kept fixed to their common values. In the test, s represented as the percentage of the whole data is swept from 1% to 100%, while the segmentation results of the MS method are studied. The data used in O are randomly chosen from the whole dataset F. Thus, to reduce the stochastic effects, every different value of s is executed 30 times independently. The results demonstrate that for higher percentages than 5%, the CC is expanded exponentially while a small enhancement in the performance of the method is perceived. As a conclusion from this study, it can be stated that the best size s of O is obtained when the number of elements is around 5% of the complete number of available data.

Therefore, only 5% of the $M \times N$ data is used to generate the group O. Such elements are randomly sampled form F. The set O involves three-dimensional elements $\{o_1,...,o_s\}$, where $s = int(0.05 \cdot M \cdot N)$, assuming $int(\cdot)$ produces as a result the integer value corresponding to its argument. On the other hand, the set of elements in $\tilde{O} = \{\tilde{o}_a, \tilde{o}_b,..., \tilde{o}_c\}$ is composed of data according to $\tilde{O} = \{a,b,c \in F | \ a,b,c \notin O\}$.

5.4.3 Operation of the MS Algorithm

5.4.3.1 MS Setting

Having produced the dataset O, the MS is applied to it. In the operation of the MS, two important parameters must be configured: the kernel support range h and the step length δ. As the MS method processes the information of a three-dimensional solution space $\left[I(x,y) \ V(x,y) \ NL(x,y)\right]$, both elements correspond to vectors of three dimensions h and δ with a magnitude for every dimension $h = [h_1, h_2, h_3]$; $\delta = [\delta_1, \delta_2, \delta_3]$ where each of dimensions 1, 2, and 3 corresponds to the intensity value $I(x,y)$, the local variance $V(x,y)$, and the non-local mean $N(x,y)$ feature, respectively. These factors are configured automatically by means of an analysis of the set O. The study considered to determine the correct configuration is based on Scott's rule introduced in [43]. Under this scheme, the extent of both elements h and δ are strongly associated with the standard deviation σ of the data in $O = \{o_1,...,o_s\}$. Every element from $o_i \in O$ is characterized as $o_i = \{o_{i,1}, o_{i,2}, o_{i,3}\}$, where $o_{i,j}$ symbolizes the j-th variable of the i-th candidate solution ($j \in 1,...,3$). Therefore, the standard deviation for each dimension σ_j is computed by Equation 5.13.

$$\sigma_j = \sqrt{\frac{1}{s}\sum_{i=1}^{s}\left(o_{i,j} - \overline{o}^j\right)^2} \tag{5.13}$$

where $\overline{o}^j$ corresponds to the averaged value such that $\overline{o}^j = \left(\frac{1}{s}\right)\sum_{i=1}^{s}o_{i,j}$.

With these values, the factors h and δ are configured as it is indicated by Equation 5.14.

$$h_j = 3.5 \cdot \sigma_j \cdot s^{-\left(\frac{1}{3}\right)}, \quad \delta_j = \sqrt{0.5} \cdot \sigma_j, \tag{5.14}$$

where $j \in [1, \ldots, 3]$.

5.4.3.2 Analysis of the Results

The MS achieves its operation through two sub-processes. First, the feature map is generated considering only the information contained in dataset **O**. Afterward, with the density map, their local optimals are identified. Therefore, it is determined a group of c attractor elements $\left\{ x_1^*, \ldots, x_c^* \right\}$ and also a list of data $X_i = \left(o_p, \ldots, o_q \right)$ for each attractor x_i^*. The list includes all the data points $\left(o_p, o_q \in C_i \right)$ attracted to each attractor point.

Assume Figure 5.5a as the image to be processed. The dimensions of the image are 214×320. Considering such an image, it is estimated that the group of characteristics **F**, which includes the grayscale $I(x,y)$, variance $V(x,y)$, and non-local mean $NL(x,y)$ magnitudes for every pixel element. Then, a set of 3,424 pixels ($o = int(0.05 \cdot 214 \cdot 320)$) are sampled randomly from **F** to generate the operative dataset **O**. By considering the elements $O = \{o_1, \ldots, o_s\}$, the MS method is applied. The MS generates as a result for each feature $F(x,y)$ a density value $\hat{f}(F(x,y))$. Therefore, we have four-dimensional data: three elements to describe the feature space and one for referring its density value. In order to visualize these results, we have used a polar technique [58,59] to represent high-dimensional data $(d_1, \ldots, d_4)$ into a two-dimensional space (u,v). Under this technique, the data are first normalized so that they vary

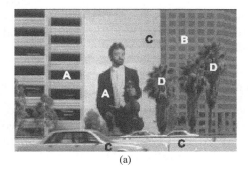

(a)

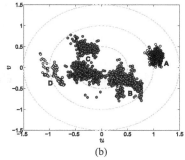

(b)

FIGURE 5.5
Visual representation of the MS results. (a) Image to be processed and (b) visualization of the MS results.

within a range from -0.5 to 0.5. Then, it is assigned to each variable d_i two different angles θ_i and $\overline{\theta}_i$. The angle θ_i is considered for positive values of d_i, while $\overline{\theta}_i = \theta_i + \pi$ is used for its negative values. The value of θ_i depends on the number of variables to visualize (dimensions). In the case of four variables, the angle θ_1 is computed as $\theta_1 = 2 \cdot \pi/8$ and $\overline{\theta}_1 = 2 \cdot \pi/8 + \pi$ for the first variable d_1. Likewise, for the second variable $\theta_2 = 2 \cdot \theta_1$, for the third variable $\theta_3 = 3 \cdot \theta_1$, and so on. With these angles, the final coordinate values (u, v) are computed by Equation 5.15.

$$u = \sum_{j=1}^{4} |a_j| \cos(\theta_j) + \sum_{j=1}^{4} |b_j| \cos(\overline{\theta}_j) \quad v = \sum_{j=1}^{4} |a_j| \sin(\theta_j) + \sum_{j=1}^{4} |b_j| \sin(\overline{\theta}_j)$$

$$a_j = \begin{cases} d_j & \text{if } d_j \geq 0 \\ 0 & \text{otherwise} \end{cases} \quad b_j = \begin{cases} d_j & \text{if } d_j < 0 \\ 0 & \text{otherwise} \end{cases} \quad (5.15)$$

By using this visualization technique, the results produced by the MS scheme are shown in Figure 5.5b. It represents the feature distribution along with the density values $\hat{f}(\mathbf{F}(x, y))$. According to this distribution, the points are divided into several sets. Each group corresponds to elements that share different similarities in the feature space as well as a certain density value. Under such conditions, elements of group **A** represent black pixels of the image. Since these points are quite homogenous, the set is compact with a small dispersion. Group **B** corresponds to gray pixels, while group **C** refers to white pixels. Finally, group **D** integrates texturized pixels or with a high variance. It is obvious that inside each group, some differences in the density values are also found. Figure 5.5 shows the relationship between the groups and sections of the image. Therefore, several local maxima can be detected. The use of this three-dimensional space makes it possible to obtain better segmentation results since different fine structures can be identified and then included in the final segmented result.

5.4.4 Inclusion of the Inactive Elements

With the results of the MS on the operative set $\mathbf{O}$, these results should be processed to add the inactive elements $\tilde{\mathbf{O}}$. In the MS method, to each, not inactive data $\tilde{o}_k \in \tilde{\mathbf{O}}$, it is designated to the cluster C_i of the nearest operative element $o_{ne} \in \mathbf{X}_i$, considering that o_{ne} represents the formulation of Equation 5.16.

$$o_{ne} = \arg \min_{1 \leq i \leq s} d(\tilde{o}_k, o_i), \quad \tilde{o}_k \in \tilde{\mathbf{O}}, \quad o_{ne} \in \mathbf{X}_i \wedge o_{ne} \in \mathbf{O}, \quad (5.16)$$

where $d(\tilde{o}_k, o_i)$ symbolizes the Euclidian distance that maintains $\tilde{o}_k$ and o_i.

Once included all inactive data from $\tilde{\mathbf{O}}$ to each group C_i ($i \in 1, \ldots, c$), all the lists $\mathbf{X}_i$ of clusters increase their number of elements as a consequence of incorporating inactive data from the dataset $\tilde{\mathbf{O}}$. Under such conditions, the new cluster lists $\mathbf{X}_i^{New}$ are updated according to the following formulation

$$\mathbf{X}_i^{New} = \mathbf{X}_i \bigcup \left\{ \tilde{o}_k \in \tilde{\mathbf{O}} \wedge \tilde{o}_k \in C_i \right\}.$$

5.4.5 Merging of Not Representative Groups

After the execution of MS, several groups are generated. Nevertheless, some of them are not visually representative. Such clusters are insignificant with regard to the number of included elements. Therefore, it is important to eliminate such clusters through their combination. The idea is to merge clusters with low concentrations with other groups that share similar characteristics in order to maintain the visual information. The objective is to keep the cluster with "enough density" while the remainder is merged.

To determine the number of data points that define a representative group is comparable to identifying the knee point in system engineering. The knee position describes the "right decision point" at which the relative magnitude of an element is no longer meaningful in terms of its contribution. There are not several methods for identifying knee points listed in the literature [60,61]. Among them, in this chapter, we employ the scheme presented in Ref. [60] due to its simplicity. In this method, a group $\mathbf{E}$ of c components are generated $(\mathbf{E} = (\mathbf{e}_1, \ldots, \mathbf{e}_c))$. Every element $\mathbf{e}_w = \left(e_w^x, e_w^y \right)$ relates the cluster information as indicated by Equation 5.17.

$$e_w^x = \frac{w}{c}; \quad e_w^y = \frac{\left| \mathbf{X}_k^{New} \right|}{\sum_{i=1}^{c} \left| \mathbf{X}_i^{New} \right|}, \quad w = f\left(\left| \mathbf{X}_k^{New} \right| \right); \quad k \in 1, \ldots, c; \tag{5.17}$$

where $\left| \mathbf{X}_k^{New} \right|$ symbolizes the number of data within the cluster C_k. $f\left(\left| \mathbf{X}_k^{New} \right| \right)$ represents a function, which calculates the rank of $\left| \mathbf{X}_k^{New} \right|$ according to the number of elements. Under this formulation, the value of one $(f\left(\left| \mathbf{X}_{high}^{New} \right| \right) = 1)$ is delivered when the group C_{high} presents the highest number of data. Likewise, the maximal index $(f\left(\left| \mathbf{X}_{low}^{New} \right| \right) = c)$ is designed to the cluster C_{low}, which contains a minimal number of elements (where $high, low \in 1, \ldots, c$). The information represented by $\mathbf{e}_w$ corresponds to the element distribution of the group density. Under such conditions, the element $\mathbf{e}_1$ represents the group with the highest density level, while the element $\mathbf{e}_c$ corresponds to the group with the lowest concentration of features (see Figure 5.6a).

Assuming $\mathbf{e}_w$ $(w \in 1, \ldots, c)$, an objective function $\mathbf{d}_w = \left(d_w^x, d_w^y \right)$ is defined. This function links the increment e_w^y in terms of the significance of the contribution e_w^x. $\mathbf{d}_w$ is estimated as indicated in Equation 5.18.

$$d_w^x = e_w^x; \quad d_w^y = e_w^y + e_w^x; \tag{5.18}$$

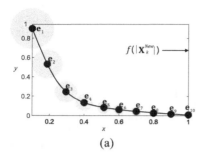 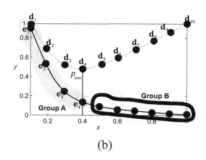

(a)   (b)

FIGURE 5.6
Estimation of the knee location. (a) Concentration of elements of each group $(e_1, \ldots, e_c)$ and (b) the clusters divided into representative (A) and irrelevant (B).

One important property of d_w^y is that it maintains only one global optimum p_{min}. This minimal value represents the knee location that is expressed in Equation 5.17 (see Figure 5.5):

$$p_{min} = \arg \min_{0 \le w \le c} d_w^y \qquad (5.19)$$

It is important to observe that there is a correction between the rank and the number of elements formulated in e_w^x and e_w^y. This correlation can also be seen in the objective function of the elements d_w^x and d_w^y. This fact is because in such formulations, the idea is to associate how an increment in rank is related in terms of the number of elements. With this association, it can be detected that the point p_{min} represents the location where an increment in the cluster rank is greater than the variation in the number of elements. p_{min} separates all groups produced by MS into two sets: (A) relevant and (B) irrelevant groups (see Figure 5.6b). Significant groups involve the clusters that contain the greatest number of pixel characteristics. For this reason, they maintain the representative visual information of the segmented image. Irrelevant groups must be merged with other nearby clusters since their elements are too few so that they cannot be considered as meaningful. Under such conditions, the groups $C_a, \ldots, C_d$ are representative, only if they are part of Group A. $(C_a, \ldots, C_d \in$ Group A). Likewise, the clusters $C_q, \ldots, C_t$ are irrelevant, in case of they are identified as a part of Group B $(C_q, \ldots, C_t \in$ Group B). Representative clusters are kept while irrelevant clusters are merged.

The idea of the merging process is to integrate a cluster C_v that is visually irrelevant (it contains so few elements) with a cluster C_z that is representative according to their number of elements. This integration is only possible when both clusters C_v and C_z maintain similar characteristics. The similarity of two clusters depends on the distance between their respective cluster centers $x_w^* - x_z^*$. Under this merging process, the elements of every irrelevant cluster C_v $(v \in$ Group B) are combined with the elements of the representative cluster C_z $(z \in$ Group A), so that the length of their respective centers $x_w^* - x_z^*$

is the smallest possible considering all the representative clusters. As a consequence, the cluster C_z absorbs the elements of C_v ($C_z = C_z \cup C_v$). Therefore, the merged versions of the clusters from group A represent the final clustering information. To represent the final segmentation results, since each cluster center x_q^* includes three dimensions, one for the intensity feature $^1x_q^*$ and two for the variance feature $^2x_q^*$ or non-local mean $^3x_q^*$, all elements of C_q are designed to have the same grayscale value indicated by $^1x_q^*$.

5.4.6 Computational Process

The MS segmentation scheme is conceived as an iterative process in which several procedures are executed. In Algorithm 5.1, these procedures are defined as pseudo-code. The MS method adopts as input an image of dimensions $M \times N$ (line 1). In the first stage (line 2), the local variance $V(x,y)$ for every pixel (x,y) by using a 3×3 window is computed. Afterward, the non-local mean characteristic $N(x,y)$ of each pixel position (x,y) is computed (line 3). Then, the feature space of three dimensions is produced by combining all features (line 4) intensity, local variance and non-local means $F(x,y) = [I(x,y) \ V(x,y) \ N(x,y)]$. Under the next step, the reduced group O is generated (line 6) by sampling different feature points of F. After this process, two groups are produced O and $\tilde{O}$. With the set O, the three-dimensional standard deviations σ_1, σ_2, and σ_3 of data O are estimated (line 7). Considering all standard deviations σ_1, σ_2, and σ_3, the configuration elements $h_1, h_2, h_3, \delta_1, \delta_2$, and δ_3 for the MS method are estimated (line 8). Afterward, MS is applied (line 9). Once the MS scheme is executed over the dataset O, it obtains a group of c cluster centers $\{x_1^*, \ldots, x_c^*\}$ and a list of data $X_i = (o_a, \ldots, o_g)$ for every cluster center x_i^* where all pixel features are defined for each cluster $(o_a, o_g \in C_i)$.

With the clustering results of MS, its partial results should be processed to involve the inactive data from $\tilde{O}$ (lines 10–14). Under this process, to each inactive data $\tilde{o}_k \in \tilde{O}$, it is designated to the cluster C_i of the nearest operative element o_a. Afterward, an objective function f is defined, which considers the rise of the number of data in terms of its significance (line 15). From the information contained in f, the knee location v_{min} is identified (line 16). Knowing the value of v_{min}, the total number of groups is divided (line 17) into two cluster elements: representative elements (Group A) and irrelevant elements (Group B). Then, in the merging procedure (lines 18–21), the pixel feature of every cluster C_j ($j \in$ Group B) is combined with the pixel characteristics of the group C_a ($a \in$ Group A), where C_a represents an element of Group A so that the length of the cluster centers $x_j^* - x_a^*$ is the smallest possible. Likewise, the pixel characteristics of C_a will also involve the pixel features of C_a ($C_a = C_a \cup C_j$). Finally, the output of the scheme is the final stored cluster elements of Group A. Figure 5.7 shows the flow chart that summarizes the computational process of the MS method. The flow chart also relates each computational step to its correspondence lines from Algorithm 5.1.

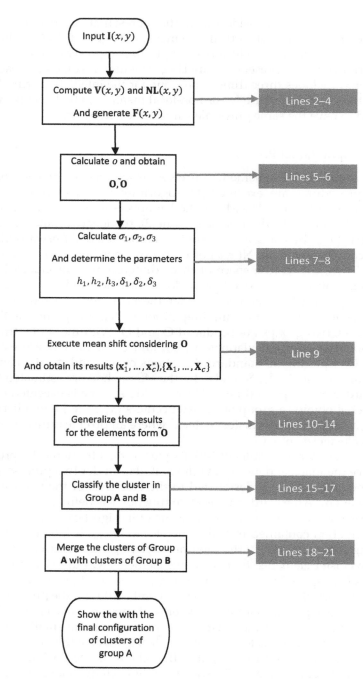

FIGURE 5.7
Flow chart that summarizes the computational process of the mean-shift method.

**ALGORITHM 5.1   COMPUTATIONAL PROCEDURE
FOR THE MEAN-SHIFT MULTI-SEGM**

1. Input: $\mathbf{I}(x,y)$ of dimension $M \times N$

2. $\mathbf{V}(x,y) \leftarrow$ **Variance**$(\mathbf{I}(x,y))$;

3. $\mathbf{NL}(x,y) \leftarrow$ **Nonlocalmeans**$(\mathbf{I}(x,y))$;

4. $\mathbf{F}(x,y) \leftarrow$ **FeatureSpace**;
    $(\mathbf{I}(x,y), \mathbf{V}(x,y), \mathbf{NL}(x,y))$

5. $o \leftarrow int(0.05 \cdot M \times N)$

6. $[\mathbf{O}, \tilde{\mathbf{O}}] \leftarrow$ **OperativeDataSet**(o);

7. $[\sigma_1, \sigma_2, \sigma_3] \leftarrow$ **StandardDeviation**$(\mathbf{U})$;

8. $[h_1, h_2, h_3, \delta_1, \delta_2, \delta_3] \leftarrow$ **MSParameters**$(\sigma_1, \sigma_2, \sigma_3)$;

9. $[(\mathbf{x}_1^*, \dots, \mathbf{x}_c), \{\mathbf{X}_1, \dots, \mathbf{X}_c\}] \leftarrow$ **ExecuteMS**$(\mathbf{U}, h_1, h_2, h_3, \delta_1, \delta_2, \delta_3)$;

10. for each $\tilde{\mathbf{o}}_k \in \tilde{\mathbf{O}}$,

11. $\mathbf{o}_a = \arg \min_{1 \le j \le o} d(\tilde{\mathbf{o}}_k, \mathbf{o}_j), \mathbf{o}_a \in \mathbf{X}_i \wedge \mathbf{o}_a \in \mathbf{O}$

12. If $\mathbf{o}_a \in \mathbf{X}_i$ then $\tilde{\mathbf{o}}_k \in C_i$

13. $\mathbf{X}_i^{New} \leftarrow \mathbf{X}_i \bigcup \{\tilde{\mathbf{o}}_k\}$

14. end for

15. $f \leftarrow$ **CostFunction**$(\mathbf{X}_1^{New}, \dots \mathbf{X}_c^{New})$;

16. $v_{min} \leftarrow$ **KneePoint**(f);

17. $\lceil$ Group A, Group B $\rceil \leftarrow$ **ClassifyClusters**$(v_{min}, \mathbf{X}_1^{New}, \dots \mathbf{X}_c^{New})$;

18. for each $C_j \in$ Group B,

19. $C_a = \arg \min_{C_w \in \text{Group A}} d(\mathbf{x}_j^*, \mathbf{x}_w^*), C_a \in$ Group A,

20. $C_a \leftarrow C_a \bigcup C_j$;

21. end for

22. Output: $\{C_q, C_r, \dots, C_t\} \in$ Group A

5.5 Results of the Segmentation Process

5.5.1 Experimental Setup

In order to determine the effectiveness of the segmentation approach by MS, it employed a dataset called Berkeley Segmentation Dataset and Benchmark (BSDS300) [62]. Each image has its own ground truth, which is provided by human experts. All images in the dataset have the same size of 481×321 pixels.

For the experimental tests, the Multi-Segm algorithm was executed in the 300 images of the Berkeley Segmentation Dataset, and its results are related to those generated by the PSO [30], the CS [38], the SFS [37], and the Fast and Robust Fuzzy C-Means Clustering Algorithm (FCM) [8]. The first three schemes represent the most popular segmentation approaches based on metaheuristic principles. On the other hand, the FCM algorithm is a state-of-the-art clustering method used for segmentation purposes. According to the literature, it presents one of the most accurate results when it faces complex segmentation problems [8,37]. In the comparisons, the configuration of every method is carried out considering its reported guidelines. In the comparative study, the configuration of each technique is set regarding their reported values, which have demonstrated experimentally obtaining the best performance assuming their reported references. The experiments have been conducted on the MATLAB® platform on a PC i7 with 6 GHz and 8 GB of RAM memory. The code of every segmentation scheme used in the comparisons has been collected from the authors and is publically avaliable. In the test, each algorithm has been executed independently while the corresponding results are registered.

5.5.2 Performance Criterion

To measure the performance of the techniques used for the study, nine different indexes have been considered: Average Difference (*AD*), Feature Similarity Index (*FSIM*), Maximum Difference (*MD*), Normalized Cross-Correlation (*NK*), Mean-Squared Error (*MSE*), Normalized Absolute Error (*NAE*), Structural Content (*SC*), Structural Similarity Index Measurement (*SSIM*), and Peak Signal-to-Noise Ratio (*PSNR*), and Computational Cost (*CC*). The first nine performance indexes evaluate the quality of the segmentation results, whereas *CC* considers the evaluation of the computational overload. These performance indexes use the ground truth **R** (Reference) of each image **I** to evaluate the quality of the segmentation for each image from the Berkley dataset.

To determine the *AD*, the AD between the segmented image **I** and its reference image is computed, thus assessing the resemblance between both images. *AD* can be computed as indicated in Equation 5.20.

$$AD = \frac{1}{MN} \sum_{i=1}^{M} \sum_{j=1}^{N} \mathbf{I}(i,j) - \mathbf{R}(i,j) \tag{5.20}$$

FSIM describes a perception-based measure that is used to compare the segmented image **I** and its reference image using a local structure by the obtention of the phase congruency (*PC*) and gradient elements (*GM*). The local similarity $S_{PC}(\mathbf{I}, \mathbf{R})$ between both images is calculated by Equation 5.21.

$$S_{PC}(\mathbf{I}, \mathbf{R}) = \frac{2 \cdot \mathbf{I} \cdot \mathbf{R} + T_1}{\mathbf{I}^2 \cdot \mathbf{R}^2 + T_1} \tag{5.21}$$

where T_1 is a small positive constant (Commonly 0.01). The gradient extent is estimated through convolutional masks for the resulting image **I** and its respective reference **R**, determining **GI** and **GR**, respectively. Hence, a local gradient map is determined by Equation 5.22.

$$S_{GM}(\mathbf{GI}, \mathbf{GR}) = \frac{2 \cdot \mathbf{GI} \cdot \mathbf{GR} + T_1}{\mathbf{GI}^2 \cdot \mathbf{GR}^2 + T_1} \tag{5.22}$$

Once S_{PC} and S_{GM} are computed, the FSIM determined using Equation 5.23.

$$FSIM = \frac{\sum_{j=1}^{2} S_{PC} \cdot S_{GM} \cdot \mathbf{I}_j}{\mathbf{GI}^2 \cdot \mathbf{GR}^2 + T_1} \tag{5.23}$$

For determining the *MD*, the maximal difference between a resulting image **I** and its reference **R** is computed by using Equation 5.24.

$$MD = \max_{\forall i, j \in M \times N} \left| \mathbf{I}(i, j) - \mathbf{R}(i, j) \right| \tag{5.24}$$

The *MSE* is used to determine the affinity of segmented image **I** regarding its reference **R** by the subtraction of the pixel intensity of the image **I** with the elements of its image **R** and then determining the averaged value of the error. The RMS is computed using the model of Equation 5.25.

$$MSE = \frac{1}{MN} \sum_{i=1}^{M} \sum_{j=1}^{N} \left(\mathbf{I}(i, j) - \mathbf{R}(i, j) \right)^2 \tag{5.25}$$

The *NAE* determines the affinity of segmented image **I** regarding its reference **R** computing the normalized absolute differences generated by Equation 5.24.

$$NAE = \frac{\sum_{i=1}^{M} \sum_{j=1}^{N} \left| \mathbf{I}(i, j) - \mathbf{R}(i, j) \right|}{\sum_{i=1}^{M} \sum_{j=1}^{N} \mathbf{R}(i, j)} \tag{5.26}$$

The *NK* computes the similarities between the resulting image **I** and its reference **R** with regard to their correlation. Thus, *NK* is estimated under Equation 5.27.

$$NK = \frac{\sum_{i=1}^{M} \sum_{j=1}^{N} \mathbf{I}(i, j) \cdot \mathbf{R}(i, j)}{\sum_{i=1}^{M} \sum_{j=1}^{N} \mathbf{R}(i, j)} \tag{5.27}$$

The *SC* uses the computation autocorrelation to evaluate similarity through. It is computed by Equation 5.28.

$$SC = \frac{\sum_{i=1}^{M}\sum_{j=1}^{N} \mathbf{I}(i,j)^2}{\sum_{i=1}^{M}\sum_{j=1}^{N} \mathbf{R}(i,j)^2} \tag{5.28}$$

The *SSIM* uses the segmented image **I** and its reference **R** to determine the similarity between both images. Considering the image $\mathbf{I} = \{p_1,\ldots,p_{M\times N}\}$ symbolizes the resulting pixels and $\mathbf{R} = \{r_1,\ldots,r_{M\times N}\}$ the reference information, the *SSIM* can be determined by Equation 5.29.

$$SSIM = \frac{(2\mu_I\mu_R + Q_1)(2\sigma_{IR} + Q_2)}{(\mu_I^2 + \mu_R^2 + Q_1)(\sigma_I^2 + \sigma_R^2 + Q_2)} \tag{5.29}$$

where Q_1 and Q_2 are two small positive values (typically 0.01). μ_I and μ_R are the mean values of the images **I** and **R** data, respectively. σ_I and σ_R symbolize the variance of both images, respectively. The factor σ_{IR} represents the covariance of the segmented and reference data.

The *PSNR* describes the highest feasible pixel value of an image *MAXI* with its corresponding similarity with regard to the *PSNR* magnitude. The *PSNR* can be determined by Equation 5.30.

$$PSNR = 20 \cdot \log_{10}\left(\frac{MAXI}{RMSE}\right) \tag{5.30}$$

The segmentation schemes compared in this study correspond to complex methods with several stochastic processes. Therefore, it is difficult to carry out a complexity test from a deterministic perspective. Under such conditions, in our test, the *CC* is considered to evaluate the computational overload. It represents the seconds invested for each algorithm during its operation.

5.5.3 Comparison Results

In this subsection, the comparison of the performance is presented considering different segmentation techniques that are used over the 300 images extracted from the Berkley dataset. The main objective is to determine the efficiency, effectivity, and accuracy of each method in the segmentation process. In Table 5.1, the average values of every examined index in the group of 300 images from BSDS300 are presented. Considering that the PSO, CS, and SFS use the number of classes to segment as input parameters, they are fixed to four levels. This number of classes has been considered to maintain compatibility with the results presented for such methods in their respective references.

TABLE 5.1

Numerical Results Produced by the Mean-Shift MULTI-SEGM and Other Considered Methods Considering the Berkley Dataset [62]

Index	PSO [30]	CS [38]	SFS [37]	FCM [8]	MULTI-SEGM
AD	53.9787	37.7108	35.3580	28.7443	**19.81472**
FSIM	0.6018	0.7384	0.7428	0.7768	**0.897327**
MD	164.1800	120.2167	121.4111	99.4666	**85.41111**
MSE	4676.7929	2349.1717	1618.4826	1674.9082	**879.4047**
NAE	0.5064	0.3696	0.3229	0.2903	**0.19051**
NK	0.5101	0.6695	0.7376	0.7763	**0.835441**
SC	8.8565	3.0865	2.1251	2.5788	**1.445604**
SSIM	0.5013	0.5796	0.5767	0.663251	**0.801375**
PSNR	12.3124	15.5141	15.9359	17.8561	**20.25181**
CC	**40.241**	80.914	97.142	85.241	50.7841

The averaged results in terms of the indexes *AD*, *FSIM*, *MD*, *NK*, *MSE*, *NAE*, *SC*, *SSIM*, and *PSNR*, and *CC* are registered in Table 5.1 for all 300 images from the Berkley BSDS300 dataset. Low values denote a better performance for all metrics except for *FSIM*, *NK*, *SSIM*, and *PSNR*, which corresponds to the opposite effect. According to Table 5.1, the *FSIM* and *SSIM* metrics that evaluate the number of structures, such as edge information of the segmented image, reveals that the MS MULTI-SEGM method presents the best performance in preserving the relevant information and significant structures present in the ground truth making it suitable for feature-related processing tasks. As can be seen from Table 5.1, our MS method obtains the lowest *MSE* elements. Low *MSE* values also determine a minimum distortion or error in the segmented image. Results from Table 5.1 demonstrate that the *PSNR* value from the MS scheme is comparatively higher, which evaluates the quality of the segmented image in terms of its noisy content. From the results, it is also remarkable that the MS method maintains one of the lowest *CC* compared with other segmentation techniques. In fact, the PSO method, which maintains the worst performance results, is the only scheme that surpasses the MULTI-SEGM algorithm. After an analysis of Table 5.1, it is observed that the MS MULTI-SEGM scheme presents the best-averaged values among the considered algorithms. The approach FCM presents second place in terms of most of the performance indexes, while the PSO, CS, and SFS produce the worst results.

In order to study the visual segmentation outcomes in detail, a group of ten representative images $I_1 - I_{10}$ have been considered from the Berkley dataset to illustrate their perceptible and numerical results. All selected images represent special cases due to their complexity, according to several studies reported in the literature [8,37]. The visual results of the five contrast segmentation schemes are depicted in Figure 5.7. They have represented in pseudo-color with the objective to contrast the segmentation results easily.

A close inspection of Figure 5.8 demonstrates that the MULTI-SEGM method maintains a better visual perception compared with the other methods. In all images, even texturized elements are clearly segmented, while the other algorithms are unable to integrate such structures. This remarkable performance is a consequence of its segmentation mechanism, which involves the use of different pixel characteristics. This extension means that texturized elements or components with bad illumination conditions can be segmented as homogeneous regions. In spite of the good results of the MS method, there are situations in which elements of a small cluster are assigned to other big clusters, producing artificial results. This fact is generated because the distance between their centers is high (even this distance is the minimal found among the representative clusters). This problem could be solved by considering a permissible threshold from which it is better to join irrelevant clusters than merge them with representative clusters.

Table 5.2 exhibits the performance results of all methods for images $I_1 - I_{10}$ from Figure 5.8. The table reports the performance indexes in terms of *AD, FSIM, MD, NK, MSE, NAE*, SC, *SSIM*, and *PSNR* and *CC* Considering Table 5.2, it is evident that the MS method presents better performance index values than the other segmentation schemes. In general terms, the approaches CS, PSO, and SFS present bad segmentation results. This fact demonstrates that these schemes require execution at different times in order to present consistent information. If they are executed only once, the probability of getting a suboptimal solution is high. As a result of this condition, these methods frequently generate inconsistent performance values. In the case of the FCM method, it presents a competitive performance in most of the indexes. Nevertheless, it exhibits worse segmentation results in comparison with the MS MULTI-SEGM method. According to Table 5.2, except for the PSO, the MS method produces the lowest *CC* compared with other segmentation techniques. Therefore, it can be said that the MS MULTI-SEGM presents the best trade-off between accuracy and velocity.

After an analysis of Tables 5.1 and 5.2, it is observed that the MS MULTI-SEGM scheme presents the best-averaged values among the considered algorithms. Its results have demonstrated that it reaches the best values with regard to the *AD, FSIM, MD, NK, MSE, NAE, SC, SSIM*, and *PSNR* indexes. The approaches the CS and the SFS present the second place in terms of most of the performance indexes, while the PSO and FCM methods produce the worst results. According to the *CC*, it is evident that the PSO scheme is the fastest method to obtain a segmented image, while the MULTI-SEGM is the method that exhibits the next best performance. On the other hand, SFS, CS, and FCM techniques obtain the highest *CC* values. The main reason for the excessive use of the computational time of the SFS, CS is the high amount of necessary iterations for obtaining a competitive result. In these approaches, a high number of function evaluations is required before convergence. Likewise, the FCM method consumes a considerable elapsed time due to the number of operations in which it divides its segmentation processes.

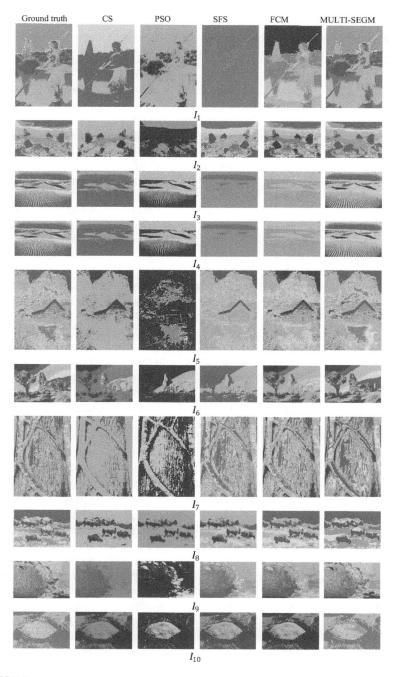

FIGURE 5.8
Visual segmentation result of a representative set of ten images from the Berkley dataset [62].

TABLE 5.2

Performance Comparison of the Mean-Shift MULTI-SEGM Regarding Other Studied Schemes Using the Berkley Dataset [60]

	Metric	PSO [30]	CS [38]	SFS [37]	FCM [8]	MULTI-SEGM
I_1	AD	109.2140	57.9052	44.9050	151.6406	**8.4597**
	FSIM	0.5804	0.7772	0.7148	0.4741	**0.9103**
	MD	200.5032	110.4832	97.1245	254.0065	**66.0021**
	MSE	17165.6436	5025.9486	2764.7810	28421.9763	**545.7747**
	NAE	0.7028	0.3726	0.2890	0.9934	**0.0544**
	NK	0.2664	0.6504	0.7354	0.0053	**0.9808**
	SC	53.8108	2.4775	1.7713	28726.4436	**1.0201**
	SSIM	0.4000	0.7138	0.7586	0.0272	**0.8828**
	PSNR	6.1438	11.8081	13.7183	3.5942	**20.7606**
	Time (s)	**5.0068**	10.0403	12.1809	12.4187	8.2478
I_2	AD	88.3786	42.5721	59.6924	137.9333	**12.4083**
	FSIM	0.5307	0.7389	0.6161	0.2633	**0.9620**
	MD	165.5432	97.2402	128.7423	252.0043	**41.8432**
	MSE	11693.4893	2961.4524	5640.3795	23172.4208	**273.7272**
	NAE	0.6350	0.3058	0.4289	0.9928	**0.0891**
	NK	0.3772	0.7233	0.5377	0.0059	**0.9455**
	SC	71.0494	1.8593	3.3783	23449.2875	**1.1076**
	SSIM	0.3837	0.7067	0.6410	0.0428	**0.9295**
	PSNR	8.4566	14.0445	10.7165	4.4810	**23.7576**
	Time (s)	**3.0068**	8.0403	12.1758	10.4060	6.8745
I_3	AD	114.1978	59.7571	65.4828	95.2079	**15.7640**
	FSIM	0.3152	0.5734	0.4422	0.3679	**0.9189**
	MD	192.1421	116.8287	130.4874	199.0003	**73.453**
	MSE	15707.2057	5350.9629	5785.1013	10001.5943	**428.9536**
	NAE	0.7197	0.3766	0.4126	0.9896	**0.0993**
	NK	0.2612	0.6266	0.5930	0.0094	**0.9185**
	SC	73.0320	3.2150	2.5343	10193.0099	**1.1727**
	SSIM	0.2748	0.6001	0.4898	0.0403	**0.9369**
	PSNR	6.3843	11.8328	10.5828	8.1301	**21.8067**
	Time (s)	**8.1067**	10.0408	12.2141	14.4352	8.2140
I_4	AD	62.9813	38.7173	59.7860	90.4985	**13.3854**
	FSIM	0.4645	0.6791	0.4424	0.1551	**0.9503**
	MD	142.1232	97.7131	128.0273	251.0075	**45.3411**
	MSE	5586.9083	2353.0781	4984.1839	10976.4842	**271.5822**
	NAE	0.6873	0.4225	0.6525	0.9890	**0.1460**
	NK	0.3858	0.6214	0.4010	0.0082	**0.8666**
	SC	18.8802	2.3820	19.3240	11158.4812	**1.3175**
	SSIM	0.2713	0.5837	0.3382	0.0403	**0.9421**
	PSNR	11.0376	15.0881	11.5842	7.7261	**23.7917**
	Time (s)	**50.0117**	80.0432	92.2719	90.4092	60.1214

(Continued)

TABLE 5.2 (*Continued*)

Performance Comparison of the Mean-Shift MULTI-SEGM Regarding Other Studied Schemes Using the Berkley Dataset [60]

	Metric	PSO [30]	CS [38]	SFS [37]	FCM [8]	MULTI-SEGM
I_5	AD	92.6520	54.323	90.2585	131.8132	**14.8896**
	FSIM	0.3862	0.5980	0.3158	0.2439	**0.9196**
	MD	161.532	105.4603	160.3254	252.0042	**45.4361**
	MSE	11057.8288	4658.77043	9845.4869	19390.4201	**391.0404**
	NAE	0.6866	0.4025	0.6688	0.9924	**0.1103**
	NK	0.3093	0.6036	0.3028	0.0067	**0.9171**
	SC	52.4815	9.6221	9.9771	19655.0466	**1.1711**
	SSIM	0.2901	0.5527	0.3065	0.0211	**0.9007**
	PSNR	8.4812	12.9948	8.1986	5.2549	**22.2085**
	Time (s)	**40.0072**	60.0406	72.2329	70.4065	43.8803
I_6	AD	65.9056	37.6423	56.9144	84.4490	**13.3444**
	FSIM	0.4671	0.6843	0.3547	0.3329	**0.9255**
	MD	139.1443	87.7211	141.3624	242.0056	**43.4502**
	MSE	6020.7029	2263.8257	4830.7467	8521.8858	**401.4386**
	NAE	0.6620	0.3781	0.5716	0.9882	**0.1340**
	NK	0.3440	0.6344	0.3690	0.0098	**0.9232**
	SC	18.1249	13.8198	6.3304	8691.7839	**1.1346**
	SSIM	0.3680	0.6746	0.4827	0.0601	**0.8592**
	PSNR	10.7244	15.6053	11.2911	8.8254	**22.0946**
	Time (s)	**30.0069**	50.0423	52.1711	60.4281	40.9397
I_7	AD	96.9601	48.7846	73.1438	139.3231	**12.7739**
	FSIM	0.2842	0.6137	0.3589	0.2047	**0.9300**
	MD	184.7211	103.3843	139.8854	254.0004	**57.9854**
	MSE	11826.5581	3701.8548	6961.6917	21955.6771	**322.1725**
	NAE	0.7025	0.3534	0.5299	0.9928	**0.0925**
	NK	0.2837	0.6605	0.4601	0.0063	**0.9221**
	SC	30.8859	2.5287	4.0044	22235.3235	**1.1633**
	SSIM	0.2203	0.5978	0.3351	0.0132	**0.9292**
	PSNR	7.7228	13.5053	9.7059	4.7153	**23.0499**
	Time (s)	**60.0067**	90.0411	92.2263	94.4126	71.0114
I_8	AD	86.1559	48.4538	72.5667	144.6709	**12.1357**
	FSIM	0.5345	0.6979	0.5461	0.3053	**0.8953**
	MD	155.8320	96.2760	132.8652	252.0022	**52.5643**
	MSE	11447.1057	3791.5835	7630.5619	25058.1594	**316.6351**
	NAE	0.5802	0.3263	0.4887	0.9931	**0.1126**
	NK	0.4271	0.6935	0.5795	0.0057	**0.9200**
	SC	44.9829	2.3527	2.2022	25348.5012	**1.1567**
	SSIM	0.4163	0.6854	0.4703	0.0329	**0.8829**
	PSNR	8.9165	13.2983	9.3058	4.1413	**23.1252**
	Time (s)	**8.0068**	12.0411	14.1637	13.4163	10.9410

(*Continued*)

TABLE 5.2 (*Continued*)

Performance Comparison of the Mean-Shift MULTI-SEGM Regarding Other Studied Schemes Using the Berkley Dataset [60]

	Metric	PSO [30]	CS [38]	SFS [37]	FCM [8]	MULTI-SEGM
I_9	AD	68.3427	40.4627	60.2085	89.2966	**9.6449**
	FSIM	0.4029	0.6488	0.2856	0.2517	**0.9284**
	MD	149.2432	94.8812	160.3654	249.4975	**35.6534**
	MSE	6098.1390	2528.9509	4949.8706	9348.8253	**196.0710**
	NAE	0.7205	0.4266	0.6347	0.9889	**0.1016**
	NK	0.3004	0.5990	0.3183	0.0094	**0.9213**
	SC	28.8975	54.1237	8.6147	9528.4186	**1.1605**
	SSIM	0.2647	0.5886	0.3723	0.0405	**0.93211**
	PSNR	10.5873	15.1627	60.2085	8.4232	**25.2066**
	Time (s)	**7.0067**	15.0412	17.1686	16.4132	10.8274
I_{10}	AD	36.1076	26.4838	42.8133	55.7475	**11.6531**
	FSIM	0.6268	0.7557	0.7952	0.2464	**0.9508**
	MD	105.82	81.04	166.38	251.00	**34**
	MSE	2573.3881	1411.6807	4503.5444	6144.8574	**210.6904**
	NAE	0.6633	0.4865	0.7865	0.9823	**0.2140**
	NK	0.4615	0.6018	0.1123	0.0090	**0.9033**
	SC	5.6639	115.6884	22.8523	6257.5956	**1.1846**
	SSIM	0.4405	0.6285	0.4103	0.2443	**0.8145**
	PSNR	14.4542	17.2941	11.5977	10.2456	**24.8943**
	Time (s)	**20.0068**	40.0404	42.1896	50.4229	30.8358

According to both tables, although the PSO maintains a small computational overload, its performance in terms of *AD, FSIM, MD, NK, MSE, NAE, SC, SSIM,* and *PSNR* indexes is the worst. Under such conditions, it can be said that the MS method provides the best balance with regard to quality and velocity. Besides the quantitative evaluation, a qualitative analysis is an important part of producing consistent conclusions when evaluating the performance of segmentation schemes. The objective of the qualitative analysis is to evaluate the visual quality and the presence of annoying distortions or other artifacts in the results attributed to a deficient operation of the used algorithms. Analyzing Figure 5.8, in general, the MS scheme is able to efficiently segment the images even in case of noise or texturized objects.

The remarkable results of the MS method are attributed to three important elements. One of them is the use of a small data set for its operation instead of the complete dataset. This mechanism allows for reducing the segmentation process without decreasing its resultant quality. As a consequence, it is possible to obtain excellent segmentation quality by investing a small amount of time (which would be required to compute the complete dataset). The second factor is the use of the MS algorithm and the Epanechnikov kernel function. With these incorporations, it is possible to obtain consistent clustering information from complex data distributions. Under such conditions, it is possible to group difficult pixel data, such as texturized regions or areas of noise. The third factor is the operation of blending clusters with a minimal number of elements. Under this operation, noise pixels can be joined to the object to which they actually belong. Therefore, the segmentation results have a better capacity to include imprecise information corresponding to pixels contaminated by common noise. In spite of its interesting results, the MULTI-SEGM scheme maintains a limitation. Such a disadvantage represents the complexity of its processes. In comparison with other schemes that consider simple histogram computations, the operations involved in the MULTI-SEGM are difficult to understand. This fact can limit its use for practitioners and application engineers. However, its segmentation results justify the use of these mechanisms, mainly when the method is used in segmentation images that demand complex clustering scenarios.

References

[1] Shi, J., & Malik, J. (2002). Normalized cuts and image segmentation. *IEEE Transactions on Pattern Analysis and Machine Intelligence, 22*, 888–905.

[2] Tian, Y., Li, J., Yu, S., & Huang, T. (2015). Learning complementary saliency priors for foreground object segmentation in complex scenes. *International Journal of Computer Vision, 111*, 153–170.

[3] Felzenszwalb, P. F., & Huttenlocher, D. P. (2004). Efficient graph-based image segmentation. *International Journal of Computer Vision, 59*, 167–181.

[4] Tan, K. S., & Isa, N. A. M. (2011). Color image segmentation using histogram thresholding-fuzzy c-means hybrid approach. *Pattern Recognition, 44*, 1–15.

[5] Cheng, H.-D., Jiang, X., & Wang, J. (2002). Color image segmentation based on homogram thresholding and region merging. *Pattern Recognition, 35*, 373–393.

[6] Arbelaez, P., Maire, M., Fowlkes, C., & Malik, J. (2011). Contour detection and hierarchical image segmentation. *IEEE Transactions on Pattern Analysis and Machine Intelligence, 33*, 898–916.

[7] Mignotte, M. (2010). A label field fusion bayesian model and its penalized maximum rand estimator for image segmentation. *IEEE Transactions on Image Processing, 19*, 1610–1624.

[8] Lei, T., Jia, X., Zhang, Y., He, L., Meng, H., & Nandi, A.K. (2018). Significantly fast and robust fuzzy C-means clustering algorithm based on morphological reconstruction and membership filtering, *IEEE Transactions on Fuzzy Systems, 26*(5), 3027–3041.

[9] Sezgin, M., & Sankur, B. (2004). Survey over image thresholding techniques and quantitative performance evaluation. *Journal of Electronic Imaging, 13*, 146–168.

[10] Zhang, X., Xu, C., Li, M., & Sun, X. (2015). Sparse and low-rank coupling image segmentation model via nonconvex regularization. *International Journal of Pattern Recognition and Artificial Intelligence, 29*, 1–22.

[11] Dirami, A., Hammouche, K., Diaf, M., & Siarry, P. (2013). Fast multilevel thresholding for image segmentation through a multiphase level set method. *Signal Processing*, 93, 139–153.

[12] Krinidis, M., & Pitas, I. (2009). Color texture segmentation based on the modal energy of deformable surfaces. *IEEE Transactions on Image Processing*, 18, 1613–1622.

[13] Yu, Z., Au, O. C., Zou, R., Yu, W., & Tian, J. (2010). An adaptive unsupervised approach toward pixel clustering and color image segmentation. *Pattern Recognition*, 43, 1889–1906.

[14] Lei, T., Jia, X., Zhang, Y., He, L., Meng, H., & Nandi, A. K. (2018). Significantly fast and robust fuzzy C-means clustering algorithm based on morphological reconstruction and membership filtering, *IEEE Transactions on Fuzzy Systems*, 26(5), 3027–3041.

[15] Han, Y., Feng, X.-C., & Baciu, G. (2013). Variational and pca based natural image segmentation. *Pattern Recognition*, 46, 1971–1984.

[16] Abutaleb, A.S. (1989). Automatic thresholding of gray-level pictures using two-dimensional entropy. *Computer Vision, Graphics, and Image Processing*, 47, 22–32.

[17] Ishak, A. B. (2017). Choosing parameters for rényi and tsallis entropies within a two-dimensional multilevel image segmentation framework. *Physica A*, 466, 521–536.

[18] Brink, A. (1992). Thresholding of digital images using two-dimensional entropies. *Pattern Recognition*, 25, 803–808.

[19] Sarkar, S., & Das, S. (2013). Multilevel image thresholding based on 2d histogram and maximum tsallis entropy-a differential evolution approach. *IEEE Transactions on Image Processing*, 22, 4788–4797.

[20] Nakib, A., Roman, S., Oulhadj, H., & Siarry, P. (2007). Fast brain mri segmentation based on two-dimensional survival exponential entropy and particle swarm optimization. In: *Proceedings of the international conference on engineering in medicine and biology society.*

[21] .Zhao, X., Turk, M., Li, W., Lien, K.-C., & Wang, G. (2016). A multilevel image thresholding segmentation algorithm based on two-dimensional K-L divergence and modified particle swarm optimization. *Applied Soft Computing*, 48, 151–159.

[22] Brink, A. (1992). Thresholding of digital images using two-dimensional entropies. *Pattern Recognition*, 25, 803–808.

[23] Xue-guang, W., & Shu-hong, C. (2012). An improved image segmentation algorithm based on two-dimensional otsu method. *Information Sciences Letters*, 1, 77–83.

[24] Sha, C., Hou, J., & Cui, H. (2016).A robust 2d otsu's thresholding method in image segmentation. *The Journal of Visual Communication and Image Representation*, 41, 339–351.

[25] Lei, X., & Fu, A. (2008). Two-dimensional maximum entropy image segmentation method based on quantum-behaved particle swarm optimization algorithm. In: *Proceedings of the international conference on natural computation.*

[26] Yang, X.-S. (2014). *Nature-inspired optimization algorithms.* Elsevier.

[27] Nakib, A., Oulhadj, H., & Siarry, P. (2010). Image thresholding based on pareto multiobjective optimization. *Engineering Applications of Artificial Intelligence*, 23, 313–320.

[28] Sarkar, S., & Das, S. (2013). Multilevel image thresholding based on 2d histogram and maximum tsallis entropy-a differential evolution approach. *IEEE Transactions on Image Processing, 22,* 4788–4797.

[29] Cheng, H., Chen, Y., & Jiang, X. (2000). Thresholding using two-dimensional histogram and fuzzy entropy principle. *IEEE Transactions on Image Processing, 9,* 732–735.

[30] Tang, Y.-g., Liu, D., & Guan, X.-p. (2007). Fast image segmentation based on particle swarm optimization and two-dimension otsu method. *Control Decision, 22,* 202–205.

[31] Qi, C. (2014). Maximum entropy for image segmentation based on an adaptive particle swarm optimization. *Applied Mathematics & Information Sciences, 8,* 3129–3135.

[32] Kumar, S., Sharma, T. K., Pant, M., & Ray, A. (2012). Adaptive artificial bee colony for segmentation of ct lung images. In: *Proceedings of the international conference on recent advances and future trends in information technology,* 2012.

[33] Fengjie, S., He, W., & Jieqing, F. (2009). 2d otsu segmentation algorithm based on simulated annealing genetic algorithm for iced-cable images. In: *Proceedings of the international forum on information technology and applications.*

[34] Panda, R., Agrawal, S., Samantaray, L., & Abraham, A. (2017). An evolutionary gray gradient algorithm for multilevel thresholding of brain mr images using soft computing techniques. *Applied Soft Computing, 50,* 94–108.

[35] Shen, X., Zhang, Y., & Li, F. (2009). An improved two-dimensional entropic thresholding method based on ant colony genetic algorithm. In: *Proceedings of WRI global congress on intelligent systems.*

[36] Oliva, D., Cuevas, E., Pajares, G., Zaldivar, D., & Osuna, V. (2014). A multilevel thresholding algorithm using electromagnetism optimization, *Neurocomputing, 139,* 357–381.

[37] Hinojosa, S., Dhal, K. G., Elaziz, M. A., Oliva, D., & Cuevas, E. (2018). Entropy-based imagery segmentation for breast histology using the Stochastic Fractal Search. *Neurocomputing, 321,* 201–215.

[38] Yang, X. S., & Deb, S. (2009). Cuckoo search via Lévy flights. In: *2009 World Congress on Nature and Biologically Inspired Computing, NABIC 2009 – Proceedings* (pp. 210–214).

[39] Buades, A., Coll, B., & Morel, J.-M. (2005). A non-local algorithm for image denoising. In: *Proceedings of the IEEE computer society conference on computer vision and pattern recognition.*

[40] Wand, M. P., & Jones, M. C. (1995). *Kernel smoothing.* Springer.

[41] Chacón, J. E. (2009). Data-driven choice of the smoothing parametrization for kernel density estimators. *Canadian Journal of Statistics, 37,* 249–265.

[42] Duong, K. S. (2007). Kernel density estimation and Kernel discriminant analysis for multivariate data in R. *Journal of Statistical Software, 21,* 1–16.

[43] Gramacki, A. (2018). *Nonparametric kernel density estimation and its computational aspects.* Springer.

[44] Cheng, Y. Z. (1995). Mean shift, mode seeking, and clustering. *IEEE Transactions on Pattern Analysis and Machine Intelligence, 17*(8), 790–799.

[45] Guo, Y., Şengür, A., Akbulut, Y., & Shipley, A. (2018). An effective color image segmentation approach using neutrosophic adaptive mean shift clustering. *Measurement, 119,* 28–40.

[46] Comaniciu, D., & Meer, P. (2002). Meanshift: a robust approach toward feature space analysis. *IEEE Transactions on Pattern Analysis and Machine Intelligence,* 24(5), 603–619.

[47] Domingues, G., Bischof, H., & Beichel, R. (2003). Fast 3D mean shift filter for CT images. In: *Proceedings of Scandinavian conference on image analysis,* Sweden (pp. 438–445).

[48] Tao, W. B., & Liu, J. (2007). Unified mean shift segmentation and graph region merging algorithm for infrared ship target segmentation. *Optical Engineering,* 46, 12.

[49] Park, J. H., Lee, G. S., & Park, S. Y. (2009). Color image segmentation using adaptive mean shift and statistical model-based methods. *Computers & Mathematics with Applications,* 57, 970–980.

[50] Fisher, M. A., & Bolles, R. C. (1981). Random sample consensus: A paradigm for model fitting with applications to image analysis and automated cartography. *Communications of the ACM,* 24(6), 381–395.

[51] Xu, L., Oja, E., & Kultanen, P. (1990). A new curve detection method: Randomized hough transform (RHT). *Pattern Recognition Letters,* 11(5), 331–338.

[52] Horová, I., Koláček, J., & Zelinka, J. (2012). *Kernel smoothing in MATLAB.* World Scientific.

[53] Cheng, Y. (1995). Mean shift, mode seeking, and clustering. *IEEE Transactions on Pattern Analysis and Machine Intelligence,* 17(8), 790–799.

[54] Fashing, M., & Tomasi, C. (2005). Mean shift is a bound optimization. *IEEE Transactions on Pattern Analysis and Machine Intelligence,* 27(3), 471–474.

[55] Buades, A., Coll, B., & Morel, J.-M. (2005). A non-local algorithm for image denoising. In: *Proceedings of IEEE computer society conference on computer vision and pattern recognition* (pp. 3–10).

[56] Paciencia, T., Bihl, T., & Bauer, K. (2019). Improved N-dimensional data visualization from hyper-radial values. *Journal of Algorithms & Computational, Technology,* 3, 1–20.

[57] Guisande, C., Vaamonde, A., & Barreiro, A. (2011). *Tratamiento de datos con R, STATISTICA y SPSS.* Diaz de Santos.

[58] Satopa, V., Albrecht, J., Irwin, D., & Raghavan, B. (2011). Finding a "kneedle" in a haystack: Detecting knee points in system behavior. In: *31st International conference on distributed computing systems workshops* (pp. 166–171).

[59] Zhao, Q., Xu, M., & Fränti, P. (2008). Knee point detection on Bayesian information criterion. In: *20th IEEE international conference on tools with artificial intelligence* (pp. 431–438).

[60] https://www2.eecs.berkeley.edu/Research/Projects/CS/vision/bsds/.[61] Luo, Y., Zhang, K., Chai, Y., & Xiong, Y. (2018). Muiti-parameter-setting based on data original distribution for DENCLUE optimization. *IEEE Access,* 6, 16704–16711.

[62] Cuevas, E., Becerra, H., & Luque, A. (2021). Anisotropic diffusion filtering through multi-objective optimization. *Mathematics and Computers in Simulation,* 181, 410–429.

6

Singular Value Decomposition in Image Processing

6.1 Introduction

In general terms, the singular value decomposition (SVD) decomposition represents a generalization of the mathematical concept of the Fast Fourier Transform (FFT) [1]. The FFT is the basis of many classical analytical and numerical results. However, its operation assumes idealized configurations or data. On the other hand, SVD decomposition is a more generic technique based entirely on data [2].

In different areas of knowledge, complex systems produce information that can be organized in high-dimensional arrays. For example, an experiment can be organized into a time series of data that represents a matrix with columns containing all the outcome measures. On the other hand, if the data at each instant of time is multidimensional, as in the case of an aerodynamic simulation, it is possible to reorganize the data in a high-dimensional matrix, forming the columns of the measurements of the simulation. Similarly, the pixel values in a grayscale image can be stored in a matrix, or these images can be rearranged into large column vectors in a matrix to represent the entire image. Although it may not seem like it, the data generated by these systems can be simplified by extracting the dominant patterns that explain the contained information, and that could make the high dimension irrelevant. SVD decomposition is a numerically robust and efficient method to extract these patterns from these data. In this chapter, we will introduce the SVD decomposition, and we will explain how to apply the SVD in images by means of several examples.

As an example, let's consider images, which contain a large number of measurements (pixels) and are, therefore, high-dimensional vectors. However, most images are highly compressible, which means that the relevant information can be represented in a much smaller subspace of dimensions. Physical systems also provide compelling examples of the low-dimensional structure that sums up a high-dimensional space. Although high-fidelity system simulations require thousands of degrees of freedom, there are often overriding structures that allow them to be reduced to just a few.

DOI: 10.1201/9781032662466-6

The SVD provides a systematic way of determining a low-dimensional approximation to high-dimensional data in terms of dominant patterns. This technique is data-driven in that patterns are discovered only from data, without the addition of expert knowledge or intuition. The SVD is numerically stable and provides a hierarchical representation of the data in terms of a new coordinate system defined by dominant correlations within the data. Furthermore, the SVD is guaranteed to exist for any matrix, unlike proper decomposition.

SVD decomposition has many applications beyond the dimensional reduction of data. It is also used to compute the pseudo-inverse of non-square matrices. In this way, solutions to indeterminate or over-determined matrix equations of the type $\mathbf{Ax} = \mathbf{b}$ are provided. SVD decomposition can also be used to denoise data sets.

It is assumed that there is a large data set such as $\mathbf{X} \in \mathbb{R}^{m \times n}$:

$$\mathbf{X} = [\mathbf{x}_1, \ldots, \mathbf{x}_m] \tag{6.1}$$

The columns of each element $\mathbf{x}_i \in \mathbb{R}^n$ can represent the values of simulations or experiments. The column values could contain the grayscale pixels of images that have been reordered into vectors. The values of these vectors could also consist of the state of a physical system that is evolving in time, such as the speed of the system at a set of discrete points.

The index i represents the set number i of measurements contained in $\mathbf{X}$. It is important to note that the dimension n of each vector stored in $\mathbf{X}$ is very large, in the order of thousands of degrees of freedom. Each vector $\mathbf{x}_i$ is known as a sample, and m is the number of samples in $\mathbf{X}$. In general, for many systems $n \gg m$, which results in a tall and tiny matrix.

The SVD decomposition is a matrix decomposition that is unique and can be extracted for every matrix $\mathbf{X} \in \mathbb{R}^{m \times n}$:

$$\mathbf{X} = \mathbf{U\Sigma V} \tag{6.2}$$

where $\mathbf{U} \in \mathbb{R}^{n \times n}$ and $\mathbf{V} \in \mathbb{R}^{m \times m}$ are defined as unitary matrices having orthonormal columns. $\Sigma \in \mathbb{R}^{m \times n}$ is a matrix consisting of positive values on the diagonal and zeros outside the diagonal.

If the condition $n \geq m$ is fulfilled, the matrix has a maximum of m non-zero elements on its diagonal, and it can be written as:

$$\Sigma = \left[\begin{array}{c} \overline{\Sigma} \\ 0 \end{array} \right] \tag{6.3}$$

With this formulation, it is possible to represent the matrix $\mathbf{X}$ using a simpler version of the SVD decomposition. This version, also known as the economic version, is formulated under the following model:

$$\mathbf{X} = \mathbf{U\Sigma V} = \begin{bmatrix} \overline{\mathbf{U}} & \mathbf{U}^{\perp} \end{bmatrix} \begin{bmatrix} \overline{\Sigma} \\ 0 \end{bmatrix} = \overline{\mathbf{U}}\, \overline{\Sigma}\, \mathbf{V} \tag{6.4}$$

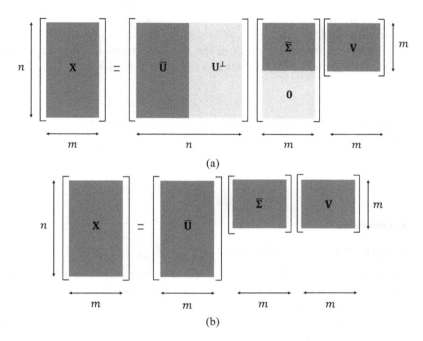

FIGURE 6.1
Process of the (a) generic SVD decomposition and the (b) simple decomposition.

Figure 6.1 visually shows the process of the generic SVD decomposition and the simple decomposition. The columns that belong to the matrix $\mathbf{U}^{\perp}$ correspond to vectors in the space that are complementary and orthogonal to the vectors that correspond to the matrix $\bar{\mathbf{U}}$. The columns of matrix $\mathbf{U}$ are known as the singular vectors on the left of the original matrix $\mathbf{X}$. On the other hand, the columns of matrix $\mathbf{V}$ are known as the singular vectors on the right, which correspond to the original matrix $\mathbf{X}$. Finally, the elements of the main diagonal of the matrix $\bar{\Sigma} \in \mathbb{R}^{m \times m}$ are called singular values. It is common to order eigenvalues from largest to smallest. An eigenvalue with a higher value implies that it better explains the variability of the original data stored in $\mathbf{X}$ than one with a lower value. The range that $\mathbf{X}$ has must be equal to the number of singular values in $\bar{\Sigma}$ distinct from zero.

6.2 Computing the SVD Elements

The SVD represents one of the most important concepts in different areas of science and engineering. The computation of the SVD is so important that most programming languages or computer packages implement a function for its extraction [3].

In MATLAB®, the svd function is the function implemented to calculate the complete or generic SVD decomposition of a matrix **X**.

```
[S,V,D]=svd(X);
```

It is also possible to calculate the simple version of the SVD decomposition using the following command:

```
[S,V,D]=svd(X,'econ');
```

6.3 Approximation of the Data Set

The most important feature of the SVD decomposition is that it allows obtaining from a high-dimensional data set **X** an optimal approximation $\tilde{\mathbf{X}}$ in a lower dimension. With the results obtained by the SVD decomposition, it is possible to obtain an approximation of rank r of the data set, which represents the result of only considering the first r different vectors and discarding the rest $n - r$.

The use of SVD decomposition has been generalized to spaces between functions. Therefore, Eckart-Young established a theorem that formulates the approximation of the decomposition through the truncation of the dimensions. The optimal approximation $\tilde{\mathbf{X}}$ for the truncation r of the data matrix **X**, in the sense of least squares, is established through the following formulation:

$$\min \left\| \mathbf{X} - \tilde{\mathbf{X}} \right\| = \tilde{\mathbf{U}} \tilde{\Sigma} \tilde{\mathbf{V}} \tag{6.5}$$

where the matrices $\tilde{\mathbf{U}}$ and $\tilde{\mathbf{V}}$ represent the first r column and row vectors of the matrices **U** and **V**. While the matrix $\tilde{\Sigma}$ contains the block of the first $r \times r$ elements of the original matrix Σ. In this way, the approximate data vector $\tilde{\mathbf{X}}$ will be defined considering only the integration of the first r elements of each matrix **U**, **V**, and Σ. This can be formulated as follows:

$$\tilde{\mathbf{X}} = \sum_{i=1}^{r} \sigma_i \mathbf{u}_i \mathbf{v}_i = \sigma_1 \mathbf{u}_1 \mathbf{v}_1 + \cdots + \sigma_r \mathbf{u}_r \mathbf{v}_r \tag{6.6}$$

where $\mathbf{u}_i$ represents column i of matrix **U** and $\mathbf{v}_i$ constitutes row i of matrix **V**. While σ_i corresponds to the value i of the main diagonal of matrix Σ. The approximation process by truncation for the SVD decomposition can be visualized in Figure 6.2.

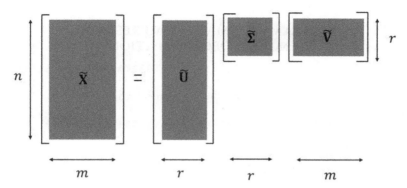

FIGURE 6.2
Process approximation by truncation of the SVD decomposition.

6.4 SVD for Image Compression

The approximation property of a data set that presents an SVD decomposition can be used to compress images [4]. This property represents the fact that large data sets maintain consistent patterns that allow approximating the total information of the set with only the presence of these patterns. Images represent large data sets with consistent patterns and redundant information. A grayscale image can be thought of as a real-valued matrix $\mathbf{X} \in \mathbb{R}^{m \times n}$, where n and m represent the number of rows and columns, respectively.

Assume the image shown in Figure 6.3. This image has a resolution of 960×1208 pixels. To observe the effects of compression, the image will be broken down into its SVD components. In this way, assuming that the image is stored in the MATLAB variable I1, the following MATLAB commands are executed:

```
X=I1;
[S,V,D]=svd(X);
```

Once the image is decomposed into its components S, V, and D, the image is approximated by truncating the matrices at different levels for these matrices. To observe the levels of comprehension, $r = 15, 50, 100$ will be chosen. To see the approximations, the MATLAB code of Program 6.1 should be executed.

There are two important elements of Program 6.1 that must be explained. The first and very important one is to convert the values that represent the pixels of the image into floating point numbers. Images are typically

PROGRAM 6.1   IMAGE COMPRESSION USING SVD DECOMPOSITION

```
%%%%%%%%%%%%%%%%%%%%%%%%%%%%%%%%%%%%%%%%%%%%%%%%%%%%%%%%%%%
%%%
% Program to calculate the SVD decomposition
% for image compression proposes.
%%%%%%%%%%%%%%%%%%%%%%%%%%%%%%%%%%%%%%%%%%%%%%%%%%%%%%%%%%%
%%%
% Erik Cuevas, Alma Rodríguez
%%%%%%%%%%%%%%%%%%%%%%%%%%%%%%%%%%%%%%%%%%%%%%%%%%%%%%%%%%%
%%%
%Acquire the image
Im=imread('I1.jpeg');
%Convert the image to grayscale
I1=rgb2gray(Im);
%Convert image to floating point
X=double(I1);
%Get SVD components
[U,S,V]=svd(X);
%The truncation point is defined
r=15;
%The approximate data matrix is obtained with only r=15
elements
Xapprox15 = U(:,1:r)*S(1:r,1:r)*V(:,1:r)';
%Converts the data array to integer
IR15=mat2gray(Xapprox);
%The image is shown
imshow(IR15)
r=50;
%The approximate data matrix is obtained with only r=50
elements
Xapprox50 = U(:,1:r)*S(1:r,1:r)*V(:,1:r)';
%Converts the data array to integer
IR50=mat2gray(Xapprox50);
figure;
%The image is shown
imshow(IR50)
r=100;
%The approximate data matrix is obtained with only r=15
elements
Xapprox100 = U(:,1:r)*S(1:r,1:r)*V(:,1:r)';
%Converts the data array to integer
IR100=mat2gray(Xapprox100);
figure;
%The image is shown
imshow(IR100)
```

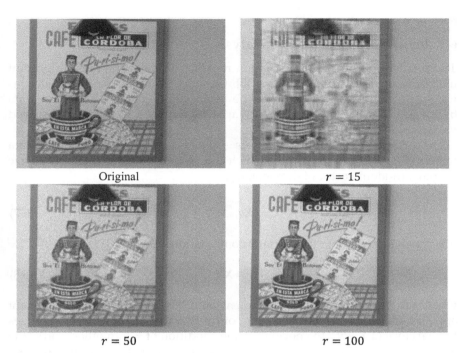

FIGURE 6.3
Returns the approximate matrices for different values of truncation *r*.

represented in a numerical format that allows each pixel to be given a value between 0 and 255. This numerical range corresponds to integers. It is for this reason that the image values are defined as integers. However, to decompose the data array into its SVD components, it is necessary to manipulate the information in the array as floating point elements. To carry out this process, the function in MATLAB of double is used. On the other hand, once the matrix has been constructed, giving approximate data $\tilde{X}$ considering a truncation level r, it is necessary to convert the data to an integer numeric type that allows the representation of images. This process is carried out by the MATLAB function mat2gray.

Figure 6.3 shows the approximate matrices for different values of truncation r. In the case of $r = 15$, it is clear that very little information has been used in the reconstruction. As a consequence, the objects in the image are hardly perceived. In the case of $r = 50$, although only 50 elements have been considered, it seems that they are enough to distinguish the objects and characters present in the image. Finally, in the case of $r = 100$, the image is already practically the original.

6.5 Principal Component Analysis

The problem of dimension reduction represents one of the most important methods of multivariate analysis [5]. Generically, it can be formulated as follows: Is it possible to describe the information contained in some data by means of a smaller number of variables than the number of observed variables?

The principal component analysis (PCA) starts from a (centered) data matrix of n rows and p columns, which can be considered as a sample of size n from a random vector of dimension p,

$$\mathbf{X} = \left(X_1, \ldots, X_p\right)'. \tag{6.7}$$

It is considered a linear (univariate) combination of $\mathbf{X}$,

$$\mathbf{y} = \mathbf{X}'\mathbf{t}, \tag{6.8}$$

where $\mathbf{t}$ is a vector of weights of dimension p. The first principal component appears as a solution to the problem of finding the vector $\mathbf{t}$ that maximizes the variance of $\mathbf{Y}$ with the normalization condition $\mathbf{t}'\mathbf{t} = 1$. In other words, the expression $\text{var}(\mathbf{Y})$ as a function of the weights $\mathbf{t}$ conducts a variational problem whose solution is the first principal component. This problem is equivalent to finding the eigenvalues and eigenvectors of the covariance matrix of $\mathbf{X}$. So that the successive principal components are obtained from the diagonalization of the covariance matrix of $\mathbf{X}$,

$$\mathbf{S} = \mathbf{T}\Lambda\mathbf{T}', \tag{6.9}$$

where $\mathbf{T}$ is a $p \times p$ orthogonal matrix whose columns are the coefficients of the principal components.

6.6 Principal Components through Covariance

In order to exemplify these concepts, assume the following covariance matrix:

$$\Sigma = \begin{pmatrix} 3 & 1 & 1 \\ 1 & 3 & 1 \\ 1 & 1 & 5 \end{pmatrix} \tag{6.10}$$

This matrix corresponds to a random vector $\mathbf{X} = (X_1, X_2, X_3)'$ of mean zero.

To calculate the eigenvalues and eigenvectors of Σ in MATLAB, you can use the `eig` function to compute the eigenvalues of a matrix.

```
A = [3 1 1; 1 3 1; 1 1 5];
eig_values = eig(A);
```

The eigenvalues of Σ, ordered from highest to lowest, are $\lambda_1 = 6, \lambda_2 = 3$ and $\lambda_3 = 2$. The corresponding normalized eigenvectors are $e_1 = (1,1,2)'/\sqrt{6}, e_2 = (1,1,-1)'/\sqrt{3}y, e_3 = (1,-1,0)'/\sqrt{2}$.

The proportion that explains the total variance of each component is specified by the vector $Y = (Y_1, Y_2, Y_3)'$. Its main components are as follows:

$$Y_1 = e_1'X = \frac{1}{\sqrt{6}}(X_1 + X_2 + 2X_3)$$

$$Y_2 = e_2'X = \frac{1}{\sqrt{3}}(X_1 + X_2 - X_3) \qquad (6.11)$$

$$Y_3 = e_3'X = \frac{1}{\sqrt{2}}(X_1 - X_2)$$

The total variance is determined by:

$$VT(\Sigma) = tr(\Sigma) = 11 \qquad (6.12)$$

The proportion of $VT(\Sigma)$ explained by the first principal component is defined by:

$$\frac{var(Y_1)}{VT(\Sigma)} = \frac{\lambda_1}{11} \simeq 54.5\%. \qquad (6.13)$$

Similarly, that explained proportions by Y_2 and Y_3 are 27.3% and 18.2%, respectively.

The representation of data from the original vector X in the plane of the first two principal components, particularly in the observation $x = (2,2,1)'$. To express X in the plane of Y_1 and Y_2, the scalar product of X must be made by the directions given by e_1 and e_2. For x, the result is the point $(y_1, y_2) = (\sqrt{6}, \sqrt{3})$

Given the data in Table 6.1, consider the variables $X_1 =$ duration of the mortgage and $X_2 =$ price and denote by X the vector $(X_1, X_2)'$.

In MATLAB, you can use the `cov()` function to compute the covariance matrix of a set of data. The function takes two inputs: the data, which should be in the form of an $n \times p$ matrix, where n is the number of observations and p is the number of variables and an optional parameter that specifies how the data should be scaled (default is `'unbiased'`).

TABLE 6.1

Data to Calculate the Principal
Component Analysis

Data	X_1	X_2
1	8.7	0.3
2	14.3	0.9
3	18.9	1.8
4	19.0	0.8
5	20.5	0.9
6	14.7	1.1
7	18.8	2.5
8	37.3	2.7
9	12.6	1.3
10	25.7	3.4

Considering that the data in Table 6.1 are represented in the matrix **X**, you can compute the covariance matrix as follows:

```
S = cov(X);
```

This will return the covariance matrix S, which is a $p \times p$ matrix, where the i, j element is the covariance between the i-th and j-th variables in the data. From the data in Table 6.1, the covariance matrix is defined as follows:

$$\mathbf{S} = \begin{bmatrix} 56.97 & 5.17 \\ 5.17 & 0.89 \end{bmatrix} \tag{6.14}$$

On the other hand, correlation in data refers to the degree to which two or more variables are related to each other. It is a statistical measure that ranges from −1 to 1, where −1 indicates a perfect negative correlation, 0 indicates no correlation, and 1 indicates a perfect positive correlation. A positive correlation means that as one variable increases, the other variable also increases, and a negative correlation means that as one variable increases, the other variable decreases. Correlation can be used to identify patterns and relationships in data.

In MATLAB, you can calculate the correlation between two variables using the `corr` function. The function takes in two vectors or matrices as input and returns the correlation coefficient. For example, if you have two vectors **x** and **y** that you want to calculate the correlation for, you can use the following code:

```
r = corr(x, y);
```

This will return the correlation coefficient r between the two vectors x and y. You can also calculate the correlation matrix for a set of variables in a matrix.

For example, if you have a matrix **A** with several columns representing different variables, you can use the following code:

```
R = corr(A);
```

This will return a matrix **R** where the element in the i, j position gives the correlation between the i-th and j-th columns of **A**. Note that the `corr` function uses the Pearson correlation coefficient by default, which assumes that the data is normally distributed and linear relationship between the variables. If your data does not meet these assumptions, you may consider using other types of correlation.

Covariance and correlation are two concepts that are closely related. Covariance is a measure of the degree to which two variables vary together. A positive covariance indicates that the variables tend to increase or decrease together, while a negative covariance indicates that the variables tend to move in opposite directions. The unit of measurement for covariance is the product of the units of the two variables.

Correlation, on the other hand, is a standardized measure of the degree to which two variables are related. It is the ratio of the covariance of the two variables to the product of their standard deviations. Correlation takes on a value between –1 and 1, with –1 indicating a perfect negative linear relationship, 0 indicating no relationship, and 1 indicating a perfect positive linear relationship.

Both covariance and correlation are useful for understanding the relationship between two variables, but correlation is generally more useful for comparing the strength of the relationship between different pairs of variables because it is standardized and independent of the unit of measurement. You can compute the covariance matrix from a given correlation matrix by using the formula

$$\mathbf{S} = \mathbf{D} \mathbf{R} \mathbf{D} \tag{6.15}$$

where **R** is the correlation matrix, **D** is a diagonal matrix of standard deviations, and **C** is the covariance matrix.

Considering that the mean $\overline{\mathbf{X}}$ value of the elements in Table 6.1 are $(19.05, 1.57)'$, the eigenvalues of **S** are defined as $\lambda_1 = 57.44$ and $\lambda_2 = 0.42$. The corresponding normalized eigenvectors are $\mathbf{e}_1 \simeq (0.99, 0.09)'$ and $\mathbf{e}_2 \simeq (0.09, -0.99)'$. Therefore, the principal components of **S** have the following components:

$$Y_1 = \mathbf{e}_1'\left(\mathbf{X} - \overline{\mathbf{X}}\right) = 0.99(X_1 - 19.05) + 0.09(X_2 - 0.42)$$

$$Y_2 = \mathbf{e}_2'\left(\mathbf{X} - \overline{\mathbf{X}}\right) = 0.09(X_1 - 19.05) - 0.99(X_2 - 0.42). \tag{6.16}$$

The variance of a principal component is defined by the eigenvalue of **S**.

$$\text{var}(Y_1) = \lambda_1 = 57.44 \quad \text{and} \quad \text{var}(Y_2) = \lambda_2 = 0.42. \tag{6.17}$$

The proportion of variance explained by Y_1 is $\text{var}(Y_1)/VT(\mathbf{S}) \approx 99\%$.

The correlation coefficients between Y_1 and X_k as $\text{corr}(Y_1, X_k)$, for $k = 1, 2$, is computed as follows:

$$\text{corr}(Y_1, X_1) = \frac{e_{11}\sqrt{\lambda_1}}{\sqrt{s_{11}}} = \frac{0.99\sqrt{57.44}}{\sqrt{56.97}} \approx 0.99 \tag{6.18}$$

and

$$\text{corr}(Y_1, X_2) = \frac{e_{12}\sqrt{\lambda_1}}{\sqrt{s_{22}}} = 0.72. \tag{6.19}$$

The fact that the first principal component (which is essentially X_1) explains a large part of the variability of the system is due to the fact that the sample variance of X_1 is much larger than that of X_2 and that makes the variance considerably larger throughout the direction given by the vector $\mathbf{e}_1$. In this case, it is convenient to standardize the data and perform a new PCA on the resulting matrix. This is equivalent to obtaining the principal components from the correlation matrix.

6.7 Principal Components through Correlation

It is also possible to calculate the principal components through the correlation matrix $\mathbf{R}$. In order to exemplify this concept, consider the data in Table 6.1. Then, by using the function `corr`, the following matrix is found:

$$\mathbf{R} = \begin{pmatrix} 1 & 0.72 \\ 0.72 & 1 \end{pmatrix} \tag{6.20}$$

$\mathbf{R}$ has as eigenvalues $\lambda_1 = 1.72$, $\lambda_2 = 0.28$ and as eigenvectors

$$\mathbf{e}_1 = (0.71, 0.71)' \quad \text{and} \quad \mathbf{e}_2 = (-0.71, 0.71)'. \tag{6.21}$$

Therefore, the principal components from $\mathbf{R}$ are calculated as follows:

$$Y_1 = \mathbf{e}_1'\mathbf{Z} = 0.71Z_1 + 0.71Z_2$$

$$Y_2 = \mathbf{e}_2'\mathbf{Z} = -0.71Z_1 + 0.71Z_2, \tag{6.22}$$

where $Z_1 = (X_i - 19.05)/7.55$, $Z_2 = (X_2 - 1.57)/0.94$, and $\mathbf{Z} = (Z_1, Z_2)'$ is the standardized vector $\mathbf{X}$.

The total variability is measured by $VT(\mathbf{R}) = \text{tr}(\mathbf{R}) = 2$, and the proportion of it is explained by Y_1 is $\lambda_1/VT(\mathbf{R}) = 1.72/2 = 86\%$. The correlation coefficients between Y_1 and the variables Z_i are:

$$\text{corr}(Y_1, Z_1) = \frac{e_{11}\sqrt{\lambda_1}}{\sqrt{r_{11}}} = 0.93, \ \text{corr}(Y_1, Z_2) = 0.93. \tag{6.23}$$

The first principal component of $\mathbf{R}$ now gives equal greater weight to the variables X_1 and X_2. As discussed in Problem 4.2, it would be more appropriate to calculate the principal components from $\mathbf{R}$.

The determination of the principal components can also be conducted through MATLAB functions. In order to calculate the principal components, the following procedure is applied (Algorithm 6.1).

ALGORITHM 6.1   DETERMINATION OF THE PRINCIPAL COMPONENTS

1. Load the data into MATLAB.

2. Subtract the mean of each column of data from the corresponding column. This is done to ensure that the data is centered around the origin, which is a requirement for PCA.

3. Compute the covariance matrix of the data. This can be done using the `cov` function in MATLAB.

4. Compute the eigenvectors and eigenvalues of the covariance matrix. This can be done using the `eig` function in MATLAB. The eigenvectors are the principal components, and the eigenvalues are the variances of the data along each principal component.

5. Sort the eigenvectors and eigenvalues in descending order of eigenvalues. This will give you the principal components in order of importance, with the first component having the highest variance.

6. Project the data onto the principal components by multiplying the data matrix with the matrix of eigenvectors.

7. You can also visualize the data in the PCA space using the scatter function in MATLAB with the projected data.

Note: PCA is a powerful tool, but it should be used with caution. It is sensitive to the scale of the data, so it's recommended to standardize the data before running PCA. Also, it can only be used on linear relationships, so it may not be appropriate for certain types of data or problems.

The code presented in Program 6.2 illustrates the necessary steps to perform the determination of the principal components from the data of matrix $\mathbf{A}$.

PROGRAM 6.2 DETERMINATION OF
THE PRINCIPAL COMPONENTS

```
% Load the data into a matrix
data = A;
% Subtract the mean of each column from the data
data = bsxfun(@minus, data, mean(data));
% Compute the covariance matrix
cov_matrix = cov(data);
% Compute the eigenvectors and eigenvalues of the
covariance matrix
[eigenvectors, eigenvalues] = eig(cov_matrix);
% Sort the eigenvectors and eigenvalues in descending
order
[eigenvalues, index] = sort(diag(eigenvalues),
'descend');
eigenvectors = eigenvectors(:, index);
% Project the data onto the principal components
projected_data = data * eigenvectors;
% Visualize the data in the PCA space
scatter(projected_data(:, 1), projected_data(:, 2));
xlabel('First Principal Component');
ylabel('Second Principal Component');
```

References

[1] Brigham, E. O. (1988). *The fast Fourier transform and its applications.* Prentice-Hall, Inc.

[2] Henry, E. R., & Hofrichter, J. (1992). [8] Singular value decomposition: Application to analysis of experimental data. In *Methods in enzymology* (Vol. 210, pp. 129–192). Academic Press.

[3] Van Loan, C. F. (1976). Generalizing the singular value decomposition. *SIAM Journal on Numerical Analysis,* 13(1), 76–83.

[4] Tian, M., Luo, S. W., & Liao, L. Z. (2005). An investigation into using singular value decomposition as a method of image compression. In *2005 International conference on machine learning and cybernetics* (Vol. 8, pp. 5200–5204). IEEE.

[5] Abdi, H., & Williams, L. J. (2010). Principal component analysis. *Wiley Interdisciplinary Reviews: Computational Statistics,* 2(4), 433–459.

Index

Note: *Italic* page numbers refer to figures.